D1822966

Under the Oak Tree

Under the Oak Tree

The Church as Community of Conversation
in a Conflicted and Pluralistic World

Edited by
Ronald J. Allen
John S. McClure
O. Wesley Allen, Jr.

CASCADE *Books* • Eugene, Oregon

UNDER THE OAK TREE
The Church as Community of Conversation in a Conflicted and Pluralistic World

Cascade Books
An Imprint of Wipf and Stock Publishers
199 W. 8th Ave., Suite 3
Eugene, OR 97401

www.wipfandstock.com

ISBN 13: 978-1-4982-1538-1

Cataloguing-in-Publication data:

Under the oak tree : the church as community of conversation in a conflicted and pluralistic world / edited by Ronald J. Allen, John S. McClure, and O. Wesley Allen, Jr.

xviii + 246 pp. ; 23 cm. Includes bibliographical references.

ISBN 13: 978-1-62032-192-8

1. Preaching. I. Allen, Ronald J., 1949–. II. John S. McClure, 1952–. III. Allen, O. Wesley, 1965–.

BV600.2 U55 2013

Manufactured in the U.S.A.

To our students:
Your conversation with us
in and beyond the classroom
helps us think more deeply
about conversation as a theological attitude.

Contents

Contributors

O. Wesley Allen, Jr., Associate Professor of Homiletics and Worship, Lexington Theological Seminary, Lexington, Kentucky

Ronald J. Allen, Professor of Preaching and Gospels and Letters, Christian Theological Seminary, Indianapolis, Indiana

Pamela D. Couture, Jane and Geoffrey Martin Chair of Church and Community, Emmanuel College of Victoria University in the University of Toronto, Toronto, Canada

David J. Lose, The Marbury E. Anderson Chair in Biblical Preaching, Luther Seminary, St. Paul, Minnesota

Donald M. Mackenzie, Retired minister of University Congregational United Church of Christ, Seattle, Washington, member of the *Interfaith Amigos*

John S. McClure, Charles G. Finney Professor of Preaching and Worship, Vanderbilt Divinity School, Nashville, Tennessee

Michael St. A. Miller, Associate Professor of Systematic and Philosophical Theology, Christian Theological Seminary, Indianapolis, Indiana

G. Lee Ramsey, Jr., Marlon and Sheila Foster Professor of Pastoral Theology and Homiletics, Memphis Theological Seminary, Memphis, Tennessee

Marjorie Hewitt Suchocki, Ingraham Professor of Theology, Emerita, Claremont School of Theology, Claremont, California

Marian McClure Taylor, Executive Director, The Kentucky Council of Churches, Lexington, Kentucky

Nancy Lynne Westfield, Associate Professor of Religious Education, The Theological School, Drew University, Madison, New Jersey

Introduction

❦ SUPPOSE YOUR CONGREGATION is in this situation or one similar to it. An Islamic community announces they plan to build a mosque down the street from your church building. A representative from a neighborhood group asks to meet with the leadership team of the congregation to invite the congregation to join the neighborhood group in opposing the building of the mosque. As the meeting begins, the leadership team, like the congregation as a whole, contains some members who support the construction of the mosque, some who oppose it, and some who are confused as to what Islam believes, its relationship to Judaism and Christianity, and the degree to which followers of Islam may be terrorists.

How does a congregation make its way through such situations? Even more importantly, how does a congregation come to generative understandings of God and of God's purposes, as well as of the purpose of the church and the relationship of the church with the larger world?

This book points to thinking of the church as a community of conversation as a way forward. A conversational approach to the church offers not only a practical way of approaching circumstances like the one just sketched but, more importantly, a way of coming to interpret the purposes of God, the church, and the world. This practical conversational ecclesiology is rooted in a vision of a God whose nature is conversational. Conversation here is more than a strategy. It is inherent in the nature of God, the church, and the world.[1]

---

1. This book grows out of ongoing conversation about conversation among the editors. With different accents, they take conversational approaches to preaching: e.g., O. Wesley Allen, Jr., *The Homiletic of All Believers: A Conversational Approach to Proclamation and Preaching* and *Reading and Preaching the Lectionary: A Three Dimensional Approach to the Liturgical Year;* Ronald J. Allen, *Interpreting the Gospel: An Introduction to Preaching,* esp. 67–118; "Preaching as Mutual Critical Correlation" in Jana Childers, *Purposes of Preaching,* 1–22; *Preaching and the Other;* John S. McClure, *The Roundtable Pulpit: Where Preaching and Leadership Meet* and *Other-wise Preaching: A Postmodern*

What Is Conversation?

Conversation has a particular meaning in this book by referring *to the act of opening ourselves to others with the possibility that we may be changed by the way in which we respond to them.*[2] Conversation differs from monological communication in which one authoritatively declares truth to others, and from debate in which one side argumentatively attempts to persuade another of its interpretation of truth. Conversation is an interactive approach in which people enter into relationship with others. All involved honor the value of both their own voices and experience and the voices and experiences of others. Key elements of conversation include being critically aware of our own perceptions and listening carefully to others so we can understand the others from their own perspectives. The other could be a person, a group, a movement, a social situation, a written text—such as a book or a poem, an expression in the media or almost anything in life.

Under the Oak Tree: An Image for the Church

The title *Under the Oak Tree* derives from Genesis 18:1–15 and suggests an image for understanding the church as community of conversation. The elderly Sarah and Abraham are camped at the oaks of Mamre. Three visitors unexpectedly approach. The couple does not know the identity of the three. Nevertheless, Sarah and Abraham enact ancient near eastern hospitality by welcoming the visitors, washing their feet, and providing food and shelter (Gen 18:2–8).

A conversation takes place. Sarah and Abraham listen to what the others have to say. The couple hears something they would not have discovered on their own: Sarah will bear a child. The encounter is not simply a divine

Ethic for Homiletics. The present work expands the conversational perspective from preaching to broader consideration of ecclesiology.

2. People in the church—including ministers and scholars—sometimes use the word "conversation" in a more limited way that *presumes* the trustworthiness of Christian tradition (or some piece of tradition, such as a biblical text). The church might then engage in give-and-take to clarify the meaning of the tradition and how it applies to today, or seek to clarify the meaning of something outside the church from the perspective of how Christian tradition leads the church to interpret that phenomenon. A preacher, for instance, often prepares a sermon under the presumption that a biblical text has a message that is applicable to the life of the church and world today. By *assuming* the validity of Christian tradition, a priori, the church is not truly open to the possibilities presented by the other. While such give-and-take often helps the church enlarge its understanding of tradition or of issues or situations, it falls short of the kind of conversation sought in this book: openness to the other that can lead to fundamental reassessment.

pronouncement but has the quality of give-and-take. Sarah calls attention to her own situation: barren. Sarah questions. Sarah laughs. God responds to the questions and laughter (Gen 18:9–15).

The encounter between the ancestral couple and the three visitors is a picture of the church as community of conversation: gathering under the oak tree and listening to others who might help the church understand the presence and purposes of God. Through such conversation, we believe the church has a good chance of coming to adequate understandings of God's purposes and of how the church can respond.

What Happens in Conversation?

After Sarah and Abraham receive God's promise, they do not settle at Mamre. They leave that camp and journey to the Promised Land (Gen 20:1). For the conversation to achieve its aim, the ancestral couple had to move out.

When we describe the church as a community of conversation to clergy and laity, people often respond, "Talk. Talk. Talk. That's what the church has always done. Where is the action?" We stress, then, that conversation is seldom an end in itself but typically takes place to help the church clarify not only God's purposes but also how to respond to God's purposes through the internal life of the community and also through relationships and mission beyond the congregation.

David Tracy expands on what happens *when the church opens itself to others with the possibility that the church may be changed by the way in which the community responds to others.* As we have already noted, "others" may be such things as people, texts, religions, cultures, world views, works of art or experiences. Using a classic (such as a novel) as an example of the other, Tracy notes, "The good interpreter is willing to put [the interpreter's] pre-understanding [of the classic text] at risk by allowing the classic to question the interpreter's present expectations and standards."[3] When conversation takes life, "we notice that to attend to the other as other, the different as different, is also to understand the different *as* possible."[4] The encounter with the other prompts us to consider how life looks from the point of view of the other. "Otherness and difference can become genuine possibility: the *as* other, the *as* different become the *as* possible."[5]

In the same way that one tries on a piece of clothing before buying it, in conversation we try on the other's interpretation of life. The encounter may

3. David Tracy, *Plurality and Ambiguity: Hermeneutics, Religion and Hope*, 16.

4. Ibid. 20. Italics in original.

5. Ibid. 21. Italics in original.

result in reinforcing or refining the perspective with which we began. The conversation may lead us to conclude that the other's interpretation of some aspect of life has more merit than our own. The other may know things we do not know, have an angle of vision that allows the other to see things that we do not see, or the other may feel things we have not felt. We may be changed by the conversation. The other may be changed by the conversation.

Listening is crucial. The church in conversation will not simply project its pre-understanding of the other onto the other. This church will seek, as fully as possible, to understand how the other wants to be understood. The church learns to respect the differentness of the other and not simply see the other as an extension of itself.

Conversation is nearly always provisional. The resolution reached by a conversation is seldom fixed in stone. Conversations re-ignite in response to fresh data, fresh perspectives, and fresh circumstances. The result of a particular conversation may become the subject of a future conversation. Consequently, Tracy cautions, "If one demands certainty, one is assured of failure. We can never possess absolute certainty. But we can achieve good— that is, a relatively adequate—interpretation: relative to the power of disclosure and concealment of the text, relative to the skills and attentiveness of the interpreter, relative to the kind of conversation possible in a particular culture at a particular time. Somehow, conversation and relatively adequate interpretations suffice."[6]

Conversation in the Church

By a conversational approach to theology, ecclesiology, ministry, and life in Christian community, then, we mean an approach that seeks to interpret God, the world, and self through reciprocal give-and-take, speaking and listening, with the full range of others in and beyond the church. This approach is based on the assumption that God and God's purposes are omnipresent and that no one person, community or culture can claim a monopoly on the experience and interpretation of God's character, ways, or will.

To be sure, this dialogical perspective honors the Bible, Christian doctrine, and Christian practice (often using these as starting points) but does not assume, a priori, either that all aspects of these expressions of the Christian faith as currently articulated should be normative or that a single interpretation of them is the only correct interpretation. The conversational church and its members attempt to listen carefully to how others within and beyond the church perceive ultimate reality and its consequences for the

6. Ibid. 23.

communities of humankind and nature, being open to the possibility that others have a grasp of God and of God's purposes from which we can learn and to which we can contribute.

Indeed, the congregation can be a community of conversation in which every aspect of the church's life is intended to facilitate many richly textured dialogues that help participants grow in their understandings of God's purposes and in their relationship with God, others, and the world. Because human perception changes in response to new angles of vision, a conversational model of doing theology does not seek to arrive at set and permanent solutions but is ever open to fresh formulations, including new perceptions of the Bible and of Christian doctrine and practice.

From this point of view, ministers are called to promote and help manage the conversations of the church in partnership with other leaders in the community, but ministers do not feel compelled to control the conversations. Ministers encourage the church to undertake important conversations in responsible and healthy ways—insofar as possible honoring the testimony and experience of all who would engage in these conversations with honesty and openness.

This approach to doing theology and being church should not romanticize conversation. Members of the community of faith who enter into this reciprocal approach to community and meaning-making risk a certain level of vulnerability. Without dictating the outcome of theological, ecclesiological, and existential conversations, and never silencing the voices of those who engage in the conversations with integrity and openness to others, minister and church must guard against repressive interaction in the community of conversation. Otherwise, the true growth and intimacy of those participating will be hindered.

An Approach for Our Time

We believe the idea of the church as a community of conversation is fundamental to the church's identity. For two reasons, it is also especially appropriate for the early twenty-first century, particularly in the United States.

First, the postmodern worldview is on the rise. Whereas the Enlightenment/modern worldview draws on empirical observation and philosophical first principles to arrive at statements of truth that are absolute and universally applicable in every time and place, postmodern thinkers recognize the relativity of all perception and the particular, contextual, and interpretive nature of all statements about God, humankind, and the world. Whereas modernism often leads to cultures that seek sameness, postmodernism values diversity and pluralism and seeks to respect the character of particular communities. The differences between modern and postmodern perspectives are at the heart of many differences in theology and church today.

Second, the early twenty-first century is a season of fractiousness, especially in politics and in matters of social and economic policy, in which people often segregate into groups that engage one another not through respectful listening to others but through polemic, sound bite, caricature, manipulation, and even misrepresentation. Churches sometimes intensify such polarization with rhetorics of superiority, exclusivism, and separation.

Conversation is not a magic pill that will resolve these issues. Nevertheless, while interplay between modern and postmodern worldviews is not settled, conversation can help negotiate the differences. Moreover, conversation, centered in respect for the other, offers a promising alternative to those who do not idolize their own self-interests and fields of power and who have patience and heart for the genuinely common good. A conversational approach to life among different groups is one of the most significant things the church can give to the early twenty-first century. Indeed, by modeling conversation in its own life and relating to the larger world through conversation, the church may be a light to the nations (Isa 42:6; Matt 5:16).

A Practical Approach to the Church as Community of Conversation

Eleven ministers and scholars contribute to this volume's practical approach to how conversation can shape the entire life of congregations and other expressions of the church. The book begins with foundational matters of theology and ecclesiology and then moves to how conversation can shape particular dimensions of the church's life and witness.

Chapter 1: the church. Ron Allen offers an ecclesiology drawing out what it means to say the church is a community of conversation.

Chapter 2: the minister. John McClure regards the basic calling of the minister to lead the community in conversation and to help the congregation carry on its conversations in theologically appropriate ways.

Chapter 3: God. Michael Miller articulates a conversational understanding of God as a theological framework for understanding conversation as a theological method.

Chapter 4: preaching. David Lose describes how a conversational perspective shapes what happens before the sermon, in the moment of preaching, and in the life of the community after the sermon.

Chapter 5: worship. Wes Allen shows how the service of worship—whether contemporary, blended, or traditional—can have a conversational character involving God, church, and world.

Chapter 6: formation (Christian education). Lynne Westfield explores how conversation can be a formative medium whether in settings traditionally associated with Christian education or in other settings.

Chapter 7: evangelism. Marjorie Suchocki deals with an aspect of the church's life that is difficult to interpret in conversational perspective: evangelism. How does the church respectfully offer its understanding of ultimate reality to others?

Chapter 8: pastoral care. Lee Ramsey examines how conversation can be a form of pastoral care in, through, and for the congregation, as well as how pastoral counseling can contain conversational elements.

Chapter 9: mission and ecumenism. Marian McClure Taylor finds not only that mission should be a natural outcome of conversation but that ecumenism in a conversational model can be an important expression of mission.

Chapter 10: social witness. Pamela Couture explores how conversation can not only play an integral role in social witness but can itself be a form of social witness with effects that are both internal and external to the witnessing community.

Chapter 11: relationship with other religions. Don Mackenzie calls for Christianity to relate to other religions in a conversational way with the goal of mutual understanding leading to mutual respect.

Each chapter follows approximately the same outline.

- Introduction to the subject of the chapter and identifying concerns appropriate to the chapter
- Brief review of typical ways the church has viewed the subject of the chapter, especially in the last generation
- Fresh look at the topic from the perspective of conversation (the heart of the chapter)

- Practical implications for ministry
- Cautions regarding the conversational perspective on the subject of the chapter
- Questions for discussion
- Further reading for those who want to explore the topic more.

Of course, writers occasionally adapt this structure in accord with the requirements of addressing particular subject matters.

Conversation in the Book about Conversation

While the contributors to this book share an overarching perception of conversation, they approach conversation with their own nuances of understanding and practice. From chapter to chapter, contributors differ in the ways they talk about conversation, in the voices to which they listen, in the methods through which conversations take place, and in the goals of conversation. From this point of view, a conversation about conversation is going on in this book about conversation. Such diversity not only befits the subject matter but expands the conversation about conversation.

The editors and contributors send this book forth with a prayer that it will help ministers and congregations come to generative interpretations of the presence and purposes of God. Such a church can be a transforming presence in the world.

PART 1

A Conversational Practical Theology

1

The Church
as Community of Conversation

RONALD J. ALLEN

❧ YOUR CAR PULLS to a stop at red light at an intersection in an urban neighborhood.[1] You notice a church on each corner. On one corner is a red brick building with white trim and a slender spire reaching gracefully towards heaven. On another corner stands a large dark stone church with stained glass windows, a dome, and large pillars. On a third corner is a former department store now used for worship. On the last corner sits a rambling two-story house with a discreet sign in the flower bed saying that a church meets there. You might surmise that the congregations occupying these buildings are pretty much the same. However, different congregations not only understand their purposes differently but have different methods for thinking about those purposes and how to carry them out.

This chapter explores what it means to think of churches as communities of conversation. This discussion pertains not only to how churches understand their purposes but also to the methods of how churches come to understand and act on their purposes. After noting that the purpose of the church derives from how a church understands the purposes of God, the chapter explores two basic methods of arriving at a purpose and of enacting that purpose: a church that *receives* and *applies* the Bible and tradition to contemporary life, and a church that has *active conversation*

---

1. I am indebted throughout to O. Wesley Allen, Jr., *The Homiletic of All Believers: A Conversational Approach,* esp. 16–38, "A Conversational Ecclesiology." Befitting a conversational approach, we sometimes emphasize different things.

with others in such a way as to open the possibility of changing some of its fundamental perspectives.[2]

A Church Derives its Purposes from its Understanding of the Purposes of God

A church should not imagine its purposes out of the blue. A church that is thinking theologically derives its own purposes from its understanding of the purposes of God for individuals, households, congregations, communities, nations, and the natural world. A church usually formulates its understanding of the purposes of God in light of how it understands the condition of the world.[3]

A church should point to the purposes of God not only for those who belong to the church, but for the wider human family, and indeed, for the created world. In the last generation, thinkers about the church have increasingly come to say that the mission of God (*missio Dei*) is the mission of the church. The mission of the church is to participate in the mission of God. O. Wesley Allen, Jr. sees a church as an institutional continuation, or an embodiment in community, of the purposes of God.[4]

Churches interpret the purposes of God differently, and hence interpret the purposes of the church differently. A church's perceptions come from the ways in which the church understands the Bible, Christian history and theology, the church's own experience, the experiences of those outside the church, and how the church views nature. Churches differ greatly on how to draw on these diverse sources. We cannot speak singularly about *the* purpose of *the* church. Different churches have different understandings of God that lead to different perceptions of the church.

The sections that follow note the roles conversation plays in different churches in coming to understand the purposes of God and of the church.

2. The taxonomy in this chapter is only one way of interpreting how churches cluster around common functions and themes. One of the most influential taxonomies is that offered by H. Richard Niebuhr, *Christ and Culture*, whose categories of Christ in relationship to culture can be extended to include the church in relationship to culture: Christ (church) *against* culture, Christ (church) *of* culture, Christ (church) *above* culture, Christ (church) and culture in *paradox*, Christ (church) *transforming* culture. Another important taxonomy is Avery Dulles' *Models of the Church*, which sets out five models of the church: institution, mystical communion, sacrament, herald, and servant.

3. For overviews of nine major theological families today, see Ronald J. Allen, *Thinking Theologically; The Preacher as Theologian*.

4. In similar fashion, how a church understands its own purposes is a window on how a church interprets the purposes of God.

All churches listen to the Bible, Christian tradition, their own members, and the culture; some churches receive and listen mainly to figure out how to apply the Bible and tradition to life today. Other churches listen with an ear that is open to being challenged not only to enlarge or reframe their viewpoints, but to fundamental rethinking. A church with a conversational emphasis falls into the latter category.

Churches that Receive and Apply the Bible and Christian Tradition to Today

Many churches believe that the Bible and Christian tradition is an authoritative inheritance waiting to be received and applied. This church assumes that its interpretation of the Bible and Christian tradition and theology contains reliable insights to guide the church in every age. A key task is to reckon how to apply the church's interpretation of those purposes to each new context.

Since many of the church's ideas are cast in language from long ago, the church must clarify the meanings of sacred traditions and must think afresh about how to express the church's historic values in forms that people in new situations can understand. Traffic runs one way on the bridge: from the past to how the present can appropriate the past afresh.

We may distinguish two "receive and apply" groups of churches. (1) One group, typically associated with fundamental and evangelical theological movements, presumes that voices in the Bible, and Christian tradition, directly apply in every time and place. (2) The other group, frequently associated with theological movements influenced by the Enlightenment and often labeled "progressive," concludes that the Bible and Christian tradition contain elements that continue to be normative but are expressed in ways that are culturally bound to the times and places in which they originated. The church, then, searches for contemporary equivalents: concepts and behaviors to correlate with ancient language and prescriptions with contemporary analogues.[5]

Snapshots of Some Receiving and Applying Churches

We now look at six snapshots of churches in the United States that seek to receive and apply the Bible and Christian tradition to the contemporary

---

5. One of the most incisive discussions of the method of correlation is still Tillich, *Systematic Theology*, vol. 1, 8, 30–31, 34, 59–60, 62, 64–66.

world.[6] Actual churches, of course, are more complex than these simple categorizations.

Elevator Lobby

Some churches are like elevator lobbies: their basic purpose is to gather people for the ride from earth to heaven. This church views today's world as sinful and corrupt; God seeks to save people from this world. In some settings, this perspective is muted, almost behind the scenes, but in many congregations it is explicit. Within these churches we often find one or both of the following two emphases: (1) winning souls for the journey to heaven and (2) preparing for the apocalypse—the second coming of Jesus. These churches listen to the culture to determine how to shape the gospel message in ways that have a good chance of appealing to people today.

Prop Up Majority Culture

Some churches assume that the world of middle and upper class Eurocentric culture in the United States is life as God intends. God's purpose, then, is to maintain that culture. Consequently, many churches in the United States associated with the middle class and upper class support Eurocentric ways of life. This support, however, often takes two different forms. (1) Some churches function as *chaplains of majority culture*. These churches assume that many dominant values and behaviors of majority Eurocentric culture are consistent with God's purposes. The church, then, passes the hand of blessing over the culture. These churches are often pillars of the local establishment and implicitly understand one of their roles to be helping people be good citizens. These churches listen to the culture to determine what they need to do to help it prosper.

(2) The church as *watchdog of majority culture* thinks that God specifically calls for the politically and theologically conservative versions of majority culture values. Some of these churches subscribe to American Exceptionalism—the idea that God has appointed the United States to be different from other countries in promoting democracy, capitalism, and Christianity. These churches keep watch over the culture to maintain and

6. These categories are influenced by Niebuhr, *Christ and Culture,* and by the attempts to bring Niebuhr's categories (which were articulated in 1951) and adapted for developments since Niebuhr's time by Carter, *Rethinking Christ and Culture.* One should also see the reservations about both Niebuhr's categories and attempts to reframe them by Marsden, "Christianity and Culture."

extend these values. These churches listen to the culture to determine when and where they need to become assertive.

Community of Support and First Aid Station

Some congregations assume that the world is ambiguous with its moments of fulfillment and struggle. God's primary purpose is to help people make their way through life with as much fulfillment as possible. Churches in the receiving and applying tradition believe that the Bible and Christian theology prescribe care that churches should provide members as they make their way through life. The church provides groups, experiences, programs, and relationships to help individuals and households on the journey from birth through growing up, the stages of adulthood, the shifting circumstances of life, and death. When crises occur—such as death or divorce—the church is a first aid station. Such churches are less concerned with public life than with equipping individuals and households to negotiate life. These churches listen to members of the congregation and to others to determine what people need to navigate life successfully.

Seeking to Change the Culture

Some churches take a receiving and applying approach to the goal of changing culture itself. We may distinguish two churches in this line whose purposes are similar but whose theological undergirding differs. (1) The *church as agent of liberation* regards various forms of oppression—such as sexism, racism, classism, heterosexism, economic exploitation, and political repression—as obstacles to the social world God desires. The Bible and Christian tradition provide the paradigm of liberation that the church applies to the culture. This church seeks to join God in liberating people from such systems. The church as receiving and applying agent of liberation listens to the culture to name oppressive persons, groups, and systems with an eye towards how such knowledge can help the church develop plans for actions that contribute to liberation. (2) Some churches hope to transform culture through direct engagement with culture. The concerns of *a church that seeks to transform culture* are often similar to those of the church as agent of liberation. For these churches, too, the Bible and Christian tradition reveal the direction transformation should take. However, while such churches share the goal of cultures similar to those advocated by liberation churches, these churches operate out of theological bases other than liberation theology. For example, some neo-orthodox churches want to transform culture often by engaging culture directly. Such churches listen to the culture to determine both points at which the culture distorts God's purposes, and timely strategies for attempting to affect the culture.

Minoritized Communities
Adopting Majority Theology and Practice

Many congregations are made up primarily of minoritized groups (to use Lynne Westfield's expression in chapter 6). While some such congregations are receiving and applying churches (discussed here), many are conversational communities (discussed below). Such congregations often believe they encounter Christian tradition when gathered with people who share their own cultural history. A receiving and applying minoritized congregation seeks to conform their experience to a particular interpretation of the Bible and Christian tradition, sometimes Eurocentric. When their cultural heritage presents figures, values, and practices that diverge from their interpretation of the Bible and Christian interpretation, they dismiss the former qualities. These churches listen to culture in order to identify things they should emphasize and excise from their own congregational practice.

Alternative (Countercultural) Community

The church has long contained congregations who regard themselves as alternative communities to the majority culture. For instance, the radical wing of the Reformation gave birth to Anabaptist movements. These churches regard culture as undermining God's purposes. Anabaptist churches see themselves as colonies attempting faithful witness in the larger culture. These colonies do not see themselves as ends (to benefit only those who live in them) but as means to witness to God's purposes for the benefit of those who live in the wider culture. Often this witness takes the form of resistance.

In the late twentieth century a similar vision of the church as countercultural community has arisen. Adherents of this new view charge that in response to the Enlightenment, many churches recast biblical and theological notions to make such notions at home in the modern mind. These postliberals reject universal rationality and universal religious experience. To them, the modern church located ultimate authority not in the Bible and Christian tradition but in the Modern worldview. They seek to displace scientific and philosophical criteria for truth with sources and criteria intrinsic to the Bible and Christian tradition.

To the faithful church the narrative of the Bible and Christian tradition is an alternate cultural world with its own language and standards for truth and faithfulness. The church evaluates the outside culture against these latter norms. The countercultural church emphasizes differences between its internal culture and the larger culture, and it often resists the larger culture. The church as alternative community respects many others outside the Christian community and even enters into partnerships with others to accomplish social goals, but its *a priori* interpretations of the Bible and orthodox Christian tradition mean that its perceptions cannot be fundamentally changed by encounters with others. The counter cultural church listens to the culture to note points at which the language and practices of the culture are in tension with the purposes of God.

Emergent Church

In the last twenty years, the diverse emergent church movement has appeared. Some representatives of this movement are in the receiving and applying tradition. Emergent communities often subscribe to postmodern values, especially dissatisfaction with Modernity and with theological and denominational divisions in historic Christian communities. This church often leaves behind traditional forms of worship, evangelism, and mission and looks for expressions more at home in the twenty-first century. Emergent churches are typically dialogical, especially in Bible study, sermon preparation, and even in the sermon itself. In the applying and receiving churches, the dialogue is to discern how to receive and apply the Bible and Christian tradition to today. The goal of the dialogue is to empower laity for missional living, that is, for individuals and groups to engage people with the gospel in day-to-day situations outside the church, embody the values of the Realm of God through community, and to witness to those values in the larger world by calling for social justice.

Churches as Communities of Conversation

Churches as communities of conversation, in contrast to the churches portrayed in the snapshots above, conscientiously seek to consider how others—including others outside the Bible and the Christian house—might prompt the church to think afresh about elements of its theology and practice. Instead of simply receiving and applying a past conversation, this community desires to participate in conversation that may lead to reinforcement, enlargement, reconsideration, or even rejection of the authority of aspects of the Bible or tradition. A conversational church respects the Bible and tradition, and listens carefully to their voices, adopting those perspectives that are life-giving while having the freedom to critique and even turn away from aspects of the Bible and tradition that work against God's purposes. The conversation includes Scripture and tradition while going beyond these two voices.

Theological Assumptions of the Church as Community of Conversation

The church as community of conversation rests on three theological assumptions, which themselves become subjects of conversation. While we list these assumptions separately, in practice they typically work together.

First, the church as community of conversation believes that God is omnipresent. That is, God is present in every moment. There is no time when God is not present. Consequently, people can become aware of God's purposes at any time and any place.[7] God was indeed present with those who shaped the Bible and tradition, but the divine presence was not limited to those individuals and communities. Such awareness is not limited to Christians. Others outside of Christian circles can be sensitive to holy leading in any moment. Indeed, others can respond positively to the divine purposes without ever recognizing that such purposes come from God.

Second, all human perception is interpretation. We never have pure, objective awareness. Hence, we always perceive God's aims through interpretive lenses. Per the preceding assumption, we can become aware of the divine presence and leading at any time, but our awareness is always colored by our ways of being in the world. From this point of view, the perceptions of the biblical writers were limited.

Our interpretive lenses are shaped by a multitude of interacting factors including such things as gender, race, ethnicity, gender orientation, national citizenship, economic and social class, cultural mores, social values, education, political views, theological commitments, personality, and mental wiring. We are not, however, entirely captive to our social locations. While we can never achieve pure and objective knowledge, we can move towards becoming significantly conscious and critical of our interpretive frames.

Third, since human perception is always interpretive and fragmentary, it follows that the church benefits from listening to diverse others, both inside and outside the Christian house. Individuals and groups whose

7. To be sure, some theologians argue that God can actually be absent from some situations.

consciousness and intuition is not pre-loaded by Christian interpretation may be in positions to identify aspects of divine leading that the church does not see. This may be the case not only with people who are affiliated with other religions but with people who are not religious. If God is omnipresent, a person or community may adopt values and behaviors consistent with divine initiative and purpose without the person or community naming or even recognizing the divine presence.

Moreover, the church as community of conversation believes that the Bible and leading elements of Christian tradition have qualities of otherness. To be sure, the Bible, affirmations of faith, Christian practices, and the wide spectrum of Christian theology typically provide helpful perspective. Yet Christians in each age are subject to limitations of perception. All thoughts and behaviors in the Christian house are historically conditioned. Expressions from the past often presuppose worldviews as well as cultural mores and practices that are quite different from those operating in North America today. Thus, people in one era or social location may be more sensitive to the divine presence and leading than people in another era or social location. The church, then, often benefits from listening to the diverse voices of others, both in the Christian house and beyond.

A caveat: others do not always open windows on God's presence and purposes. Others are also limited. But, the act of considering the viewpoints of others may help the church clarify its own viewpoints.

What Happens in Conversation?

What happens, in practical terms, when the church engages others in real conversation? From a formal theological point of view, we may describe what takes place in conversation as a mode of mutual critical correlation.[8] Paul Tillich articulated a theology of correlation which seeks to correlate contemporary questions and experience with traditional theological concepts. This method assumes the trustworthiness of tradition, and envisions the church as applying the tradition to its new contexts via correlation. Many churches and theologians who do not adopt the specific content of Tillich's program of correlation nonetheless follow a similar pattern of analogy in seeking to apply tradition to today.

The method of mutual critical correlation arose in response to a growing awareness among some in the church that not only has the church

---

8. Full descriptions of this theological method are found in Tracy, *Blessed Rage for Order*, 45–47, 79–81; and his *The Analogical Imagination*, 371–72, 405–11, 421–23; as well as his "Theological Method," esp. 52–59.

sometimes received and *applied* elements in Christian tradition oppressively, but occasional elements of Christian tradition *are* oppressive.[9] Additionally, from contemporary points of view, some ancient assumptions about the world (expressed in ancient worldviews) are not simply historically conditioned but are mistaken. Simply to apply such elements to today's situation is to go against the grain of God's purposes. The church needs not just to correlate the tradition with the present but also to consider the degree to which a particular element of tradition is consistent with God's purposes.[10]

On the one hand, when a voice in tradition seems to speak in behalf of divine leading, the church can regard it as authoritative. In such situations the voice from the tradition may criticize the life of the church and point the church to change. On the other hand, when a voice in the tradition seems to encourage the church to depart from divine purposes, the church needs to criticize that voice and point to understandings and behaviors that are more consistent with God's purposes. The church, of course, is ever in conversation about how to name and describe divine purposes.

Such a conversation has the character of *mutual critical* correlation because the correlation and the criticism are mutual: the traffic runs both ways on the bridge: from the tradition to the present, *and* from the present to the tradition. The tradition can be critical of the present church and world, and the present church and world can be critical of the tradition.

In the process of mutual critical analysis, the church's perception of the tradition may change, and the tradition may prompt the church to reassess the church's perception of its present life and witness. The church may discover points at which an element of tradition misrepresents God's purposes, points at which the church's perception of the tradition has always been on target, or points at which the tradition provides unexpected guidance. A voice in tradition may prompt the church to discover points at which the church misuses the tradition in repressive ways, points at which the tradition can continue to live in continuity with the tradition, and points that prompt the church to imagine aspects of its life and witness in new ways.

9. The word "critical" here refers not simply to making negative judgments but, as in the work of a movie critic, to summarizing a viewpoint, drawing out its implications, and assessing its strengths and weaknesses. As a consequence of identifying the weak points of a perspective, a mutual critical correlation might conclude that the original perspective is mistaken. However, a critical analysis could also conclude that an original perspective is commendable.

10. Although mutual critical correlation as a theological method has been around for a generation, ministers are only sometimes aware of it, and only sometimes subscribe to it. But whether or not a church and its leaders recognize the term "mutual critical correlation," or consciously operate in its mode, the spirit of mutual critical correlation typically describes what happens in a real conversation.

Such an approach presumes two things. First, the interpreting community needs to have existing normative understandings of God's purposes and a set of criteria for identifying those purposes by which to *begin* critical discussion with the tradition and others. Second, since these normative understandings are only the *beginnings* of conversation, the community needs to have awareness that conversation itself may prompt the community to reconsider aspects of its pre-existing understandings and criteria.

For example, many churches believed for a long time—and some still do—that God did not permit women to be ordained as ministers of word and sacrament. Churches supported this viewpoint by appealing to such things as select passages of the Bible that claim women should be subordinate to males, to the fact that Jesus and the twelve apostles were male, to historical precedent in the history of the church (women were not ordained for centuries), and to the idea that women were a "weaker sex." Over the last two generations, a conversation with respect to women has ensued in which the church listened to the Bible, history, and experience in fresh ways. Many churches have become increasingly aware that the Bible and tradition are not univocal in pressing women to subject themselves to males, but also contain many instances of women who transcended the limitations placed on them and who lived in ways that point to partnership and equality. Moreover, the actual experience of women indicates that women are often as strong as or stronger than males, and often have insight into the Bible, tradition, and life that particularly qualify them for ministerial leadership. As a result of this conversation, many churches have embraced the ordination of women.

Method and Purpose in Churches as Communities of Conversation

Instead of receiving and applying the Bible and tradition, the general purpose of the church as community of conversation is to engage tradition in ongoing conversation in order to renegotiate and rearticulate an adequate understanding of the purposes of God and appropriate responses to those purposes. Response includes formulating appropriate strategies of mission as well as patterns of church life. The church as community of conversation seeks an adequate understanding of what the church most deeply believes, and an adequate determination of what the church should do.

From this point of view, conversation is more a method of church life than a single, specific purpose. Indeed, some of the churches from the categories above approach the Bible and Christian tradition in a conversational mode (e.g., churches seeking to change culture, minoritized churches, and emergent churches). Based on the authority they assign to the Bible and Christian tradition, some churches cannot be conversational in the way conversation is described here. Elevator churches, for instance, are committed to the priority of their interpretations of the Bible and Christian orthodoxy.

Community of Support and First Aid Station

Some churches that operate in this vein believe that sources outside the Bible and Christian tradition can offer perceptions of the fulfilled life—and obstacles to the fulfilled life—that are not found in Scripture and tradition. Furthermore, such churches may conclude that elements of the fulfilled life as described in parts of the Bible—such as the prescription for wives to be subject to their husbands—are actually obstacles to God's purposes. Such churches, then, need to help their communities reinterpret God's aims.

Churches Transforming Culture

The *conversational church as agent of liberation*, like its receiving and applying counterpart, seeks to participate with God in efforts to liberate people from systems of repression. A primary difference between receiving/applying and conversational churches is that the latter are willing to question and possibly reconceive some of their fundamental ideas, values, and practices as a result of encountering others who are oppressed, others who oppress, and others otherwise related to specific situations. Some churches that *hope to transform culture through direct engagement* with culture can also be conversational. This church is open to being transformed by its encounters with others.

Minoritized Community

Many minoritized congregations are conversational communities as they bring dimensions of racial and ethnic culture into dialogue with elements of the Bible and Christian tradition so the church may rethink the relationship of these two important bodies of perception. While conversation may lead the church to think that some elements of its cultural heritage should be supplanted by perspectives from the Bible and theology, the conversational community may also conclude that elements of its cultural heritage are more authoritative than the Bible and Eurocentric interpretation of

Christian tradition. Some minoritized conversational congregations reso-
nate with liberation themes (per above).

Emergent Church

While sharing many of the characteristics of applying and receiving emergent churches cited above (e.g., postdenominational, pluralistic in theology,
oriented to missional living with emphasis on personal evangelism and
social justice), conversational emergent congregations are open not only
to learning from others but to reshaping elements of Christian theology in
response to others. The emergent churches not only respect diverse interpretations of the Bible, Christian tradition, and ethical perspectives, but also
see conversation as essential to interpreting God's leading and to identifying
appropriate forms of mission for particular contexts.

Conversation Can Lead to Fresh Understandings of the Purpose of the Church

Some churches that are communities of conversation cannot categorically
state their immediate purposes in the ways just described. The church as
community of conversation rethinks its relationship to culture in accord
with changing cultural dynamics, and articulates accordingly. Conversation
helps the church reveal the character of the culture in a particular era. A
fundamental intention of the church's conversations is not only to help the
church come to an adequate understanding of God's purposes but also to
help the ecclesial community identify how it can join those purposes as they
are coming to expression. At times, for example, conversation may lead a
church to think that God's purposes in a moment resemble those of the
church as agent of liberation, or community of support. A significant difference, of course, is that the conversation keeps going so the church may be
open to fresh perceptions of how it can join God's purposes.

Voices in the Conversation

The number of voices in ecclesial conversations is limited only by the number of inhabitants in the cosmos. The church seeks to identify what each
voice asks the church to believe and do, and reflects on the degree to which
that voice invites the community to believe and do things that are consistent
with the congregation's deepest convictions concerning God, as well as the

degree to which that voice reinforces or challenges the church's perceptions of what is appropriate for the church to believe and do. A representative list of voices includes the following.

- The diverse theological perspectives of the Bible. From a conversational perspective, the Bible is less a book and more a library of diverse theological points of view.

- The history of the church. These voices include affirmations of faith (creeds), statements of doctrine, perspectives from different denominations and theological movements, and viewpoints of individual theologians.

- Today's congregation, denomination, or ecumenical setting. Conversational churches attend to the experience of other Christians and churches who differ in social location.

- Others beyond Christian community. This vast body includes not only other religions, but people who are not religious, the various sciences, arts, philosophy, and, of course, individuals and communities.

- The experience of immediate participants in the conversation. The experience of the conversationalists can add important data to the conversation. Furthermore, we need to be cognizant and critical of our own experience and preassociations so they do not unconsciously distort the conversation by inappropriately filtering what we hear from others and even from ourselves.

From the perspective of a conversational church, some of these voices articulate points of view resulting from earlier conversations. Such perceptions are historically conditioned. A conversational church seeks not only to be clear about why particular perspectives emerged in their originating settings but seeks to explore the degree to which such points continue to be at home in the world today.

Conversation Takes Multiple Forms

Conversation can take multiple forms, among them:

- Face-to-face interaction with give and take. People in the same physical space can talk with one another in one-to-one conversations, in small group settings, in large church councils and assemblies. Through electronic media, such as Skype, face-to-face interactions can occur across long distance.

- Between people and written texts (such as the Bible and affirmations of faith). The text is an other. Conversation can also be prompted by other modes of expression, such as electronic media.

- In assemblies and classes. Conversation here is sometimes monological in form (one person speaking) but dialogical in character (the one voice prompts participants to encounter others).

- Experiences. The things that happen to us—such as mission trips—often bring Christians into encounters with others.

- With oneself. We can sometimes be other even to ourselves. Conversations can take place within the mind. Indeed, some of my best conversations occur when I am talking with myself.

Regardless of the form, in real conversation the church listens to others and considers possibilities for life, even while presenting its own possibilities to others.

When Conversation Fails

Conversations do not always arrive at conclusions. In such cases a workable resolution (provisional) may be for participants respectfully to let their points of view stand alongside one another in the marketplace of ideas. If one viewpoint must have legislative power over others, people associated with that viewpoint should continue to listen to others. Even when conversation does not make it possible for differing individuals and groups to come together in common perspective, conversation could lead to mutual understanding and tolerance.

The situation is more difficult when quality of life is at stake, or when individuals and groups with divergent perspectives will not enter into real conversation but only seek to persuade others into their perspectives. It is most difficult when others attempt to impose their will on church and culture. In such cases, the church's internal conversation may lead it—with a heavy heart—to conclude that the most timely approach is for the church to articulate its own position forcefully. Even so, the church should offer the possibility of conversation to those whom the church resists.

Practical Implications for Thinking of the Church as Community of Conversation

The following are among practical implications that result from thinking of the church as a community of conversation. These implications are not unique to this church, but they are distinctive.

Listening, Really Listening, to Others

Listening is one of the most important skills of this church. At base, listening means hearing the point of view of the other from the perspective of the other. A temptation for the listening community is to impose their categories on the individual or group to whom they listen. We often hear what we want to hear. If we are predisposed favorably toward others, we tend to hear them as echoes of us. If we are predisposed negatively towards others, we tend to hear them defensively or antagonistically. A conversational church needs to make an ethical commitment to discipline itself to hear the other as other.

Of course, the ways in which the other *wants* to be understood are not always the way in which the listening community *can or should understand* them. On the one hand, the other may not be aware of dynamics in the situation that affect the other's perception. Insofar as possible, the church needs to listen to the story behind the story at work in the world of the other. On the other hand, the church should not use such subtexts as an excuse for casually dismissing the voice of the other.

Given the relativity of all awareness, we can never perceive the other in a pure and objective way. But we can become as conscious and critical as we can of our perception of the other.

Regarding Others with Respect

The early twenty-first century is a time of fractiousness in human community. While polarization and rancor are particularly evident in politics, suspicion and antipathy affect many other sectors of life. Individuals and groups frequently regard others with disrespect. Sadly, churches too often mirror these larger cultural patterns.

Showing respect for others does not mean that the church agrees with the theological and ethical commitments of others. Indeed, a conversation may lead the church to conclude that others are mistaken in particular attitudes or behaviors. To maintain its integrity, the church may need to criticize the prescriptions of others. Yet the church needs to honor the conviction that others are created in the image of God. Disagreement should not allow us to reduce others to caricature, much less to attempt to manipulate them or to silence them.

Respectful conversation among others is a gift the church can bring to the early twenty-first-century world. While the church does not have a monopoly on such interaction, the diversity of the body of Christ makes the church especially amenable to becoming a model for how people who see things differently can live together in community-encouraging ways.

Ready to Live with Discomfort

Conversation is often effervescent as conversation partners make exciting discoveries. But, conversation can be hard when individuals and communities have the courage to say difficult things to one another and to be open to things that are difficult to hear. Some of our cherished values and behaviors can come into question in ways that make us nervous. Conversation can be hard when we come face to face with people in painful situations. Conversation can be hard when we must dialogue with people to whom we respond in negative, visceral ways.

The blunt fact is that conversation sometimes leads to discomfort. Nevertheless, naming the causes of such discomfort can be an important part of the encounter with the other. Not only does it bring honesty to the conversation but it can provoke us to recognize and claim things about ourselves we need to face.

A Provisional Attitude

The twin factors of (1) acknowledging the relativity of all perception and (2) of continually being open to the fresh perspectives of others, combine to mean that church as community of conversation has an experimental attitude. That is, the church does not regard its resolutions—about doctrine, ethics, mission, church organization, cooperation with others—as permanent conclusions, but as the best we can do at present, with the understanding that we will re-evaluate such concerns in light of fresh encounters.

A provisional attitude does not mean the church has no convictions or that everything is up in the air all the time. It means that we do not take our interpretations so seriously as to make them absolute, even idolatrous. The church should keep a window open to catch fresh breezes of otherness blowing through the culture.

Humility

The various relativities at work in the church as community of conversation mean that this church should live with humility. Humility means (1) acknowledging one's identity as a finite creature whose perspectives on life are limited and (2) respectfully engaging others in search of adequate understandings of God's purposes. In a culture in which there is much arrogance, braggadocio, and dismissiveness towards others, humility means taking oneself and one's own group with full seriousness but not in such a way as to make our own perspectives imperial.

Humility can also play an important role in the church's relationship with others. Others—especially from outside the church—are more likely to take conversation with the church seriously when they sense that traffic can run two ways on the bridge. Some individuals and groups outside the church have the impression that from the church's point of view, the traffic runs one way: from the church to the culture, often in the form of the church passing judgment, or in attempting to impose the church's will on the larger order, or in the church simply being irrelevant to real life today. Such perceptions can be barriers to the willingness of others to interchange with the church. A posture of humility in which the church indicates openness to others may help others be open to interacting with the church.

Nimble and Open to Reconceiving (Most) Aspects of Its Life

In conversation about the church as conversation, William B. Kincaid of Christian Theological Seminary pointed out that in the optimum situation, a conversational church needs to be nimble, that is, able to make adjustments in its life fairly quickly in response to changing circumstances and compelling insights. This nimbleness pertains to what the church believes about God, Christ, the Spirit, and Christian doctrine as well as to the church's relationship with others in the larger world. It also pertains to how the church goes about such things as worship, preaching, education, leadership, mission, and even matters of church organization.

A Conversational Spirit throughout the Church

Despite the effervescent claims of this chapter that all aspects of the life and witness of the church are open to conversation, churches sometimes feel locked into particular patterns of ecclesial life that are hierarchical and even authoritarian. In such cases, a church may nevertheless bring a conversational spirit to aspects of its life. For example, the Roman Catholic Church, the Episcopal Church and various Wesleyan bodies are partly defined by having bishops. In these churches, bishops can approach their leadership from a conversational perspective that begins by listening to others (e.g., priests, ministers, and congregations). Congregations can seek to initiate conversation with bishops.

Critical Reflection on the Church as Community of Conversation

Every way of understanding the church has both strengths and weaknesses. We conclude with critical reflection on the notion of the church as community of conversation.

Making God into Our Own Image

Every church struggles with the impulse to make God into its own image. This danger is particularly strong in the church as community of conversation since this church recognizes that all constructs—including those about God—are open to reconsideration. A conversational church is tempted to remake our understanding of God in our own image, thereby losing transformative possibilities that come from encountering God as the great other. Of course, the church can never have pure and objective perception of God. But when we perceive God to be little more than an extension of ourselves, such a God can offer us little more than our present life. When our perceptions of God begin to look too much like the faces we see in the mirror in the morning, we need to engage in conversation with others about this great other.

Using Conversation to Serve Our Own Ends

Ideally, conversation is an encounter with others that provokes us to become clearer about the other, ourselves, and the possibilities for our relationships.[11] However, participants in a conversation can use conversation to serve their own (often prejudged) ends. This phenomenon can occur unconsciously or consciously as we seek partners, ask questions, and pose possibilities that point to the outcome we desire. We can exaggerate some voices and ignore

11. Note the similarity between these ideas and the "scripted conversations" that Lynne Westfield describes in this volume, pages 123–26.

or silence others. While we may begin a conversation hoping for a particular destination, a genuine conversation means that we are genuinely open to how it might unfold and where it might go.

An ideal conversational situation might be monitored by someone familiar with the participants and the issues but not directly involved, and who does not have a vested interest in the outcome. Good consultants, for instance, play this role when a congregation, agency, or denomination seeks to rethink itself. Since an outside consultant is beyond the reach of many expressions of the church, ministers and leaders can try to play a comparable role, declaring "time outs" for the church to pause and reflect on the conversational process.

Too Selective in the Voices to Which the Church Listens

A church seeking to be a community of conversation is finite; hence that church cannot listen to all of the infinity of others in the world. Because of its finitude the church must be selective in the others to whom it listens in connection with a particular issue. Nevertheless, the church is sometimes too selective in the others to whom we listen. In the press of an urgent conversation, we may overlook voices that do not immediately come to our attention. The church may lean towards listening to those who are sympathetic to our existing viewpoints or who promise to confirm directions we might like to go. I confess that I would often prefer to avoid conversations and conversation partners that make me feel uncomfortable. While a finite church cannot listen to the infinity of others, the church can develop a regular rhythm of listening to voices that could prompt questions, insight, and reconsideration.

Anxiety in the Church

Many people today seek certainty, especially in the anxiety-strewn early twenty-first century. Conversations of the kind described in this book may leave some folk feeling anxious. "What can I really believe? What can I count on? What can I not count on?" The conversation itself can spark anxiety. A minister or congregation moving in the direction of becoming a conversational community needs to deal pastorally with such uncertainty and anxiety.

We can seldom be free of all anxiety. Nevertheless a theologically appropriate way to frame a response to conversation-anxiety is also a good place to end this chapter. The conviction that we are in community with

God and with one another can carry us from the present moment when we see in part to that great time when we see God face to face. We are not alone. Indeed, from the perspective on God articulated by Michael Miller in chapter 3, the community of conversation is not only a means of mutual support but is itself a sign of the divine presence.

Questions for Discussion

1. Describe how the church of which you are part understands its relationship to the cultures in which it lives (neighborhood, community, national, and global)? For example, does your church see its relationship to the culture as largely negative, positive, ambiguous?

2. How do you see the actual purpose of the church of which you are a part? Does it manifest one (or more) of the purposes mentioned in this chapter? In this regard, is your church more applicational or conversational? What would you like to see as the purpose of your church?

3. When thinking about its identity and purpose, to what voices does your church listen most attentively? The Bible? Voices from Christian tradition (affirmations of faith, denominational history, particular theologians, etc.). Voices within the congregation? Voices of others outside the Christian house?

4. Are there voices to which your church gives less attention than it should? What are some practical steps you might take to help your church listen to them?

5. If you see yourself as a member of a church that is a community of conversation, what might you say to people who say the following:

   a. "Your church has abandoned the clear and authoritative word of God, especially as it is found in the Bible and orthodox Christian tradition."

   b. "Your church uses conversation to formulate a version of Christian faith that is to your own liking. You simply make the gospel and the church into your own image."

   c. "Your conversational church is too timid. The church is to be the contemporary prophet—exposing injustice, denouncing evil, and organizing resistance."

Further Reading

Allen, O. Wesley, Jr. *The Homiletic of All Believers: A Conversational Approach*. Louisville: Westminster John Knox, 2005.

Allen, Ronald J. "Preaching as Mutual Critical Correlation through Conversation." In *Purposes of Preaching*, edited by Jana Childers, 1–22. St. Louis: Chalice, 2004.

———. *Thinking Theologically: The Preacher as Theologian*. Elements of Preaching. Minneapolis: Fortress, 2008.

Dulles, Avery. *Models of the Church*. Expanded Edition. Garden City, NJ: Doubleday, 1987.

Küng, Hans. *The Church*. 1976. Reprinted. New York: Continuum, 2001.

Kysar, Robert. *Stumbling in the Light: New Testament Images for a Changing Church*. St. Louis: Chalice, 1999.

Minear, Paul S. *Images of the Church in the New Testament*. Philadelphia: Westminster, 1960.

Niebuhr, H. Richard. *Christ and Culture*. New York: Harper & Row, 1951.

Williamson, Clark M., and Ronald J. Allen. *The Vital Church: Teaching, Worship, Service, Learning*. St. Louis: Chalice, 1998.

———. *Way of Blessing, Way of Life. A Christian Theology*. St. Louis: Chalice, 1999.

2

The Minister as Conversation Partner

JOHN S. MCCLURE

☙ MOST MINISTERS HAVE in mind an image for themselves as minister. Although ministers are sometimes intentional and self-conscious when choosing and adopting a ministerial model or image, often this image emerges naturally over time out of personal, social, missional, theological, liturgical, educational, pastoral, or denominational commitments. Scholars have attempted to cluster these images into categories. Donald E. Messer, for instance, identified six such images: wounded healer, servant leader, political mystic (prophet), liberator, practical theologian, and good shepherd.[1] William Willimon identifies another set: media personality, political negotiator, therapist, manager, resident activist, preacher, and servant leader.[2] Robert Dykstra traces images for the minister in the works of Heije Faber (minister as circus clown), Alasdair Campbell (minister as "wise fool"), James E. Dittes (minister as "ascetic witness"), before developing his own image of the minister as "intimate stranger."[3]

For most of us, our ministerial self-image is developed in response to perceived needs or issues within the Christian community. If the situation seems rife with personal and social illness then the "wounded healer" makes sense. If the community is suffering an overdose of authoritarian leadership, then the "servant leader" image may be best. If one's context is perceived as an unjust social system, then the minister may be attracted to images such as "political mystic," prophet, or "political negotiator." In each instance, one's

1. Messner, *Contemporary Images*.

2. Willimon, *Theology and Practice*.

3. Dykstra, *Images of Pastoral Care*.

25

image for ministry derives from one's perception of the current condition of the church in the world.

Minister as Counterculturalist

In the current generation, by far the most compelling and popular image for the minister might be labeled "minister as counterculturalist." William Willimon is perhaps the strongest proponent of this view, taking many of his ideas from the work of theological ethicist Stanley Hauerwas.[4] Charles Colson, Walter Brueggemann, Rodney Clapp, and John Howard Yoder are other prominent spokespersons with different theological perspectives who have articulated a similar view of the minister.[5]

For those who adopt this image, the minister is a countercultural leader. Ministers are "aliens and exiles" (1 Pet 2:11) who march to the beat of a different drummer. They understand the current-situation as post-Enlightenment, post-Christendom, and post-denominational. In this situation, the church is freed from its overly comfortable co-optation by the dominant culture, and can now recover and express its true countercultural genius. The minister will not look or act like anyone else (managers, therapists, etc.) because the minister is ordained to be an utterly unique person whose actions and words will always seem odd according to prevailing cultural standards and mores. The gospel demands radically distinct forms of behavior and speech, including pacifism, nonviolent resistance to principalities and powers, an insistence on the oddness of biblical language, the rejection of any attempt to translate biblical language and categories into cultural terms, and an inculturationist or catechetical approach to liturgics, preaching, and evangelism.

The idea of the minister as counterculturalist is built on a particular kind of narrative theological method sometimes called the "Yale school" of narrative theology.[6] Ministers attracted to this theological method believe that all religions, denominations, and cultural worldviews are defined by the way that they narrate the world. In today's context, larger "metanarratives" such as the metanarratives of Enlightenment, Socialism, Capitalism, and Christianity, have been reduced in size and importance and now take their place alongside other cultural and social narratives. These narratives are like games, or "language-games," generating very different worldviews.

---

4. Hauerwas and Willimon, *Resident Aliens*; Willimon, *Pastor*.

5. Colson, *Countercultural Christians*; Brueggemann, *Prophetic Imagination*; Brueggemann, *Cadences of Home*; Brueggemann, *Journey to the Common Good*; Clapp, *Peculiar People*; Yoder, *Politics of Jesus*.

6. See Comstock, "Truth of Meaning," for a summary of this school of thought.

In this situation, ministers are *radical pluralists*. They believe that the rules and concepts for one game cannot be translated into the rules and concepts of another. The world is a pluralistic arena of competing language games or worldviews, some religious and some not. The Christian minister is obliged to represent the Christian language game as forcefully and conspicuously as possible. The odd grammar of the Christian language game, provided by Scripture and tradition, must be made larger, more consistent, and more univocal.

For those who adopt the image of the minister as counterculturalist, the idea of Christian "practice" and "best practices" has become very important as a means of shoring up Christian identity. Through careful historical and ethnographic study, ministers can seek out best Christian practices for work, play, dying, hospitality, worship, pastoral care, healing, preaching, and so on. Best practices cannot be discerned by talking with those from other disciplines, traditions, or worldviews. They can only be discovered through analysis of what Christians do uniquely and best, especially those aspects that appear to be distinct from cultural influences, or the influences of other worldviews. Because of this, ministers are wary of secular theories of rhetoric, communication, or composition when learning to preach, reject much of what is learned in psychology textbooks when learning to provide pastoral care, and are suspicious of anthropological methods of cultural and social translation when engaging in evangelism. Ministerial leadership can only be learned by observing carefully what ministers do when living out the countercultural narrative of the Christian Scriptures and tradition. The current situation and context of the church is one of competing postmodern narratives, and the ministry as a set of internally adjudicated best Christian practices designed to shore up the church's singular narrativity.

This thumbnail sketch of the minister as counterculturalist is painted in broad strokes, designed to push into the foreground the basic *habitus* or "feel for the game" inherent in this image for the minister. Many scholars and some practitioners will adopt a more nuanced countercultural stance. This basic approach to ministry, however, with its very large body of literature, its excellent spokespersons, and its popularity at ministerial conferences and retreat centers, has become the dominant image for the minister in our time.

Conversation Partner, Not Counterculturalist

This chapter will suggest a very different situation in the world today, in need of a very different image for the minister. This situation is one of divisive, and increasingly violent *cultural-narrative entrenchment*. The church's current social and political context and its inner life has become a potentially dangerous and divisive climate of competing and mutually exclusive narratives and monologues. Entrenchment within different and competing cultural narratives is destroying the fabric of life both inside and outside the church, creating a situation in which "countering" others has been turned into a force for division across religions and cultures that has tremendous destructive potential.

In today's popular media, countering opposing narratives has become the prevailing model for political rhetoric. Increasingly media outlets are adopting strict, consistent ideological/narrative frameworks. It is now evident that "counter-speaking" is what sells. People tend to seek out like-minded, self-referential news sources that are defined by their stances *against* certain others. In a nutshell, counterculture has been commodified and largely co-opted by the prevailing culture. Paradoxically, counterculturalist ministry mirrors this prevailing cultural norm, in which competing monologues vie for control and power as commodities within the marketplace of ideas. For ministers to adopt the image of minister as counterculturalist is to adopt the predominant cultural image for courage and "authenticity" within popular culture itself.

I do not wish to wade into arguments regarding whether, in fact, it is possible to be untainted by other cultural currents—whether in fact a counter-cultural posture is even possible. Kathryn Tanner has demonstrated adequately the difficulties inherent in all culturally separatist thinking.[7] Neither do I wish to argue against the importance of standing up to unjust or potentially violent cultural or religious ideas of impulses. A critical posture to dangerous or violent worldviews is a crucial component of any minister's identity.

I only wish to argue that in our present context it takes more courage, and requires more genuine Christian authenticity to adopt what may, at first glance, seem to be a less exciting image for the minister: the *minister as conversation partner*. What is needed most in this generation are not theological narrativists, but theologically informed pragmatists and public theologians. In a situation of competing cultural narratives or worldviews, what is needed are not those who are focused on further cultural-narrative entrenchment, but those who are able to relate and connect worldviews, and negotiate shared meaning and truth *across* differences on behalf of the common flourishing of all.

---

7. Tanner, *Theories of Culture.*

Another way of putting this is to say that we need ministers who are *dynamic pluralists*, not radical pluralists. The dynamic pluralist, like the radical pluralist, agrees that each worldview or religion has to some extent a narrative quality including rules, practices, and symbols often shaped by a long internal history. Where the dynamic pluralist disagrees with the radical pluralist is on the possibility of communication and correlation across worldviews. For the dynamic pluralist, there is much to be learned from strangers who are living according to the rules, practices, and symbols of other religious and non-religious language games. In fact, the dynamic pluralist sees all of us as constantly conversing between, correlating, and re-framing multiple worldviews. This is not to completely de-center the Christian worldview. Rather, it is to insist on the permeability of the boundaries of that worldview, and to seek to honor the way in which Christianity is, in fact, always "othering" itself—seeking its deeper identity through creative relationships with those who are different.

In what follows, the words "conversation" and "partner" are closely associated. Partnership was an important idea in the New Testament church. In the book of Philippians (1:5; 4:15) Paul uses the idea of partnership (*koinonia*) to describe his ministry. According to New Testament scholar John Koenig, the early Christian community became partners in ministry with a host of wandering itinerants.[8] Congregational ministers such as Barnabas, Phoebe, Philologus, and Julia were in constant conversation with others within and beyond the community in ways designed to build up an ever-expanding partnership or *koinonia* in the gospel. Ministry, therefore, is a process of becoming ever-better conversation partners in service to the gospel. It is this image of minister as conversation partner that is needed in our current situation in which our obsession with living into wholly consistent narratives or worldviews is driving wedges between people in the church and in the larger society. With this argument for the minister as conversation partner in mind, let me identify several themes that this image brings to the table that illustrate its timeliness.

Key Themes for the Minister as Conversation Partner

From Fear to Love

The current social and cultural climate is rife with fear of others. The so-called "culture wars" pit liberals against conservatives, and the politics of identity pits women against men, race against race, and persons of differing

8. Koenig, *New Testament Hospitality*, 109.

sexual orientations against one another. Immigration policy is becoming more xenophobic and aggressive. Fear of persons of Islamic faith is on the rise. School de-segregation policies established in the sixties and seventies are being overturned. Children are instructed from an early age to be fearful of "strangers." In this situation, the rhetoric of isolation, conflict, intimidation, prejudice, hatred, and distrust thrives.

Learning how to hold conversations, instead of only debates, across different worldviews, narratives, and languages is needed desperately in order to help reverse this trend. Perhaps more than ever before, we in the church and in the larger culture need to learn how to approach those who are different from us in love, with the business of seeking new ground that will move in the direction of creating communities of mutual support in mind. The image of the minister as conversation partner suggests a community shaped by mutual honor, listening, reconciliation, compassion, and mercy.

An Ecclesiology of Welcome

One of the key reasons for embracing the image of the minister as conversation partner is to build a genuine community of welcome. Many children of the evangelical megachurch generation, sometimes called post-evangelicals, are leaving the churches of their childhood, finding these congregations stifling of thought and narrow in perspective. Many of these churches were founded on principles outlined by the Church Growth Movement, especially the principle of homogeneity, whereby churches were designed to resemble market niches to attract people with very similar backgrounds and interests. Young post-evangelicals find that genuine diversity is missing; not merely demographic diversity, but diversity of leadership, diversity of engagement with other religious traditions, denominations, and ideas, and diversity of theological and ethical perspectives. As they see it, the welcome mat for many of these churches is closely guarded by gatekeepers who are largely unresponsive to their interests and social-ethical commitments.

At the same time, many who were raised within liberal, mainstream denominations express a similar concern that the welcome of the church has been constricted. Progressive social ideals and Christian faith have been woven into a seamless cloth, and identifying different perspectives or rationales for faithful practice within the biblical witness is not welcomed. This tends to create an unwelcome atmosphere for many, especially those with more evangelical commitments.

In this context, a ministry of conversation promises an honest dialogue in which the most difficult and substantial differences (of doctrine, race and ethnicity, culture and class, worldview, etc.) are welcomed and, in fact, deemed *essential* to the nature and witness of Christian community. The minister as conversation partner welcomes such difference as the very key to growth in the life of faith. Embracing difference is not based on an enlightened commitment to egalitarianism, acceptance, and tolerance. Rather, it is based on a more fundamental theological commitment to the *ecclesial-communal nature of Christian truth*. Within this perspective, welcoming all perspectives on the great Subject in our midst (gospel) is more likely to yield truer knowledge of that Subject. Only by coming into complete community with God's truth can that truth be known.

A Witness to Unity

Another reason for embracing the image of the minister as conversation partner is its power to promote unity within the body of Christ. Unity is something quite different than homogeneity. One of the fundamental issues for those who observe Christianity today is the massive disunity within and across the churches. Congregations and denominations are antagonistically divided on issues such as the leadership of women, abortion, homosexuality, multiculturalism, and doctrine. Interactions among Christians of different viewpoints (liberal and conservative, mainline and evangelical, Protestant and Catholic) can be quite hostile. By contrast, at the heart of the ministry of conversation lies an enduring focus on *partnership*, even in the face of serious disagreement. The more churches can shift their mode of relating from mutual exclusion to conversation, the more a deeper witness to unity will emerge within the church as a whole. Disagreement can be re-framed as difference between ongoing conversation partners who are committed to one another, rather than as difference that marks off insiders from outsiders.

Relational Authority

In today's late modern context, authority is increasingly de-centered and disseminated among a plurality of influences, experts, and resources within a network of connections and relationships. In human terms, this means that people are less willing to accept the authority of hired professionals or gate-keepers (academics, clergy, religious leaders, etc.) on the one hand, or institutions and traditions on the other. Authority is re-located at the intersection of pluralistic, multi-perspective, situated conversations in which clergy, and the institutions and traditions they represent, are only one voice.

A conversational model of ministry works well in this situation, because it allows authentic, authoritative norms for faith and practice to emerge within a broad network of resources, including the complex knowledge represented by educated clergy. The ministry of conversation is grounded in what Jackson Carroll calls "the relational dimension of authority."[9] Authority, in this model, is a function of the relationship one has with others in the exploration of this huge range of resources for the life of faith. Relational authority comes from developing intentional relationships and fostering a sense of a shared human quest for Christian truth and values. It is built-upon trust and the genuine belief that all are working together in ministry to plumb the depths of as many resources as possible in the search for the meaning of the gospel in today's world.

Looking Afresh at the Past While Living towards the Future

Another reason for adopting this image for the minister is the need in most churches for renewed conversation with their past and future. The minister is not only a conversation partner with those in the present moment but is also one who brings the community of faith into conversation with its past and future. The past is constantly re-opened and forms of counter-memory are consulted. In this process, memory retrieves the wisdom of all of those whose voices may have been silenced throughout the denomination's or congregation's history. Past practices, traditions, doctrines, and warrants for the faith are always open for re-assessment. This brings about a new form of *anamnesis* or memory within the community of faith, one that is open to change and revision.

At the same time, conversation within the community of faith looks forward, striving to hear the voices of those yet to come. Will our current thoughts and practices cause suffering for future generations? What do their voices tell us to heed? This encourages the church to consider how its past and present have serious implications for the future, and opens the future up to new possibilities. In conversation with the communion of saints to come, the community of faith realizes that the future projected by the present may be problematic, but this can be changed. The future doesn't have to look like the present or the past. New choices can yield a new and better future.

Before deciding that anything is true or worthy of commitment, the community of conversation examines whether an idea has caused unnecessary suffering in the past, or might cause suffering in the future. The present is not the final measuring rod for truth or practice. Truth-claims are both

9. Carroll, *As One with Authority*, 58–70.

anamnestic and eschatological in nature, open to revision based on voices from the community's past and future.

Reclaiming the Public Realm

Another good reason for the image of the minister as conversation partner lies in its great potential to restore a public dimension to ministry. The public realm is where diverse people come together to deliberate about the common good. In the late modern period, spaces where this kind of public deliberation can take place have receded as the private realm (home theatre, family, social network) has grown larger. For some people, the congregation has even become a kind of private realm. At the same time, impersonal systems of exchange and power (bureaucracy, political parties and lobbies, technologies of investment, payment, and exchange) have also become larger and more invasive, encroaching on the public realm.

Ideally, the public realm is a place where people of all sorts make decisions *together* about how systems will be structured and function on their behalf. Public discourse and deliberation is increasingly difficult, however, as the public realm is shrinking and replaced by mediated public debate on television, radio, and the internet. As already suggested, this debate is largely monological, univocal, and oppositional in nature, which limits public reasoning to the sparring of political opinion leaders.

In this context, the ministry of conversation becomes a training ground for public discourse across difference. Churches become places where a uniquely compassionate form of civil discourse is learned. Within these conversations, theological ideas are weighed as decisions are made in service to the common good. Instead of politicizing religious and theological ideas, these ideas are explored critically for their usefulness in shaping and articulating public values, policies, and actions.

Characteristics of the Ministry of Conversation

Having identified reasons for the image of minister as conversation partner it is now time to discuss with more particularity the practical characteristics of ministry understood as conversation.

Motivated by the Love of Christ

The ministry of conversation is motivated by the love of God demonstrated in the life, death, and resurrection of Jesus Christ. This love is a gift. As *agapic* love it is unconditional and exists outside of the logic of exchange, or "this-for-that." It does not live under the shadow of expectations of either reward or punishment. Informed by *agapic* love, the Christian minister desires relationship and communication for their own sake. Conversation is not primarily a means to an end. Rather, it is a good gift that we share as those who belong to a community of faith and the community of truth-seekers across faiths. It is its own end and is experienced in the first instance as a gracious gift that brings people of good faith together.

Governed by the Guest-Host Rhythm of Hospitality

For the Christian minister, conversation becomes a form of hospitality. Hospitality to strangers or those who are different from us is rooted in a biblical tradition that instructs members of the community of faith regarding the redemptive rhythm that can exist between welcoming hosts and responsive guests. This guest-host rhythm is found in many stories of hospitality throughout the Bible. From Sarah and Abraham, hosting angels unawares, to the disciples hosting a very special guest on the road to Emmaus, ministry is shaped by conversations in which strangers are first hosted, and then, in a surprising twist of affairs, become hosts who bring special gifts to us. In one moment we are hosts welcoming others. Then, as we attend more deeply to guests, we discover that we have become guests, hosted by someone with unique and important spiritual wisdom. The roles of host and guest are constantly shifting. The ministry of conversation, therefore, is energized and moved forward by difference, by constantly shifting asymmetries of knowledge, experience, and authority.

Energized by the Spirit to Discover "New Ground"

Conversation and ministry converge when the Holy Spirit and the human spirit join together to create new grounds for understanding between two or more persons. According the Lutheran theologian Regin Prenter, the Holy Spirit is Creator-Spirit or *Spiritus Creator*.[10] The book of Genesis tells us that God's Spirit brooded upon the waters and brought forth new ground upon

---

10. Prenter, *Spiritus Creator*.

which we all could live together. This creative work continued throughout the history of the people of God, as new forms of community and new possibilities for life and redemption were discovered time and time again. In each instance, the Spirit worked with the human spirit to create something new.

Religious educator James E. Loder argued for an analogy between the creative human spirit and creative Holy Spirit.[11] This analogy is most often active when a conflict or problem of profound existential and spiritual proportion is engaged and eventually solved. When solving such problems the Holy Spirit helps the human spirit through a creative "getting outside the box" or re-framing of the problem in order to discover a new insight or a way forward. In like fashion, the Holy Spirit and human spirit work together in ministerial conversation searching for new grounds. When we respond to the Spirit's creative, inventive power, conversation becomes co-creative with God's Spirit of new ways to become the people of God together in today's world.

One of the most powerful dynamics in ministerial conversation occurs when a topic or issue is re-framed in a way that is redemptive. As the conversation proceeds a new perspective can begin to emerge that places a different and often unexpected frame onto a topic, issue, or concern. We see this over and over again in the gospels, whether it is a re-framing of the meaning of greatness, who is neighbor, who is sinner, or the meaning of resurrection. What was initially seen as a problem is suddenly seen as an opportunity. What was seen as accepted practice is suddenly seen as potentially harmful. What once seemed righteous is suddenly unrighteous. What people thought they understood well is suddenly a barrier to understanding rightly. In many ways, the ministry of conversation is a constant process of framing and re-framing the core values, beliefs, assumptions, and aspirations held by the minister, congregation, and community.

Plurivocal, Not Univocal

One of the most remarkable aspects of the biblical canon is its plurivocality: the rich diversity of writers who contribute to its composition. In a similar fashion, the ministry of conversation is plurivocal rather than univocal in nature. Univocal or single-voiced speaking is the often the norm in today's society. The political arena in particular is dominated by mutually exclusive monologues. Univocal speaking of this type tends to create insider-outsider, us-them, center-margin dualities that divide and fragment the arena of public discourse.

11. Loder, *Transforming Moment*.

The ministry of conversation disrupts this rhythm of competing mono-logues, thus modeling speaking-with, rather that speaking-at/to, as the best way to determine what it true, right, and best. Instead of being univocal, truth is plurivocal, multi-voiced, interactive, and co-inventive. Truth is always a matter of seeking *new* ground, rather than insisting on *my* ground.

The Yes in Every No, and the No in Every Yes

The minister as conversation partner operates very differently than the counterculturalist when it comes to affirming or denying the truth of an idea or situation. Although there are some theological truths that can be un-equivocally affirmed, and some evils in the world that should be univocally rejected, most ministerial situations contain a great deal of ambiguity and require a certain amount of humility. The minister as conversation partner is not afraid to say "no" or "yes." But within each "no" or "yes," the minister is aware of grey areas and limitations that may exist. This means that hy-perbole, overstatement, and "one-way for all time" statements are usually avoided. When affirming an idea, the minister learns to ask, "Where is the 'no' in this?" When rejecting an idea, the minister learns to ask, "Where is the 'yes' in this?"

Empowering Others

When reading the gospels, it is exhilarating to watch as ordinary women and men are empowered through conversations with one another and with Jesus to become witnesses to the Reign of God. The ministry of conversation empowers others by sharing the power to speak. It invites others to assume responsibility for the direction of their own lives as people of faith or as those in search of God. It strives to give everyone an active role in the in-terpretation of their situation and in making decisions about their spiritual well-being. This is sometimes called *hearing others into speech*. This idea, first articulated by Nelle Morton, refers to the kind of patient listening that is designed to help another person find and claim their own subjectivity and personhood before God.[12] Hearing into speech involves creating spaces in which there is a certain kind of silence aimed at allowing and inviting others to venture forth with thoughts and ideas about themselves and about God. If as ministers we are always talking, telling our story, pushing our agendas, asserting the superiority of our ideas, setting forth our plans, or proffer-

12. Morton, *The Journey Is Home*, 205–6.

ing our evaluations, it is impossible to make this kind of space available. Hearing into speech is a practice that involves maximizing silence without interference, taking in what another says without appearing disquieted or troubled, or rushing in to comfort or escape what is difficult or painful. The goal is to allow and encourage another person to find their own voice in matters pertaining to both self and God.

Centered on God's Emergent Word

Ministers are often considered special ambassadors *bringing* God's Word to a congregation, either as heralds of God (messengers) or as witnesses on the congregation's behalf. Although this is partly true, a conversational view of ministry shifts away from these metaphors toward a view of the interpretation of the Word of God as constantly *emerging* in the give-and-take of conversations among human beings who are genuinely seeking to discern God's truth in today's world. The ministry of conversation is grounded in a "subject-centered" *epistemology*. Coming to an interpretation of God's Word for today is neither a minister-centered, nor congregation-centered process, but is centered on the great Subject in our midst: sometimes called God's Word. This Word is an active, living Subject pursued by both minister and congregation together. In this pursuit, the minister is, of course, a steward of the tradition and Scripture, as well as one who ensures that conversations are inclusive, safe, and redemptively focused. All participants, however, bring essential insights into the pursuit of this Subject, and believe that, if diligently sought, this Subject will emerge in their midst.

Intentional and Timely

In the early church, a range of issues called for sustained and broad-based conversation, such as: divisions in the church, offering food to idols, the role of women and men in worship, the nature and practice of the Lord's Supper, spiritual gifts and speaking in tongues, false teachers, the relationship between new believers and Gentiles to the Jewish law, the meaning of the resurrection, persecution and suffering, and the relationship between the church and imperial Rome. The list goes on, of course, and many of these conversations continue into our day and age. Ministers in every generation are aware of the crucial issues and concerns in the church and community, and facilitate conversations that will respond.

In our pluralistic generation, ministers must facilitate conversations with other religious traditions and denominations, conversations focused on the meaning of Scripture and doctrine in a post-Enlightenment world, conversations with experts and artists regarding prevailing intellectual and cultural resources and ideas, conversations with global theological partners, as well as conversations within the local congregation and community regarding theology, ethics, and a host of other immediate issues and concerns. All of these conversations are central to furthering the mission of the church. The ministry of conversation, therefore, requires awareness and intentionality, because there are certain conversations that may not be initiated without the minister's self-conscious facilitation.

Entering Congregational Conversation at the Point at Which People Are Ready

Ministers who follow a conversational model will seldom simply set the agenda for a congregational conversation and launch the interaction on the minister's terms. Before directly entering a conversation, the minister needs to listen to the community to discern the core conversations already taking place and the various places people are with respect to those conversations. In a sense, the minister follows the lead of the congregation into issues. The pastor can then think critically about how to enter the conversation in a way that is likely to promote continuing conversation and not to polarize or otherwise derail genuine interchange. Ministers will not give up their integrity in making such moves, but can usually shape their entry into a conversation in a way that invites participation. With this in mind, it is important for ministers to be aware of the thoughts of those around them. Indeed, the minister becomes attentive to the perceptions of others in the field of conversation, is responsive to their topics and takes into account the concerns that are most important to them, whether or not the minister agrees with the others. Once in the conversation, the minister takes an active part in shaping the conversation even while being responsive to developments in the unfolding conversation.

Valuing Partnership When Consensus Fails

Consensus and partnership are two distinct qualities of unity fostered by conversation. Whereas consensus is a unity at the level of ideas, partnership is a unity at the level of relationship in spite of divergences at the level of ideas. Consensus can become a blessing when achieved, but consensus is not always possible, nor is it always necessary for there to be unity and solidarity as human beings and as Christians. This is an absolutely crucial distinction and goes to the very heart of the meaning of the ministry of conversation.

In other words, in the ministry of conversation, it is possible to disagree and to challenge another person's position without questioning their faith or status as a follower of Christ. At the level of ideas, we may be pushed to the very brink of separation, especially when the positions of our conversation partners are injurious to ourselves or others. At the level of ideas, divergence, and even strong disagreement can occur. Within a genuine ministry of conversation, however, partnership, or remaining in conversation with one another survives.

A Brief Summary

I have attempted to define several of the most important ways conversation and ministry converge. To summarize, the ministry of conversation maintains the following qualities:

- It is motivated by love.
- It is governed by the guest-host rhythm of hospitality.
- It is energized by the Holy Spirit to seek new ground.
- It is plurivocal (seeking new ground, not my ground).
- It empowers others.
- It is centered on God's emerging Word.
- It is intentional and timely.
- It is able and willing to follow the lead of others.
- It re-frames values and ideas with more theological and spiritual depth.
- It values partnership when consensus fails.

Cautions

Given the complexity of ministry, no single model does justice to it or is without its shortcomings and potential for abuse. There are several cautions that accompany the idea of the minister as conversation partner. First, a conversational view of ministry should not be used as a way to avoid the difficult work of getting to know one's Christian tradition and narrative deeply and consistently. In order for points of contact between worldviews to be discovered, comprehensive knowledge and practice of one's own traditions and worldviews is required. The best points of contact are always found at deeper and more profound levels.

Building on the first caution, it is important to emphasize, secondly, that a conversational approach to ministry does not imply an abdication of ministerial authority. Although relational authority is central, the minister retains an official authority given by the church to act as a steward of the church's Scripture, doctrine, tradition, practices, and polity. Conversation partner does not simply mean "facilitator." Ministers bring important expertise and wisdom, and are responsible partners *in* conversation, not simply those who facilitate conversations.

Third, an emphasis on hospitality can sometimes lead to disregarding safety concerns—for both guests and the hosting community. Ministers who host conversations are cautioned, therefore, to embrace dual responsibilities. First, we have a responsibility to protect the safety of those who are welcomed into conversation, insuring that, regardless of age, race, sexual orientation, and religion, their voices are heard and honored. At the same time, we must protect the safety of the community, insuring that guests welcomed into conversation do not intend harm. When such intentions are discovered, the minister as conversation partner must intervene to protect the safety of the conversation itself.

Fourth, some conversations are not meant for everyone or every place. Ministers must detect which conversations are likely to involve forms of self-disclosure that are better pursued privately and which conversations are likely to involve ideas that should be pursued among adults. All conversations require a place and time that is appropriate.

Fifth, it is crucial that new and difficult topics are introduced slowly and incrementally. Ministers as conversation partners must learn how to introduce troubling topics in a way that can be heard and engaged by all who have strong thoughts on the matter. Often it is a good idea to begin with topics that are related in subject matter in order to prepare the way for a difficult subject. When emotionally loaded topics are involved, the safety of all participants must be kept in mind, as well as the task of empowering all to speak.

Finally, the minister as conversation partner will need to cultivate generosity, patience, and careful interpretation among those still operating in the older framework of competing worldviews. When the Presbyterian Church (USA) created a multi-year study group to discuss homosexuality and ordination, many who participated in the group's process were transformed in attitude and perspective. New ground was clearly achieved for participants. Partnerships in ministry were built across differences, minds were changed, new relationships were built, commitments to new forms of speaking and living were forged. When those on the inside of this process tried to speak about it to those outside, however, the new ground they had achieved was not easily understood. The results seemed ambiguous, amorphous, or overly spiritualized to outsiders. This is likely to be the case often for the minister as conversation partner. Those outside key conversations will only understand the results based on older patterns of thinking. The minister, therefore, will need to learn forbearance, patience, and generosity toward those individuals. At the same time, the minister will need to think carefully about how to interpret what has occurred in order to bring everyone on board as much as possible.

Practical Outcomes for the Minister

In this final section, I focus on everyday practical outcomes for the pastor who follows a conversational approach to leadership. The minister can approach almost every setting in ministry with the question, "In this situation, does a conversation need to happen? If so, as the minister, what can I do to facilitate the conversation?" If a conversation is already happening, the minister can think critically about when and how to enter it.

With this model in mind, here are some examples of ministerial practices that follow from the ministry of conversation. Each of these is discussed very briefly, and is meant to be suggestive in nature—a paradigm of the kind of practical results that might be expected by adopting the image of ministry as conversation.

- A hospice chaplain engages in conversation with Muslim families and rethinks current best practices for grieving in her Christian tradition.

- A minister seeks out conversation with the most troublesome member of the church board, simply to engage in conversation for its own sake and to indicate mutual belonging to one another in Christ.

- A minister leaves the pastor's study and brainstorms sermons in a variety of locations, with a variety of different people, some Christian, some not.

- A minister takes a two-day retreat and lists the key conversations in the congregation, community, and global context, and prays about the appropriate role to take in these conversations as a minister of the gospel.

- A college chaplain creates a Facebook page for the campus ministry. In this cyber environment, the chaplain intentionally cultivates the posture of "guest" when engaged in conversations with students—listening for the spiritual wisdom they possess and taking note of what can be learned from this wisdom.

- A minister insures that a broad range of members of the congregation and community are engaged in prolonged conversation as the congregation's governing board deliberates on the denomination's ordination polity regarding sexual orientation.

- A minister invites members of other Christian denominations and congregations to speak in Sunday School about their worship practices. Later the class visits those congregations.

- A Christian educator creates a class in which participants share music playlists as a way of identifying and learning from religiously attenuated worldviews at work within popular culture.

- A minister in a liberal, social-justice minded congregation invites evangelicals into conversations regarding the Bible and social witness.

- A minister in an evangelical congregation invites those within mainstream liberal churches into conversation about how to interpret the Bible today.

- A minister institutes a monthly "praying for partnership" worship service, which is entirely focused on praying for conversations as partners among those with differing and sometimes violently conflicting worldviews, whether Palestinian and Jew, pro-life and pro-choice, liberal and conservative, Sunni and Shia, etc.

- A minister organizes a congregational retreat on "Conversation Among the Communion of Saints." At this retreat the goal is two-fold: 1) to re-open the church's past, lamenting past actions that may have caused suffering, while discovering other voices to learn from that were not recognized or celebrated in the past; 2) to open the church's present decisions, positions, policies, and trends to the future, asking what might be re-considered or re-framed in light of conversation with generations yet to come.

- A minister invites the youth group to create "sermon mashups" and posts them to the congregation's Facebook website. Using digital audio and video software, the youth group cuts and pastes snippets of audio from the sermon into conversation with other clips of audio from songs, videos, or other pop cultural sources.

- A minister enters a conversation that engages the voices of those whose lives have been touched by disabilities of many kinds, seeking new ground for ministry that would be welcoming and create partnerships among those of differing abilities.

- A minister involves the congregation in conversation with members of the local synagogue and mosque designed to develop relationships and to learn from one another about theology, worship, and understandings of the relationship between religion and society.

- A minister involves the congregation in a conversation with a variety of social service agencies in an urban area, some religiously oriented, some supported by city government, and others supported by nondenominational charities, in an effort to develop a joint mission statement for serving the city's homeless population.

- A minister invites psychologists and other experts into conversation with pastoral staff and members of the Congregational Care Committee to discuss best practices for ministering to and with victims of sexual or domestic violence.

- Insofar as possible, a minister needs to help conversations in the congregation be safe. For example, when participating in a conversation regarding chaperoning the youth mission trip, the minister may need to dismiss a known childhood sex offender from the conversation.

As this list indicates, the ministry of conversation keeps the church engaged in those spaces between worldviews, where new ideas for life together are desperately needed. Ministry in these places will challenge the church to claim its own identity, but not in a way that reserves that identity for its own edification and redemption. Rather, that identity will be constantly broken open, stretched, re-framed, repaired, and renewed in each generation, in conversation with others. In the end, there are endless adventures to be had in this between space—adventures that will invite the churches to re-engage their creative powers and join the Spirit in the business of creating new ground for ministry in each generation.

Some Possibilities for Using Social Media in This Aspect of Ministry

As noted previously, a minister needs to know what conversations are taking place in the congregation. In addition to listening to people in live situations (e.g., at church, in their homes, encounters in the grocery store), a minister can send emails to particular individuals, households or groups soliciting their direct input. Without "lurking," a minister can pay attention to the Facebook pages (and similar expressions) maintained by members of the congregation. These pages often reveal concerns, questions, issues, joys that are important to the people who maintain those pages and communicate through them. Material posted on Facebook, after all, is public.

Many congregations are experimenting with congregational Facebook pages. These pages are not only good places to post announcements but also provide a space for people to post comments about the congregation, their own lives, and the world. It a good idea, of course, to have someone moderate this page, insuring the safety of children and those who wish to protect their privacy. Other, more specialized "group" pages can also be maintained from time to time in order to promote conversation regarding specific topics or issues.

A growing number of ministers write their own blogs. The best blogs typically provide opportunities for readers to respond, thus moving the blog from a simple form of self-expression on the part of the preacher to becoming an ongoing conversation with respondents. As time permits, such blogs are a good place to post short sermon audio or video clips or "remixes" of one's sermon (no longer than 122 seconds).

To increase efficiency in communication and planning, many church groups communicate via email, list-serves, and similar technology. Indeed, sometimes members of a task force will say things in print in these contexts that they would hesitate to say in a face-to-face committee meeting.

Using Skype and other video-conferencing technologies, a minister can convene a group to talk over an important issue. With a minimum of technological fuss, people on a committee can be in their homes or offices or even on vacation while being able to see and hear one another in real time on the screen. Such gatherings can save people time and can lessen the environmental footprint of such a gathering as participants do not have to drive cars. This approach is particularly promising for members of congregations scattered over large urban or rural areas.

A congregation's website can be configured not only to pass along information about the congregation, but to provide opportunities for congregational interaction on discussion boards and other means. The congregation can set up password-protected areas so that only members (and other holders of passwords) can log onto the site.

Enterprising ministers can also run electronic surveys to determine where a congregation's center of gravity might be on a particular issue. For example, a few questions on *SurveyMonkey* can ask members of the congregation what they think and feel. A comment box gives survey participants the opportunity to express themselves more fully with just a few strokes on the keyboard.

In one respect, ministers need to be careful. In some situations, there is no substitute for face-to-face interaction. Many ministers who are introverts and find such interactions draining or even threatening sometimes hide in the office and think that by shooting emails all over creation they are fulfilling their pastoral calling. However, there are some moments when ministry calls for a look from eye to eye or the touch of hand to hand.

Of course, a minister and a congregation need to account for the fact that some people today resist the use of social media. Aristotle once said that a speaker seeking to convince an audience to adopt a particular viewpoint or take a particular action should use all available means of persuasion. In a similar vein, a minister or congregation needs to use all available means of communication in order to try to connect with all members. Digital communication should never entirely eclipse making calls in the home or office, using the telephone, writing letters, and sending paper documents.

Questions for Discussion:

1. Discuss the diagnosis of the crisis in our generation in this chapter: cultural-narrative entrenchment. What impact does this entrenchment have on your life? Your community? Your congregation?

2. What do you make of the author's solution to this crisis: the ministry of conversation? Which reasons for the image of the minister as conversation partner are most compelling for you? Are there other reasons for this image?

3. Which aspects of the ministry of conversation are most important for your congregation and why?

Further Reading

Creps, Earl. *Reverse Mentoring: How Young Leaders Can Transform the Church and Why We Should Let Them*. New York: Wiley, 2008.

Elmer, Duane. *Cross-Cultural Conflict: Building Relationships for Effective Ministry*. Downer's Grove, IL: InterVarsity, 1994.

Gornik, Mark R. *To Live in Peace: Biblical Faith and the Changing Inner City*. Grand Rapids: Eerdmans, 2002.

Kiefert, Patrick. *Welcoming the Stranger: A Public Theology of Worship and Evangelism*. Minneapolis: Fortress, 1992.

Koenig, John. *New Testament Hospitality: Partnership with Strangers as Promise and Mission*. 1985. Reprinted, Eugene, OR: Wipf & Stock, 2001.

Mackenzie, Don, Ted Falcon, and Jamal Rahman. *Getting to the Heart of Interfaith: The Eye-opening, Hope-Filled Friendship of a Pastor, a Rabbi, and a Sheikh*. Woodstock, VT: Skylight Paths, 2009.

McClure, John. *Other-wise Preaching: A Postmodern Ethic for Homiletics*. St. Louis: Chalice, 2001.

———. *The Roundtable Pulpit: Where Leadership and Preaching Meet*. Nashville: Abingdon, 1995.

Palmer, Parker. *The Company of Strangers: Christians and the Renewal of America's Public Life*. New York: Crossroad, 1983.

Tanner, Kathryn. *Theories of Culture: A New Agenda for Theology*. Guides to Theological Inquiry. Minneapolis: Fortress, 1997.

3

God as Conversational

Michael St. A. Miller

A FOUNDATIONAL PRESUMPTION of Christian community is that what we believe about God shapes how we understand ourselves and the world. This means that what we observe in human life and the life of the world can give us important clues about God. Given the prominence of communication not only in our day-to-day life but also in the ways in which God is pictured in the Bible and by many voices in Christian tradition, we generally assume that a personal God is in ongoing communication with human beings, influencing them and being influenced by them. Sometimes communication involves direct speech, but often it involves other modes of expression. Regardless of the mode of communication, conversation is at work.

I will make the case that key considerations in the Bible and in life hint at a personal God who not only desires human life to be built around conversation but who is conversational in character and whose quality of life is affected by conversation. To exclude conversation from characteristics attributed to God would be a contradiction in terms, and to exclude conversation from any aspect of the church would run counter to its calling to be a community that models God's ideals for the world.

Biblical Testimony in Support of a Conversational God

In the earliest narratives the Bible portrays God in conversation with Adam and Eve (Gen 2:3). The rest of the Hebrew Bible contains a number of episodes that picture God, not only making demands and giving orders, but acceding to persuasive argument (e.g., Gen 18:16–33; Exod 32:7–14). God communicates with humans with the hope that they will listen (Jer 26:3), and learns about the character of humans from the way they respond to God's communications (Jer 3:7, 19). In the Gospels and Letters the injunction to pray for what one desires from God also presumes the ability to influence God (e.g., Matt 11:24, 25; Acts 10:31; Eph 6:18; Phil 4:6). Surely this presumption is epitomized in Jesus' prayer in Gethsemane (e.g., Mark 14:32–42). In that prayer/conversation, the conditional "not what I will, but what you will" acknowledges God's freedom to respond in light of God's desires, just as much as "if anyone hears my voice and opens the door" in Rev 3:20 suggests freedom on the part of humans.

Classical Theism: The Most Important Challenge to a Relational-Conversational God

Although biblical episodes like the ones just cited are striking in their portrayal of a conversational God, the approach to religious knowledge by a number of important Christian thinkers challenged their significance in this regard. A defining challenge to the idea of a conversational God comes from Augustine, whose thought is a high point of theology in the first five centuries. Augustine objected to anthropomorphizing God, an objection with implications for describing God as speaking. Augustine's view is that by means of an ascending hierarchy of capacities the believer is directed away from the external realm of the senses to the internal realm of contemplation and reason. In other words, our best awareness of God comes not from observing human beings and the world but from logical arguments derived from pure reason. This is the path to "incorruptible truths" and thus to the most appropriate conception of God.[1] In developing this position Augustine initiated the form of Christian rationalism popularly called classical theism that found its most sophisticated expression in the work of Thomas Aquinas, and continues to influence a range of contemporary theologians within and outside of Catholicism.

Thomas Aquinas and the Core of Classical Theism

While Aquinas was less suspicious of the material world than Augustine, he was clear that we cannot draw conclusions about God from its impact on us. To do so is to engage in inadequate anthropomorphism. We need to progress toward more adequate conceptions resulting from logical intellectual

---

1. Augustine, *On Free Choice of the Will*, 44–52.

analysis of the idea of God. While the truths of faith are superior to intellectual truths, the theologian, convinced that the intellectual capacity was
given by a creator God, will seek after the greatest level of correspondence
between the two.

With this conviction as background, Aquinas formulated what he
considered the most rationally appropriate statements to make about God.
His efforts further disqualified the absolute ultimate from being a personal
God who by character and desire is relational and conversational. This God,
similar to Aristotle's unmoved mover, has the power to affect the world, but
cannot be affected by things people say.

Aquinas thought that, given God's categorical uniqueness as creator/
first cause, the usual means of determining the nature of things in the world,
by locating them in a genus and species and observing differences, was not
appropriate. We could not observe people and extrapolate from them positive ideas about God. By observing people, we can only establish negative
differences between humankind and God,[2] because the effects of an infinite,
ultimate, and categorically unique God are radically disproportional to
their cause. Nevertheless, for Aquinas there were some clues regarding the
nature of God available from the fact of the relation between God as cause
and the world as effect, even as we work at eliminating illusions regarding
the true nature of our knowledge of God.[3] Aquinas extended Aristotle's correction of the Platonic dualism between form and matter by arguing that
existence had priority over essence, that is, the "what" of a thing (its particular character as matter and form) is only actualized in its instantiation
(the "that") as a particular entity/existence. For example, while the notion
"humanness," in terms of which we are assigned a particular species within
the genus "animal," is a real concept, it is only a potentiality when compared
with actually existing humans.[4] At the heart of this discussion is Aquinas'
classification of God as simple being; that is, unlike created beings God's
essence *is* God's existence. From this point of view, God is not just devoid of
component parts; God's attributes should not be distinguishable from God's
essence and thus from each other.

The challenge posed for the idea of a conversational God becomes
most vivid when Aquinas' analysis of the relation between *esse* and *ens*
leads to the claim that God as *esse* is "pure act" with no potentiality. This is

2. Aquinas, *Summa Theologiae* 1a.2–11, [1a.3.2], 27 (translated 1963).

3. Ibid., [1a.3.3], 31.

4. Aquinas sums this up in his *Summa Theologiae* 1a 3.4. He declares: "It follows
then that, if a thing's existence differs from its nature, that existence need be externally
caused. But we cannot say this about God, whom we have seen to be first cause. Neither
then can we say that God's existence is other than his nature."

dramatized when Aquinas embraces Boethius' claim that "The divine substance is being itself, and from it comes being."[5] Neo-Thomist David Burrell is clear that this is the meaning of simpleness for Aquinas.[6]

Therefore, as simple being, God is complete in Godself. God is perfect in the sense of lacking nothing. God is immutable, that is, God cannot change or be changed. This God can cause things to happen, but cannot be affected by humans (or other beings) whose existence is contingent on God.

There is nothing in these ideas that lead naturally to a claim that the One classified as *esse* is the personal God with whom Christians have intimate relationship, pray to, worship, and more so, the one who is involved in the kind of conversation which is mutually impactful.

Tillich's Ground of Being

Aquinas' formulation points to the notion associated with Paul Tillich's ontological question: "What is being itself? What is that which is not a special being or a group of beings, not something concrete or something abstract, but rather something that is always thought implicitly, and sometimes explicitly, if something is said to be?"[7] Tillich's explication of Being itself/ Ground of Being or better yet "creative ground of essence and existence"[8] is quite impressive. However, like Aquinas' *esse*, Tillich's ultimate is not an actual entity of any sort. Some will quickly remind me that Ground of Being, symbolically represented as "God," is personal in the sense that God is "the ground of everything personal."[9] However, this is not the same as a personal God who intentionally relates, engages in mutually beneficial communication, and, as such, establishes conversation as a necessity for ecclesiology.

Is Trinity the Solution?

I am mindful that the idea of God as *esse* did not stand by itself in Aquinas' scheme. Like many other representatives of Christian orthodoxy, he was committed to the notion that God is Trinity. Many in recent times have championed this doctrine claiming that the conception of God as community, that is, constituted by relations between Father, Son, and Spirit is reflected in the

---

5. Aquinas, *Summa Contra Gentiles*, book 1, 116–21 (translated 1975).

6. Burrell, *Faith and Freedom*, 8.

7. Tillich, *Systematic Theology*, vol. 1, 163.

8. Ibid., 205.

9. Ibid., 245.

constitution of the cosmos. Being God's creatures and coming to be in a relational world, the human is intrinsically relational. This, for Trinitarians, is the grounding of any argument for conversation as a necessary feature of human life, the church, and ultimately for wholesome existence.

Discussion of Trinity with a Focus on the Essence of God

By Aquinas' time the doctrine of the Trinity had developed in sophistication from Tertullian's well-known declaration: *una substantia, tres person* (one substance, three persons). Aquinas embraced this concept as compatible with his position on divine simplicity. He argued that "The persons (*hypostases*) of the Trinity are distinguished by their relations to each other."[10] The persons have the same essence and their differences are discernible by the way they relate to each other: the Father is Father of the Son; the Son is eternally begotten from the Father; the Spirit eternally spirates from the Father and Son.

In support of this agenda Aquinas modifies Boethius' definition of person. Rather than a person being *naturae rationalis individua substantia* (an individual substance of a rational nature) it is *subsistens distinctum in natura rationali* (a distinct subsistent of a rational nature).[11] Here it is important to recognize that Aquinas held that, while persons are not individual substances, they must be complete substances.[12] The contrast is between that which exists in and of itself and that which exists in as much as it participates in relationship in the divine nature.

Bearing divine simplicity in mind, it is unclear to me how there can be distinct subsistents in the One nature. However, Aquinas' explanation seems to be governed by what he accepts as a truth of faith. As such, we are left with a "picture" of interpersonal relationships that have no resemblance to anything in the dynamics of human experience from which the idea of relationship emerges and which gives clues about what to look for when the word is used in any context. I will delve further into this limitation by examining the theological legacy that formed the background for Aquinas' discussions. Contemporary proponents of the Social Trinity trace this legacy back to the Cappadocian fathers of the fourth century CE.

---

10. Aquinas, *Summa Theologiae* 1a.33–43, [1.40.3], 147–48.
11. Moltmann, *The Trinity and the Kingdom*, 146.
12. Webb, *Jesus Christ, Eternal God*, 189.

Discussion of Trinity with a Focus on its Social Dimensions

This is not the place to go into the linguistic problems that emerged in the early centuries of the church as thinkers from its Eastern and Western streams struggled to explicate the Trinitarian character of God. Most important for us is the recognition that the Nicene claim that Jesus the Christ was *homoousios* (of the same substance) with the Father necessitated new understandings of the being of God.[13] Colin Gunton reminds us that up to the time of the Cappadocians, *hypostasis* in distinction from *ousia* translated as the concrete particularity of the Father, Son, and Holy Spirit. With the influence of the Cappadocians it was no longer adequate to translate this term to mean individual. Instead Father, Son, and Spirit were persons, "beings whose reality can only be understood in terms of their relations to each other, relations by virtue of which they constitute the being (*ousia*) of the one God."[14] In his representation of the shift, Leonardo Boff shows how this relational shift constituted a radical revision of Tertullian's formulae. As he put it: "They took not the unity of the divine nature but the three divine persons as their starting point, seeing them as the basic reality. The unity that forms the essence of the persons springs from the communion and relationship between them."[15]

Social Trinitarians encourage us to take serious note of the implications of this move for what can be said about other things, especially human community. They emphasize that to think of persons is to think of relations, that is, a person is neither an individual defined in terms of separatedness from others nor one swallowed up in the collective. At the socio-political level, there is first the claim that "monotheism supports strict monolithic identities and authoritarian forms of government in which power is held exclusively by a single leader or group." In contrast to this, they claim, Trinitarianism is "associated with egalitarian politics and respect for diversity within community."[16] As such, the Trinity in which each person is necessary to the being of the other is most reflective of the true character of wholesome human society.

---

13. Gunton, *The Promise of Trinitarian Theology*, 8.

14. Ibid., 39.

15. Boff, *Trinity and Society*, 54.

16. Tanner, "Trinity," 322.

Why the Doctrine of the Trinity Is Not Necessary for a Conversational God

Kathryn Tanner sows seeds of doubt regarding the capacity of the doctrine of the Trinity to support the kind of conversational ethos proposed in this book when she suggests that "much of what is said about the Trinity simply does not seem directly applicable to humans: human society could take on the very shape of the Trinity only if people were no longer human."[17] I add that typical Trinitarianism also promotes the kind of sovereign freedom that has compatibility with Aquinas' pure act, in the sense that, while God relates to the world, God's life is already fully satisfied in the internal life of the Trinity. The members of the Trinity have complete relationships with one another. This intensifies the difficulties associated with Tanner's reminder that "the Trinity easily suggests the appropriateness of rule by three absolute co-rulers."[18] In the next paragraphs I will go even further to argue that the very structure of the Trinitarian formulation is flawed and as such cannot provide an adequate support for the kind of human sociality in which free, mutually beneficial conversation between persons is central.

On the assumption that the idea of the individual rejected by the Cappadocians and contemporary Social Trinitarians is grounded in a Boethius-like substantialism, I declare my support for their move.[19] That being said, the alternative chosen to protect the integrity of the Godhead seems to undermine the foundation for the very relationality by which authentic personhood is established.

Without doubt sociality is fundamental to personhood, but personhood is also not realizable without the creative tension between sociality and individuality. Here I recall Aquinas' view that, while our thinking about God unavoidably begins in the realm of finite beings, it should take us to the place where we recognize that what is last epistemologically is first ontologically. I suggest that, while this may well be so, we should not delude ourselves into thinking that concepts we apply to establish God as personal can have any real meaning that is not informed by the framework in which they were first derived; that is, human life in the world. As such, I assert that there is nothing in our human frame of reference that enables us to justify talk of authentic relations that do not involve I–thou[20] interactions between and among

---

17. Ibid., 325.

18. Ibid., 322.

19. Here substance refers to the underlying reality of an entity of which everything else about the entity is predicated, while substance is itself not predicated of anything else.

20. This notion was made popular by Rudolf Otto in his work, *The Idea of the Holy.*

individuals. These relations are grounded in the shared essence of all individual persons, that is, our common humanity. Applying this to a tri-personal God I would claim that, even if one were to accept that the relations between the persons are properties of one divine essence or substance, they must be pursued as individual persons to be authentic inter-personal relations.

Any talk of relationships that precludes I–thou interactions between individuals must be referring to relations between concepts or propositions. As such, I propose a scenario in which, as I imagine it, Christian thinkers deduced concepts from the life of an actual human person (Jesus), and then by theological subtlety developed them into a Trinity of persons constituting Godhead.

Christotheism and other Factors at the Heart of Trinitarianism

Driven by soteriological concerns Jesus of Nazareth who called God *Abba* came to be seen as the God-human who on our behalf was ransom, recapitulator, victor, or substitute. Jürgen Moltmann highlights the weight of the soteriological concern in his claim that "the meaning of the cross of the Son of Golgotha reaches right into the heart of the immanent Trinity." From the beginning, he suggests, "no immanent Trinity and no divine glory is conceivable without 'the lamb that was slain.'"[21]

Thus, against the background of belief in one God, there emerged a situation in which the move to establish Jesus as God resulted in a number of unavoidable consequences. Firstly, at the level of affective spirituality (where the soteriological concern is grounded) "Christotheism" emerged whereby Christ the Eternal Son, in effect, supplanted the God of Israel as the ultimate grounding of Christian faith. Secondly, at the level of rational explanation (where the logic of ultimacy has precedence) the principal actors in the soteriological work, with the Eternal Son as the necessary presupposition for Jesus as God-human at the center, were portrayed as relating in a way more like concepts do, that is, as a network of logical relations between them, while being characterized as actual persons.

In this regard Basil of Caesarea, speaking about the Father, suggests that "Unbegotteness expresses how God is, not what God is." Analyzing the relative names of Father and Son, Basil expands on the idea that persons derive from "relations of origin," with these relations being/constituting modes of being persons. As such, the "Father is defined by relation to Son,

---

21. Moltmann, *The Trinity and the Kingdom*, 159.

and not just the absence of all relation to an antecedent term. The notion of Father necessarily includes the notion of Son."[22]

I suggest that it was exactly Christotheism, in which the idea of the Eternal Son incarnate in Jesus presupposes an ingenerate Father, which ensured that the doctrine of the Spirit would often be neglected. In Augustine's case, I am tempted to suggest that it was the elevation of the Son to center stage that generated ideas that later led to the inclusion of the *filioque* clause (and from the Son) in the Latin translation of Nicene-Constantinople creed. I also suspect that this might well be the reason he argued that the Spirit is the communion or love between the Father and Son and their common gift to humans.[23] Indeed, it is quite telling that when he depicts the relationship between the immanent Trinity and the economic Trinity through his well-known formula *Omnia opera trinitatis ad extra indivisa sunt* (All the actions of the Trinity outward are undivided)[24] we are again pointed to a scenario in which the Eternal Son incarnate in Jesus of Nazareth is at center stage.[25]

Casting our eyes to more recent times we find that, even as Moltmann adopts the position that the Spirit proceeds from the Father, Christotheism is very evident in his declaration that "The first person of the Trinity is the Father, but only in respect of the Son—that is to say, in the eternal generation of the Son. God the father is always the father of the Son." He proceeds to say, "In salvation history he is exclusively 'the Father of Jesus Christ,' and it is through Christ the Son and in the fellowship of this 'first born' among many brothers and sisters that he is our Father too."[26]

Evidence suggests that the Cappadocians did struggle to reconcile the Trinity and unity of God. LaCugna describes how, in order to hold together a strict monarchy and the idea of a common *ousia* (substance) shared by three hypostases, the Cappadocians, and Gregory of Nyssa in particular, sought to establish a distinction between the absolutely unknowable and incomprehensible *ousia* of God and the manifestation of God through divine

22. LaCugna, *God for Us*, 61.

23. Augustine, *The Trinity*, [15.17], 491–96.

24. It is interesting to see how Augustine explicates this position in his Sermon 52 on the Trinity, found in *The Works of Saint Augustine*, 51:65.

25. Gunton is quite strident in his critique of Augustine, claiming that he caused the Trinity to seem irrelevant to the ways of God toward us in time. I am of the view that, despite what Augustine felt required to hold in regard to the triune nature of God, he was probably certain that if God is one then all activities associated with God should, in the final analysis, be attributed to this one God. Conversely if the immanent Trinity is not constituted by individuals with distinctions that correspond to their individuality (not just their relations) it is not appropriate to attribute unique operations to the economic Trinity understood to be ultimately grounded in the immanent Trinity.

26. Moltmann, *The Trinity and the Kingdom*, 183.

energies.[27] This has spawned an approach to the Trinity seen by some as an alternative to the Social Trinity.

LaCugna is critical of the way this move suggested "either that the divine *ousia* is to some degree independent of the hypostases or that *ousia* is incomprehensible in a way that the hypostases are not." Her view is that what the Cappadocians should have insisted on "is that the incomprehensibility of God is due to the fact that God comes to us in this way in the economy, that is, through the Son in the power of the Holy Spirit." As such, the divine energies should be seen as the proper subject matter of theology. She delves into other critical evaluations of the spirituality that emerged from this apophaticism, but what interests me most at this point is her claim that, in the end, the Cappadocians' position allowed "Trinitarian distinctions and relations to fall somewhat into the background."[28]

LaCugna's analysis, following from my assessment of Social Trinitarianism, displays vividly the difficulty of justifying a Trinitarian position and using it confidently as the foundation for human sociality that expresses itself in conversation. I also remind the reader of the earlier case made for the inappropriateness of the conception of God as simple being.

So then, where do we go from here? What is a plausible conception of God that avoids the weaknesses of divine simplicity and Social Trinitarianism, while honoring God as ultimate being, supports a robust soteriology, and justifies the kind of God-world relation that undergirds conversation as a vital feature of human life and God's life? The answer to these questions lies in the next section.

A Church as Community of Conversation is Grounded in a God Who has Mutually Influential Relations with the World

The first step in answering the questions just posed is the recognition that the doctrines of sin and salvation, which required Jesus of Nazareth to be identified with the Eternal Son and as God, are not the only viable ways to speak about God's redemptive presence in the world or the place of Jesus in God's relationship with humankind. Other paths open better possibilities for understanding a God who has mutually influential relations with the world.

27. LaCugna, *God with Us*, 72.
28. Ibid.

Reinterpreting the World: Not Simply Fallen but Ambiguous

Contemporary insight into cosmic development suggests that rather than a fall in a single act from a state of wholeness and communion with God to one of discord and corruption, the human species has been emerging over the course of just over a million years. This process has involved various stages of biological, cultural, and psychological development that have produced a species which, among other animals, has a level of mentality, subjectivity, and autonomy that warrants the characterization "free, partially self-creating, self-determining creatures"[29] The process in which humans engage in decision-making is such that the integration of causal factors and the act of decision-making itself result in outcomes that are not always fully explainable by the sum of these factors. This scenario points to an element of freshness and innovation that can never be predetermined and which is an expression of creativity at the heart of existence. We are not simply a "fallen" species. From this process of ongoing development and creative expression has resulted both horrendous acts and exalting achievements. Therefore, rather than requiring a God-human as atoning sacrifice, the way is opened up for the idea of a God who engendered the creative process from which has emerged wonderful and potentially terrifying co-creating creatures who over time have come to recognize that individuality-in-community is a critical expression of our character.

The Idea of God

Following the dominant emphasis in Christian tradition, I classify this God as creator. This basic claim opens the way for me to suggest that however one might struggle in regard to the character of a self-existing perfect God, the belief that God was moved to create without external persuasion implies that when we contemplate "God," we must presuppose a creative drive that further presupposes the metaphysical principle of creativity.[30] If creativity is essential to God's being, it can be reasonably claimed that as long as God has been God, God has been expressing God's self creatively. And the self-existent One of orthodox theism would not have been creating Godself, but something other than self, that is, some world of actualities. As such, we can rationally embrace the idea that God has never been without a world with which God has been relating in myriad ways.[31]

29. Williamson, *Way of Blessing, Way of Life*, 107.

30. Miller, *Reshaping the Contextual Vision in Caribbean Theology*, 340.

31. Miller, *Freedom in Resistance and Creative Transformation*, 238.

This being the case, the traditional claim that God's perfection means that God does not need a world for self-fulfillment, is replaced by the recognition that a God with creativity as a central characteristic finds fulfillment in creating, desires to see creative processes unfold, and seeks to be as close as possible to the dynamic outworking of these processes. As such Keith Ward is correct when he suggests that the universe in which humans are situated can be seen "as a particular contingent expression of the imaginative creativity of God."[32]

God's Sovereignty is God's Unending and Universal Influence on the World

Nothing in this proposal undermines the dignity of God as sovereign. Among the ways in which God is distinctive from that which God has created is that God is never confronted by a world "whose" coming to be antedates God's existence. Everything that influences God has always been influenced by God. Human beings and other creatures in the world, on the other hand, are influenced by our pasts with which we have had nothing to do.[33] God's relatedness to others is radically unlike humanity's in being itself not merely relative, but wholly absolute. What "absolute" means here is radically different from its meaning among classical theists. It establishes God as the eminently incarnate and relative One whose sphere of interaction is the whole universe of contingent entities, with each one of which God's relation is unsurpassably immediate and direct,[34] even though as finite creatures God's presence is experienced as mediated immediacy.[35] God's relatedness to other beings is itself relative to nothing, because God is the ground of any and all real relationships. In this scenario, the sovereignty of God does not mean that God has absolute power over every other entity but that, whereas other entities come and go, God is perpetually related to all other entities and has the power to invite them into higher possibilities of being and relationship.

32. Ward, *Divine Action*, 35.
33. Hartshorne, *The Divine Relativity*, 30.
34. Ogden, *The Reality of God*, 60.
35. Hodgson, *Winds of the Spirit*, 129.

God as Personal Ultimate Who Influences
and is Influenced by Other Personal Entities

This characterization of God is not completely incompatible with Aquinas' notion of the One whose essence is existence and Tillich's creative ground of being. However, it is most consistent with Alfred North Whitehead's ontological principle which, in one of its representations, suggests that "the reasons for things are always to be found in the composite nature of definite actual entities."[36] Consistent with this principle, Whiteheadeans characterize God as constituted by a primordial nature, a consequent nature, and a superjective nature.

Keith Ward helps with the explication of the first of these characterizations as he critiques some British atheists who, among other explanations for the fact of a world, suggest that the present world is simply one actualization of the total set of possible worlds. Ward suggests that these persons are referring to nothing more than "possibilities of existing,"[37] and as possibilities they must be present in something actual.[38] In this regard we can imagine the self-existent God as an infinite mind that contained the sum totality of possibilities for existence. At the same time, if this is the imaginatively creative God already described, God has always been bringing into existence some of these possibilities. Thus we must also imagine another side of God's character, required for ongoing relations with these extra-divine existents. When we include in the scenario the emergence of entities, like human beings, with freedom, and the fresh possibilities resulting from our creative expressions, there is little difficulty conceiving of a God-world relationship in which God influences and is influenced, provides new insights for human life in the world, and receives new insights from the actual outcomes of human creativity. It is the conviction that influences from the world occasion real changes in God, which affect God's subsequent relations with the world, that informs the idea of a superjective nature.

Jesus Exemplifies both the Possibilities God Offers
the World and How Human Beings Can Respond

God's abiding presence is traditionally referred to as the Spirit of God; this presence manifested concretely in a variety of ways from the level of primal energy fueling the processes of evolution to God's ongoing wooing of

36. Whitehead, *Process and Reality*, 19.
37. Ward, *Why There Almost Certainly Is a God*, 71.
38. Ibid., 70.

individual persons and communities of individuals that we experience as redeeming, restoring, and perfecting/maturing. Inspired by Peter Hodgson I portray Jesus as a unique "shape" of God's self-communication in the sense that in Jesus' life the gracious transforming, renewing, maturing power of God's involvement at the heart of life was evident in a uniquely focused way—exemplifying rich possibilities for human life with God, fellow human beings, and the world. Jesus, as the Word made flesh, represents God's call and God's desire for an answer. He also represents the capacity of human beings to hear and answer that call. With the conviction that what fuels God's interaction with the world is some analogue of love as humans understand it, we can conceive of identification between the Spirit of God and the Love of God. And with the conviction that this love was reflected in the way Jesus lived his life and his willingness to give up his life, I am able to appropriate Augustine's formulation of the Spirit as the love between Father and Son and the joint gift of Father and Son to humanity for the sake of the world.

Implications for Church and World: Conversation at Ground Level

Conversation Generates Fresh Possibilities

The structure of God's relationship to the world as we have described it is also the pattern for all healthy relationships. This structure involves identity (self), difference (other) and mediation (mutually beneficial interaction). Through mediation selves experience a level of fulfillment that is not possible in isolation, no matter how complex one's internal processes might be. In considering the fulfillment that God experiences through interaction with a world of actualities, which includes human beings and other elements of the created word, I am inspired by Charles Hartshorne to suggest that God's perfection should not be assessed in terms of reaching a completed maximum but in seeking unlimited progress.

From this point of view, God is, by nature, open to being changed by conversation with the world and God's perfection would involve the inexhaustible capacity to listen, learn, and to respond in ways that are appropriate to each and every situation in both their uniqueness and their relation to all other situations. Thus when we say that God is love, that God loves the world, and that God's purposes are for all to live together in love it should be understood that God will express God's love for us as unique persons in unique situations in relation to God's unique expression of love for every other entity (human beings and other elements of creation), and God's unique expression of love for the cosmos as a whole.

Therefore, each conversation will always be part of a complex network of interactions, and the "transcendence" of each individual self in conversation should be appreciated through the recognition that a self is always more than any other person can see of it or contribute to it. Indeed, a self is always more than it can see of itself or draw from itself[39] because it is always realizing fresh possibilities for existence as a result of its communion with an infinite and absolutely relative God, and with an interconnected world of human beings and other co-existents.

Christian Community as Conversational Community

We have here the foundation for approaching all aspects of life within the Christian community as a creative partnership in which each engages the other with the recognition that their unique individuality is fundamental for an authentic community of persons. In the language of the introduction to this book, each self is an other with its own integrity that should relate to other selves with respect for their integrity. As such, individuality should be encouraged with the recognition that the complex riches of life come to expression from the creative interaction of individual persons (presence, ideas, and feelings) and communities of these persons who share a common grounding at a place infinitely deeper than can be portrayed by sectarian labels or religious categories.

Yet, we should not romanticize the experience of community from this point of view. This partnership, when healthy, involves challenge and nurture; judgment and forgiveness as selves explore ways to honor the selfhood of each while relating with one another in genuine community. Sometimes the fresh possibility for a particular moment involves saying and doing some hard things.

It must also be appreciated that as finite creatures our relationship with any other (God and other humans) is always characterized by "mediated immediacy."[40] There is also an unfathomable mystery that is intrinsic to God's categorically unique being. As such, vagueness and ambiguity will not be eliminated by God's immanence or our intimacy with other human beings. Operating in the midst of vagueness and ambiguity, we will sometimes hurt others and hurt ourselves. Yet this recognition also constitutes an invitation and challenge to enter more deeply into each other's lives, to

39. Levinas, *Totality and Infinity*, 180.
40. Hodgson, *Winds of the Spirit*, 129.

become more sensitive to the dynamics of our own lives, and to be discerning of clues regarding God's presence in the world at large.

Dynamics of Conversation in Christian Community

There is no question that some within the church, whether by socialization or formal training, will be more equipped in particular areas than others. However, it makes a radical difference to the way these advantages are expressed when all others are recognized as persons who have as much access to God as we do, and that in honoring this recognition by encouraging mutual interaction that engenders and nourishes imaginative creativity and fosters the welfare of each and all we are imitating the way God relates to the world. In addition we contribute to the fulfillment of the imaginatively creative God who delights in creative-humanizing interactions, mourns when they are destructive, and learns from the fresh outcomes that result from them.

Among the implications for church leadership is that there should be emphasis placed on structures and opportunities through which members are enabled to pursue the deepest possible interpersonal engagement in which people share discernments and are exposed to clarifying and applicative scrutiny, instead of simply gathering *en masse* to be inflicted with one person's discernments and analysis or to be given directives. This being so, a high priority should be that every member of the church becomes the best biblical scholar, theologian, historian, explorer of interdisciplinary ideas, and ethicist that it is possible for he or she to be. This process of learning would be an expression of devotion to God, and a component of a developing sense of a person's individual significance and the value of what they have to contribute to others.

A Community of Diverse Perspectives

There is everything right about each member of the Christian community having her own theological center as long as she does not fetishize that center, thus becoming idolatrous. Given our inclination to this form of idolatry, the church should make a constant effort (individually and corporately) to formulate and refine norms to guide and assess resources, discernments and claims. These guidelines, of course, are always themselves subjects of conversation. The church also has the crucial task of nurturing the capacity for effective communication in its narrow sense of talk and the broad sense, which involves the utilization of varied communicative devices as lures to increase and refine perception, strengthen interpersonal and intra-communal participation, and encourage recognition of relationships within the church and as citizens of a complex world. This requires that, along with the presence of guidelines to give direction to conversation, there needs to be a clear vision of what conversation means theologically and socially in each context in relation to other contexts. Surely these concerns, if taken seriously, would influence everything about church life, from the way sermons are preached, Bible studies and other educative processes are conducted, to the way decision-making is pursued.

Regarding Conversation beyond the Christian Community

I am empathetic to Christians who doubt whether it is possible to have fruitful conversation with those who are not within the church, and, by extension, whether insights from outside of the Christian sphere should be utilized in the development of doctrine. Stephen Bevans is spot on: "Reality is not just 'out there;' reality is 'mediated by meaning,' a meaning that we give in the context of our culture or our historical period, interpreted from our own particular horizon and in our own particular thought forms."[41] Stanley Grenz is also on target when he suggests that to be part of the church of Jesus Christ is to be involved in a unique cognitive framework, characterized by a set of fundamental categories through which we view and experience ourselves and the world.[42]

World and Church Inherently Influence One Another

Still, I remind those who identify with Grenz's stance that they too must face the challenge posed by Bevans' claim. The emergence of contextual theologies and postcolonial theologies, informed by Bevans-like commitments, have highlighted the ways the particularities of our "situations" influence our directions and our procedures, as well as the tools utilized in theological analysis—thus affecting the ways common Christian claims are interpreted and applied to life.

That being said, the Christian cognitive framework, of which Grenz speaks, is not as discrete as his pronouncements suggest. Those who are part of the church are still simultaneously members of a wider community,

---

41. Bevans, *Models of Contextual Theology*, 4.
42. Grenz, *Theology for the Community of God*, 423–24.

constituted by a variety of overlapping cognitive schemes. As such, operating as a Christian in a nation, geographical region, community, or intellectual epoch, ensures that one is always entangled in a network of influences that by virtue of their overlapping nature will have also inter-permeated each other. This will be so even if one scheme appears dominant. Over time, obvious and not so obvious paths of interchange, rules of negotiation, and forms of allegiance develop within and outside of the Christian community. Thus, even as we take seriously the need to respect the otherness of the other, these insights should begin to clear the path for the consideration of intentional communication between members of the Christian community and those who are not a part of it.

God is in the World beyond the Church

The most significant influence on my approach to conversation beyond the Christian community is the very idea of an imaginatively creative God who, being absolutely relative, operates at the heart of existence from the level of primal energy to the level where free, partially self-creating, self-determining creatures explore life's mysteries, wrestle with what it means to be human, creatively imagine new possibilities for life, and harbor hopes for the future. Our belief that God's presence is universal should enable us to accept that God works not only in and through the church but throughout the world at large. Others, outside the church, can sometimes help the church perceive God's presence. While some of these may use the name "God" others may portray the effects of God's presence without recognizing that presence or naming the presence "God."

I assert that those who perceive themselves as special agents of God must be willing to engage life as a whole and other human beings wherever and whenever it is possible for God to be present, to have influence and be influenced, and to enhance the welfare of the world. A special vocation of the church, then, is to help its own membership as well as the larger world to be attuned to God's influence—even when such influence is not explicitly labeled "God at work here"—and to respond appropriately. Even as the church seeks to help people name God's presence and purposes, so the church needs to listen to others (including those outside the church) for their help in these regards.

In this regard, I find interesting Hodgson's characterization of the power of God's presence that was evident in Jesus. He suggests that the "the Christ gestalt [reflected in Jesus, but not reducible to Jesus] fans and flames out from Jesus to the ecclesial community and thence to the world as a whole, to other communities both religious and nonreligious where it interacts with other shapes of God's presence."[43] Given that those of the church carry the characterization "Christian" it is imprecise to use the term to describe God's presence elsewhere. That being said, Christians need to develop reasonable clarity regarding what is unique about our community, and, as such, what we have to offer to the complex overlapping scenario to which Hodgson alludes. This clarity will also inform our attitude to the contributions of others. Serious pursuit of the intra-church conversation I have described will contribute to this clarity.

Closing Comments

For the sake of internal and external conversations, we need to become multilingual where possible, and be willing to utilize the services of translators and interpreters where necessary, recognizing that cultures (religious, socio-political, ethnic, intellectual) are not static and that some levels of internal meaning will always be elusive. There will always be dimensions of the other to which we do not have access and which we cannot fully understand. Embracing Hodgson's words, I suggest that conversation "does not deny that circularity exists between beliefs and norms by which they are judged." However, conversation "prevents this circularity from becoming a static, self-enclosed system by insisting that it is possible to bring alternative traditions into productive encounter with each other, thus keeping them dynamic, growing, open to transformation." Conversation "involves a spiraling toward new and always open possibilities."[44]

Finally, conversation should be pursued with the appreciation that God communicates God's ideals for each individual and community in relation to God's ideals for all individuals and communities, and the cosmos as a whole. God has the infinite capacity to be in conversation with all persons and groups at the same moment. Through these conversations God seeks to influence them all in the direction of creating a cosmic community in which every self and every community maintains its distinct "selfhood" while living in relationships of respect and support with other communities. The more human communities take seriously the divine conversational relationship with the world as the model for conversation involving, individual human beings and groups (including elements of nature), the more likely the

43. Hodgson, *Winds of the Spirit*, 49.
44. Ibid., 101.

world will become such a place. What we believe about God shapes the kind of world in which we live.

Questions for Discussion

1. Which, if any, of the conceptions of God discussed in the chapter are most compatible with your present theological stance? Do you feel drawn to aspects of the other positions discussed?

2. With whom would you be willing to explore the positions on God, theological anthropology, and the work of Christ that have been discussed, and why? With whom would you not be willing to explore them, and why not?

3. What would need to change in your community for it to become the kind of setting described in the chapter? Is the intention worth the effort it would take and the potentially disruptive consequences?

4. What are some of the possibilities and pitfalls associated with the dialog outside of the church community, with religious and nonreligious groups?

5. What guidelines do you think are necessary to heighten the chances of productive conversation? Would the same ones be applicable for conversations within the Christian community and those with persons who are not a part of it?

   a. What would be the role of culture, ethnicity, gender, and sexual orientation in the structuring of conversational interactions?

   b. What do you think about the idea of conversation as a spiritual discipline?

Further Reading

Knitter, Paul. *Jesus and the Other Names: Christian Mission and Global Responsibility.* Maryknoll, NY: Orbis, 2001.

LaCugna, Catherine Mowry. *God for Us: The Trinity and Christian Life.* San Francisco: HarperCollins, 1973.

McCormack, Bruce, and Kimlyn Bender, editors. *Theology as Conversation: The Significance of Dialogue in Historical and Contemporary Theology.* Grand Rapids: Eerdmans, 2009.

Miller, Michael. *Freedom in Resistance and Creative Transformation.* Lanham, MD: Lexington Books/Rowman & Littlefield, 2013.

————. *Reshaping the Contextual Vision in Caribbean Theology: Theoretical Foundations for Theology Which Is Contextual, Pluralistic, and Dialectical.* Lanham, MD: University Press of America, 2007.

Ott, Daniel. *The Church in Process: A Process Ecclesiology.* Claremont, CA: Claremont Graduate University Press, 2006.

Pinnock, Clark. *Most Moved Mover: A Theology of God's Openness.* Grand Rapids: Baker Academic, 2001.

Placher, William. *Unapologetic Theology: A Christian Voice in a Pluralistic Conversation.* Louisville: Westminster John Knox, 1989.

Williamson, Clark. *Way of Blessing, Way of Life: A Christian Theology.* St. Louis: Chalice, 1999.

PART 2

The Tasks of Ministry

4

___

Preaching as Conversation

David J. Lose

❀ Ask almost any church-goer about the degree to which he or she experiences preaching as a conversation and you are likely to receive a puzzled look in response. Conversational? But only one person is talking.

Indeed. Given that the overwhelming majority of sermons given across the church's long history have been monologues, the question appears at first glance nonsensical. Consider one of the earliest descriptions of preaching, found in Justin Martyr's *First Apology*: "And on the day called Sunday, all who live in cities or in the country gather together to one place, and the memoirs of the apostles or the writings of the prophets are read, as long as time permits; then, when the reader has ceased, the president verbally instructs, and exhorts to the imitation of these good things."[1]

What is striking about Justin's description, authored around 150 CE, is how accurately it describes not simply the preaching of those living a generation or two after the writers of the New Testament but also the preaching of our own day. Though we no longer read the Bible "as long as time permits," but instead limit ourselves to three or four passages, I suspect that most parishioners might nod their heads in agreement that in the sermon the preacher "instructs and exhorts to imitation of these good things." How, then, are we to imagine preaching that stands in any kind of relation to the larger tradition of Christian proclamation as a conversation?

Historically, the answer has rested not in the sermon proper—consistently viewed and practiced as a monologue—but rather in preaching's place and role in the larger liturgy. Preaching, that is, exercises a particular

___

1. Justin Martyr, *First Apology*, 287.

function in the larger "holy dialogue" that is Christian worship, both announcing God's Word to the people as well as prompting their joyful response in creed, song, and life.[2]

While this view of preaching has dominated the homiletical imagination over the centuries, in recent years various preachers and scholars have sought to heighten and extend the conversational dimension of preaching, some by stressing the importance of a communal dimension of the preacher's *preparation*, others by noting the significance of the dialogical character of the preacher's *language* and *pastoral authority* in relation to the congregation. Both of these movements share a common desire to help preaching invite and prompt a more conversational experience of worship that starts in, but also continues beyond, the sanctuary.

Most recently still, the premise that preaching facilitates a larger liturgical dialogue has been challenged and extended by a few voices who believe that preaching itself should actually *be* a conversation, a place where Christians play an active role in the interpretation of Scripture. Though not by any sense uniform in theory or execution, these various approaches to preaching share a commitment to empower a genuine sense of shared responsibility for the preaching and worship of the church among those gathered.

In order to explore the possibility for a vibrant understanding of preaching as conversation, I will initially recall the dominant way preaching has been understood—as a provisional monologue that is part of the larger dialogue of worship. I will then explore the work of those who seek to make preaching more collaborative, and conclude by engaging the more recent subversion of the notion that preaching should *prompt* conversation in favor of one that advocates preaching that is *intentionally* conversational and participatory.

Preaching as Provisional Monologue

Since Jesus sat in the synagogue to preach on Isaiah as recorded in Luke's Gospel (4:16–30), preachers have strived to be provocative in their preaching. While perhaps not looking for quite the same outcome Jesus received, preachers nevertheless hope to provoke their congregation to a faithful response, both in the liturgy and beyond.

From this point of view, preaching plays a particular role within the larger "holy dialogue" that is worship. Traditionally, as Justin's early description of Christian worship attests, the preacher interprets the Scripture just read. The "instruction and exhortation" is meant to make the biblical

2. See O.W. Allen's essay in this volume, "Worship as Conversation," 93–112.

reading both understandable and applicable. The sermon, then, is both a response to the reading and also an extension of it.

During the Reformation, preaching continues to follow after and flow from the biblical reading, but the emphasis shifts from instruction to proclamation. Reformation preachers accent the imperative not just to teach but to announce the *kerygma* of the gospel to the expectant hearers.[3] In response to having heard the word of proclamation, congregation members are then prepared to confess their faith in turn by joining in the common confession of the faith with the words of one of the ecumenical creeds, singing a hymn, and making their offering to care for the congregation and community.

Preaching, from this classic point of view, is a "provisional monologue" in which one person speaks for a time, not simply to deliver a message but to prompt and nurture a response.[4] In this way both preacher and congregation are caught up in the divine dialogue and drama of worship in a manner reminiscent of Kierkegaard's comparison of worship to theater and, in particular, to the three agents of theater: audience, actor, and prompter (the one who aids the actor to speak his or her lines). Most congregants, Kierkegaard assumes, approach worship as if they are the audience, the preacher is the actor, and God is the prompter nudging the preacher to a better performance. Kierkegaard, however, insisted that God is the proper recipient of our prayer and praise and is therefore the audience. The congregation members are the actors, and the preacher is the prompter, guiding and aiding their performance.[5]

Kierkegaard's metaphor captures well the instinct of those preachers who have sought to emphasize the sermon's distinct and integral role in the holy conversation of worship. The sermon, understood along these lines, is certainly still responsive to Scripture, but it is also provocative, even catalytic, in its attempt to elicit a confession of faith in word and deed from the community.

---

3. Luther's assertion is paradigmatic of the Reformation sentiment: "It is not enough or in any sense Christian to preach the works, life, and words of Christ as historical facts, as if the knowledge of these would suffice . . . Rather ought Christ to be preached that faith in him may be established and that he may not only be Christ, but be Christ for you and me, and that what is said of him and is denoted in his name may be effectual in us. Such faith is produced and preserved by preaching why Christ came, what he brought and bestowed, what benefit it is to us to accept him." "On Christian Liberty," 357.

4. The term "provisional monologue" comes from Mikhail Bakhtin. See his "The Problem of Speech Genres," esp. 67–82.

5. Kierkegaard, *Purity of Heart*, 180–81.

Collaborative Sermon Preparation

In recent years, scholars of preaching have moved in two related directions to extend and clarify this notion of provisional speech. Each direction assumes a monological sermon but approaches the sermon as dialogical in character.

Imagining the Congregation in Sermon Preparation

The first extension takes seriously preaching as a communal word and focuses on methods of biblical study and sermon preparation that reflect that communal reality of the sermon. As Thomas Long writes,

> When preachers go to the scripture, then, they must take the people with them, since what will be heard there is a word for them. . . . We must self-consciously embody the needs and situations of others, especially those who are different from ourselves. Some preachers find it helpful, as part of the process of interpreting the scripture, to visualize the congregation that will be present when the sermon is preached. They survey the congregation in their mind's eye, seeing the familiar faces and the lives behind them. . . . When preachers turn to the scripture, all these people go with them.[6]

While preachers may therefore do all the speaking, they do so not on their own account or authority but rather on the behalf of, and authorized by, the congregation. Long, and other homileticians like Fred Craddock, imagine the role played by preachers as a sympathetic task, anticipating and imagining how their people might hear, question, wonder about, and ultimately be encouraged by the biblical passage at hand.[7] Indeed, the "inductive" method of preaching so identified with Craddock is itself a largely sympathetic endeavor as the preacher invites hearers to follow along the journey the preacher traversed—as opposed to merely hearing it recounted—that they might discover and own for themselves the insights of the sermon.[8] Such an approach also allows a broader understanding of "conversation" to include not just the preacher and the local congregation, but also, as Ronald Allen writes, "God,

6. Long, *The Witness of Preaching*, 55–56.

7. Preachers, according to Craddock, are invited to listen in—both actually and imaginatively—to the conversations of those all around them. See *Overhearing the Gospel*, 101–19.

8. See, in particular, Craddock's *As One Without Authority*, where he outlines the need, rationale, and execution of inductive preaching.

the gospel, the Bible, Christian tradition . . . the wider Christian community, [and] the world."[9] All of this and more is available sympathetically to the
preacher while preparing the sermon.

Actual Collaboration with the Congregation

In the preceding approach, the preacher *imagines* how hearers might engage the biblical story but doesn't actually ask them to contribute directly
to the preparation of the sermon. Recently, however, several scholars have
proposed that such engagement with the community of hearers does not
need to be theoretical and sympathetic only, but rather can and should take
place in the form of actual and ongoing collaboration. Preaching, while it
may be an activity exercised by one person at a time, should nevertheless
be a thoroughly communal endeavor. As John McClure writes in his book
The Roundtable Pulpit, preachers are responsible for both promoting and
representing the ongoing conversations of the community from the pulpit:

> The goal of collaborative preaching is to *engage in* and *influence*
> the ways that a congregation is "talking itself into" becoming a
> Christian community. The preacher does not present sovereign
> declarations of the purposes and goals of the church from the
> pulpit (You must, or You ought), or take the congregation on an
> inductive journey through which certain goals or purposes can
> be experienced and owned. Instead the preacher collaborates
> with members of the congregation, galvanizing in the pulpit
> the actual talk through which the community, in response to
> the biblical message, is experiencing and producing in its own
> congregational life and mission.[10]

In her book, *Sharing the Word: Preaching in the Roundtable Church*,
Lucy Rose articulates one of the core convictions of collaborative and communal preaching: "Fundamental to my experiences of and reflections on
preaching is the conviction that the preacher and congregation are not
separate entities but a community of faith."[11] Preaching is no longer simply
a matter of declaring, teaching, or witnessing, but rather is designed and
executed with the intent of "gathering the community of faith around the

---

9. R. J. Allen, *Interpreting the Gospel*, 71.

10. McClure, *The Roundtable Pulpit*, 50.

11. L. A. Rose, *Sharing the Word*, 89.

Word where the central conversations of the people of God are fostered and refocused week after week."[12]

This kind of preaching, its advocates suggest, is not simply appropriate to our time, but more accurately reflects the biblical witness. As Rose reminds us, "The Greek word *homily* means 'familiar conversation' similar to the exchange of the two apostles on the road to Emmaus, as they 'talked with each other about all these things that had happened.'"[13] The goal of such an approach, according to McClure, is to create an encounter in which other—often very different—people engage one another in such a way as to become aware of the possibilities for interpreting faith and life via the shared conversation mediated by the preacher:

> Collaborative preaching is designed to place before an entire congregation, each Sunday morning, an ongoing, core-conversation. All members of the congregation can participate in this conversation. They can do so directly, by signing up to join the sermon brainstorming group (the sermon roundtable) or indirectly, by providing feedback to someone who is currently a member of this group.[14]

The Preacher becomes Host and Steward

To conceive of preaching in this way is necessarily to re-imagine the role of the preacher not simply as authorized witness (Long), or experienced guide (Craddock), but rather as both a generous and engaged host of the congregation's ongoing conversation and a faithful steward of the Christian tradition. As McClure writes, "The preacher is a host who opens access to the pulpit to those whose interpretations and experiences may be very different. The preacher listens, reflects, argues, and agrees, satisfied all the while to be the 'last' instead of 'first' at the roundtable to receive and communicate the divine Word."[15]

Leonora Tubbs Tisdale takes the metaphor even further. Advocating a method of biblical engagement and sermon preparation that takes the context of the hearers—their situation, history, experiences, struggles, and more—as seriously as the context of the biblical passage, Tisdale inviting preachers to imagine themselves as folk dance leaders:

12. Ibid., 93.
13. Ibid., 94.
14. McClure, *The Roundtable Pulpit*, 50.
15. Ibid., 51.

Contextual congregational proclamation on Sunday mornings is a lot like folk dance. The preacher, functioning both as dancer and as leader in the dance, stays close to the ground of the local community, inviting and encouraging others to join in the circle dance of faith. The sermon itself is a participatory act in which the preacher models a way of doing theology that meets people where they are, but that also encourages them to stretch themselves by trying new steps, new moves, new patterns of belief and action. In this dance, as in the circle dance, the leader must always be alert to what is happening in the life of the community—sometimes correcting, sometimes encouraging, sometimes guiding, sometimes pushing toward new vistas—as the need arises.[16]

What unites these distinct proposals is their common commitment to engaging hearers in an activity that is variously described as collaborative, conversational, and participatory. Each, that is, seeks to invite hearers into the process of preparing a sermon so that the proclaimed Word draws them into the ongoing conversation of faith that constitutes the Christian life. The sermon is a "provisional monologue" in that it is not the last word but rather seeks both to reflect previous conversations of faith and to prompt and provoke future ones. The goal, ultimately, is to create not simply a conversational sermon but a community conversation where the preacher, as O. Wesley Allen, Jr., notes, "is one of many conversation partners in the church."[17]

Conversational and Confessional Sermon Language

A closely related—and often overlapping—strand of recent homiletical work draws attention to the distinct nature of conversational preaching and the consequent demands *such preaching places on the language and form of the sermon and on the attitude and authority of the preacher.*

Reconsidering Language and Sermon Form in Conversational Preaching

If the sermon is to be truly conversational, it needs at least to reconsider, if not also relinquish, traditional forms of homiletical authority. As

16. Tisdale, *Preaching as Local Theology and Folk Art*, 125. While Tisdale's approach in many ways leans closer to the sympathetic engagement of Long, Craddock, and others, her overall contextual homiletics lends itself and adds to the collaborative, conversational approach advocated more directly by McClure and L. A. Rose.

17. O. W. Allen, Jr., *The Homiletic of All Believers*, 39.

McClure reminds us, "Conversation does not necessarily imply collaboration. . . . Conversations can be dominated by certain parties and used to reinforce divisions or hierarchical power relations within a congregation. For this reason, we need to identify a form of conversation that is commensurate with collaborative leadership and the task of sermon preparation and delivery."[18]

Preachers wishing to foster a collaborative and conversational approach to preaching must therefore be wary of sermon forms and language that separate the preacher from the community, as such always bear the marks of a hierarchical model of preaching. In contrast, the goal of a provisional monologue that arises from a conversational homiletic seeks to bridge and eventually erase such divides. As Rose writes,

> In conversational preaching, this sermonic conversation is grounded in solidarity—a shared identity as the believing people of God, a shared priesthood before God and within community, and shared tasks of discerning and proclaiming God's Word.[19]

This conviction makes demands on the language and form a preacher chooses. As Tisdale notes, preaching that seeks to nurture congregational conversation "exhibits a preference for the simple, plain, conversational speech of the local congregation."[20] The preacher, that is, needs to sound like the parishioners. Even more, as McClure points out, preaching that seeks to be collaborative must also reflect the actual conversations the preacher has had with congregation members: "The language of the collaborative sermon . . . will either describe the dynamic as it took place at the sermon roundtable or it will imitate directly one of those dynamics."[21] Most simply put: if participants are going to believe the preacher values the conversations she is having with her parishioners, then the preacher must represent those conversations in the sermon.

Much of the same can be said about sermon form, which must itself be more conversational, imitating the give and take of the conversations the preacher has had with congregation members in preparing the sermon. This doesn't necessarily rule out traditional sermon forms that may at first glance seem more didactic than conversational. Even a verse-by-verse expository sermon can reflect the insights and contributions parishioners made during

---

18. McClure, *The Roundtable Pulpit*, 50.
19. L. A. Rose, *Sharing the Word*, 95.
20. Tisdale, *Preaching as Local Theology and Folk Art*, 127.
21. McClure, *The Roundtable Pulpit*, 73.

the discussion leading up to the sermon. What is crucial is faithfully representing the content and value of such contributions and conversations.

Further, the form must also recognize the ways of being, thinking, and believing of a particular congregational culture. As Tisdale notes, a highly didactic form may suit one congregational culture very well but fail another altogether. Similarly, a highly stylized sermon that deeply moves a congregation that privileges the fine arts, for instance, may not prove nearly as effective in another context where personal stories might be more effective.[22] What is at stake throughout is that the preacher chooses sermonic forms that honor both the actual conversations leading up to the sermon and the culture and "learning style" of the hearers. As Tisdale repeatedly emphasizes, the sermon—in its content, language, and form—must be fitting to the congregation as well as faithful to the tradition.[23] In short, congregants must hear and see themselves in the conversation the preacher hosts in the sermon if they are expected to participate in it.[24]

Shared Authority in the Conversational Sermon

The stakes of authentic conversational preaching, however, are often higher than identification (Tisdale) and representation (McClure). Indeed, concerns about the language and form of conversational preaching usually stem from deeper convictions about the nature of both *authority* and *truth* in a twenty-first-century, post-Christian, postmodern world.

In this kind of environment, where traditional hierarchical roles have been at least called into question if not rejected altogether, the preacher's authority is being negotiated anew. In previous generations the preacher's authority rested in his or her (though predominantly it was "his") ordination or appointment as *the* interpreter of Scripture and teacher and preacher of the faith. All this changes, however, if the preacher's goal is not simply to impart or apply biblical truth but rather, as we heard Rose state, to gather "the community of faith around the Word where the central conversations of the people of God are fostered and refocused." With this understanding of the role and purpose of preaching in the larger life of faith, the preacher must give over a certain amount of authority. It is quite different, after all, to be the authorized interpreter than it is to be a welcoming host.

---

22. Tisdale, *Preaching as Local Theology and Folk Art*, 133–43.

23. Ibid., 33.

24. As R. J. Allen writes, "A sermon is conversational when the congregation recognizes itself in the sermon" (68).

If all the voices of the community are to be valued, then the preacher must eschew previous conceptions of homiletical authority and resist the urge to "trump" diverging or even dissenting voices in both the conversations leading up to the sermon and in the sermon itself. As Rose writes, "Conversational preaching in part grows out of and reflects the ongoing conversations between the preacher and members of the congregation in which the preacher is not the one-in-the-know but an equal colleague in matters of living and believing. Instead of impeding these conversations with a final or single answer, the preacher fosters them by explicitly acknowledging a variety of points of view, learning processes, interpretations, and life experiences."[25]

As most preachers know from experience, this is not always easy to do. To share a personal example: when I suggested in an online preaching resource that pastors invite a "roundtable discussion" *in* the sermon rather than before it, one preacher shared in the comments his fear that when his parishioners "got it wrong" he would have to correct them and that would be "shaming." This particular preacher voiced, I suspect, the concerns of many. After all, we preachers have been well trained in exegetical methods and generally—though not by any means always—know more than our parishioners about the social and historical setting of biblical texts as well as about the history of their interpretation. We are, in short, the experts, called, set apart, and trained for this purpose. We may therefore fear promoting "bad"—or at the very least unhelpful—interpretations of the text than our less-trained parishioners may offer.

There is good warrant for this concern. The church has been harmed by the poor interpretations of its people (and, far more frequently, its leaders!) in the past. More recently, however, many of us are preoccupied by a greater fear, one expressed well by Richard Nysse and Donald Juel: "while many [preachers] have been convinced that sound method is a way of avoiding mistakes, in most cases the greatest danger is not wrong answers as much as lack of engagement."[26] Most simply put, many preachers are increasingly worried that our emphasis on "right interpretation" and our role as the trained arbiters of what constitutes such interpretation may lead our people to lose confidence in their ability to read the biblical text and, over time, even to lose interest in trying. A conversational homiletic for this reason negotiates and shares authority for interpretation with the rest of the faith community, seeking over time to build a community of faithful collaborators where each member is conversant in the faith.

25. L. A. Rose, *Sharing the Word*, 96.
26. Nysse and Juel, "Interpretation for Christian Ministry," 353.

Conversational Sermon as Tentative Yet Bold Interpretations

But concerns for shared authority do not reflect only a particular commitment to egalitarianism or even a desire to build up the body; they also stem from an understanding of *truth* that is simultaneously more tentative and more dynamic than that of a previous generation.

This understanding of truth is more tentative in that it believes that all human knowledge, inquiry, and apprehension are inherently limited. To borrow from the Apostle Paul, this side of the eschaton we will always "see in a mirror dimly" and "know only in part" (1 Cor. 13:12). This has immediate implications for theology and preaching. As Rose writes, "If all human knowledge is inexact and incomplete, revelation is incomplete and inconclusive." Even, "the truth of the Gospel, as the content of revelation, remains fragmentary, uncertain, and approximate. Revelation is also incomplete and uncertain because God is finally ineffable." For this reason, all "human speech about God is a 'gesture' toward God . . . never a formula delimiting God."[27]

Given this understanding of truth and revelation, Rose chooses to pass over previous terms like "proclamation" to describe preaching and instead chooses more provisional language: "Preaching is about tentative interpretations, proposals that invite counter proposals, and the preacher's wagers as genuine convictions placed in conversation with the wagers of others."[28]

But while this understanding of truth, revelation, and preaching is more tentative, it is also more dynamic, in that truth and revelation are no longer static terms or settled things that we simply refer to. Instead, truth is emergent, arising from the clash of inquiry and conviction, assertions and counter assertions, questions and insights of the community. Revelation itself, from this point of view, turns out to be dialogue, a "dynamic, ongoing exchange that always requires interpretation and reinterpretation."[29] For this reason, she re-imagines how a traditional theological and homiletical category like "*kerygma*" might itself be dynamically renewed:

> In conversational preaching the *kerygma* is no longer the unchanging core of the gospel, grounded in the apostles' preaching as once-and-for-all revelation. Instead, the *kerygma* might designate a temporary formulation of a slice of God's activity in the world that is critical for the contemporary church and that

27. L. A. Rose, *Sharing the Word*, 99, working particularly off of the thought of Robert E. C. Browne in *The Ministry of the Word*.

28. Ibid., 100.

29. Ibid., 101.

is grounded in revelation as an ongoing conversation with God, the Word, and biblical texts.[30]

Sharing Tisdale's concern for a contextual homiletic, Rose concludes that the "*kerygma* for one generation in one corner of the church might be human freedom; it will be different in a different generation in a different corner of the church."[31]

While some might fear surrendering the certainty of Christian truth and preaching in such a formulation, I think that it not only better fits the skepticism of our postmodern age but also more aptly reflects the character of Christian faith. In my own attempts to formulate a homiletic that is both faithful to the biblical witness and responsive to the postmodern age in which we preach, I concluded that many of our fears are not only unfounded but indeed misplaced. It is not so much that we must surrender truth, but rather our exclusive claim to *proving* truth. In this refusal to have the last word, we not only invite others into the conversation but force ourselves to live, once again, by faith alone.[32]

In language similar to Rose, I have therefore also called for preachers to adopt language that is simultaneously tentative and bold in order to offer confessions of faith that seek to elicit a response from the hearers.[33] Terms like confession, proposal, and wager aid a conversational homiletic, I believe, in that they make room for the hearer to respond with questions, further conversation, doubt, and also genuine belief—belief that stems from a dynamic interaction with the living Word rather than a static and dutiful repetition of the truths handed down by a previous generation. In order to nurture such belief, adopting terms like confession and wager invite preachers to surrender a certain degree of authority and to guarantee their hearers their unconditional regard regardless of how the hearer responds to our confessions. Such a guarantee creates the safe space in which hearers may freely contemplate and respond to the preacher's wagers and confessions and come to their own dynamic and relevant convictions.[34]

In this way, both the preacher and the community of faith are drawn week after week into a conversation in which truth reveals itself as something that can be *confessed* and *professed* but never fully *possessed*. Such truth emerges in the interplay of faithful conversation, confession, and wager and is characterized by equal measures of confidence and humility as it beckons

30. Ibid., 103.

31. Ibid.

32. Lose, *Confessing Jesus Christ*, esp. 62.

33. Ibid., 206.

34. Ibid., 201–2.

hearers and preachers alike into an uncharted and unknown future that is imagined and secured only by the promises of God.

Moving beyond Monologue to Actual Dialogue in the Sermon

At various points in her book on conversational preaching, Lucy Rose imagines that the preacher not only makes space for the perspectives of all members of the community but also invites them, upon occasion, into the pulpit to preach.[35] While the sermon would still be a monologue, such a practice would make it at least a communally shared monologue where various members of the community take their turn, so to speak, at the microphone. Near the very close of her book on conversational preaching, she also entertains the possibility of making space for congregational responses to the sermon both around and during the actual worship service:

> Conversational preaching welcomes a variety of personal responses to every sermon. Many communities of faith include either within the worship service or afterward opportunities for reflection and personal sharing. These communities model ways of legitimizing a variety of personal experiences, interpretation, and convictions as primary ingredients in the community's ongoing conversations.[36]

While this suggestion may have seemed fifteen years ago a fitting and innovative extension of the work of Rose and other advocates of more collaborative preaching, today's skeptics might point out that this is as close to an actual conversation as "conversational" preaching apparently gets. Similarly, while preachers may greet suggestions of conversational roundtables before the sermon or discussion groups after with gratitude, they may also wonder about the potential for bringing that dynamic directly to the moment of preaching.

There is good reason to consider doing so. Living in a social media-saturated culture, where our interaction with movies, books, television programs, and almost every other form of communication has become increasingly participatory, the one-way monologue of preaching seems

---

35. As L. A. Rose, *Sharing the Word*, 123, writes, a "nonhierarchical ethos perhaps leads those who are ordained to resist monopolizing the pulpit and to re-envision their role as ensuring that preaching occurs. This ethos perhaps leads the community of faith regularly to invite others, particularly laity, to preach."

36. Ibid., 129.

increasingly out of step with the culture. For this reason, more and more preachers question the unidirectional nature of historic preaching.

The inclination to move to a more interactive style of preaching, however, does not stem simply from an urge to mimic the culture. Rather, it flows from a desire to have preaching and the larger worship service itself more closely reflect and connect to the daily experience of most North American Christians. As Doug Pagitt, one of the leading advocates for a more truly conversational style of preaching, writes,

> This is the age of Pandora, where I tell an online radio station what to play. It is the age of the app store, where a major corporation essentially hands control over to an open-source network of ordinary people. It is the age of Wikipedia, where anyone can help decide what a word or concept or cultural touchstone means. It is the age when a bunch of college kids create a social network and seven years late it has more than 500 million users.
>
> It is the age of ownership and customization and user-created content.
>
> The impetus behind all of this personalization isn't narcissism. It's the longing to attach meaning to experience.[37]

Echoing concerns first articulated by the "dialogue preachers" of the late sixties, Pagitt and others assert that hearers today are less inclined to receive the meaning imparted by authority figures—whether preachers or political pundits—and more interested in making meaning themselves.[38] Little wonder that beneath the 2012 presidential debates ran a constant report of Twitter-users or that some of the larger news stories after each debate were various reactions generated on Facebook. We are increasingly an interactive culture, as our contact with almost all media is ever more colored by our desire to participate as *co-creators* of the content we simultaneously receive, produce, consume, and share. Indeed, as Frank Rose, editor at *Wired Magazine* and author of *The Art of Immersion*, writes, "even the concept of audience is becoming outdated; participants would be more like it."[39]

---

37. Pagitt, *Preaching in the Inventive Age*, 5–6. Pagitt's book, it should be noted, is actually a slightly revised edition of his 2005 *Preaching Re-Imagined*.

38. Earlier attempts at dialogue preaching animated by a similar concern to invite hearers to make meaning for themselves include Reuel Howe's *Partners in Preaching* and William Thompson and Gordon Bennett's *Dialogue Preaching*.

39. F. Rose, *The Art of Immersion*, 6.

Preaching Redefined?
New Ways of Understanding Preaching for New Days

In today's environment, the "crisis" of preaching decried by scholars of preaching of all stripes in the seventies seems almost passé. Or, to put it another way, to imagine that preaching is in a crisis is to imagine it's something we can fix, that there is some flaw in the execution of a fundamentally sound practice. The challenge, in this case, is to reform or revise or even re-imagine a form or style or method of preaching while assuming the foundational tenets of the practice. This assumption accounts for the history of the latter portion of the twentieth-century, North American, and primarily Anglo homiletics—the move from didactic and deductive forms of preaching to narrative and inductive forms and eventually to collaborative and "conversational" ones.

But what if preaching does not need to be revised or re-imagined but rather redefined? As Pagitt's notes, "There was a time when I felt my ability to deliver sermons was a high calling that I sought to refine but didn't need to redefine. Those days are gone. Now I find myself regularly redefining my role and the role of preaching."

Why? Because, as Pagitt continues, "I find myself wanting to live life with the people of my community where I can preach—along with the other preachers of our community—but not allow that to become an act of speech making. Instead, I want it to be a living interaction of the story of God and the story of our community being connected by our truth telling, our vulnerability, and our open minds, ears, and eyes."[40]

Toward this end, Pagitt develops a method of preaching that he calls "implicatory progressional dialogue," but which might be more easily and simply described as a facilitated conversation on the biblical readings chosen for the worship service. Such a dialogue shifts hermeneutical authority and meaning-making agency from the pastor to the congregation so that the congregation draws its own implications rather than receiving simply the "applications" of the pastor.[41] Such a progressional dialogue is, in many senses, the roundtable method McClure describes moved from the fellowship hall to the sanctuary. Pagitt contrasts this kind of sermon with a form of preaching he calls "speaching," traditional preaching that is characterized by a monologue akin to the typical speech.[42]

---

40. Pagitt, *Preaching in the Inventive Age*, 9–10.

41. Ibid., 96–99.

42. Pagitt describes "speaching" in ibid., 41–43.

Pagitt's work is largely descriptive, offering the method of preaching he employs at his emergent congregation for more popular consumption and imitation. Because almost all of his examples come from his own distinct context (he is the founding pastor of his congregation), it is sometimes difficult to assess how his ideas might work in a non-startup, non-emergent setting. Despite these limitations, however, he advocates a model of preaching that in many ways takes the guiding principles and core convictions of the "provisional monologue" to its natural conclusion. Such an approach invites a style of preaching that reflects the ways in which people today make meaning and construct identity. As O. Wesley Allen notes, "Citizens of the postmodern culture make meaning in a conversation manner, giving and taking from the myriad of 'conversation' partners we have in today's world."[43]

Further, there is ample warrant, I believe, to experiment with this and other homiletical forms that help to move us from what I would describe as a largely *performative* model of preaching to one that is more intentionally *participatory* and *formative*. Briefly put, performative preaching represents the monologue sermon that has dominated the imagination of preachers over the centuries. I choose the word "performative" neither to over-emphasize nor downplay the performative elements of preaching as public speech, but rather to draw attention to the fact that in the traditional, monologue-style of preaching, the preacher is the primary performer in that he or she typically is

- the only one that speaks,

- the sole interpreter of the biblical witness,

- the one charged with making connections between faith and life, and

- the one expected to share his or her faith publically (that is, in the sermon).

Perhaps most importantly, the mark of competence in a performative model is degree to which the *preacher* excels at these tasks.

While this style of sermon has served the church remarkably well over the centuries, it flourished in a culture that had some knowledge of and sympathy for the Christian story. In a post-Christian era, however, and when time is at a premium for persons besieged by more information, more opportunities, and more obligations than ever before, it is no longer enough, I believe, that ministers perform these central tasks of the faith for their people. Rather, each member of the community of faith must develop the capacity to use the Christian story and faith to make sense of their lives.

43. O. W. Allen, *The Homiletic of All Believers*, 17.

That this has not happened is demonstrated by several recent and alarming trends describing the decline of Christianity in North America.[44] Viewing these trends and the contributing factors behind them, we might assert that our primary challenge is that we preach to people—to borrow from Walter Brueggemann—for whom God is no longer an active character in the drama of the world or their lives.[45]

Indeed, recent research has suggested that the primary reason for the decline of mainline Christian traditions is not that they are too liberal or disconnected from traditional creedal Christianity—an explanation regularly suggested—but rather because they have failed to provide a coherent and compelling religious identity that not only informs but also guides and enriches the lives of their congregants. When people stop coming to our churches, that is, it is typically not because they have chosen to go to more conservative churches but simply because they have decided no longer to go to church.[46]

In this kind of environment it is imperative that Christians participate in worship and the sermon not simply because they are used to participating and making meaning in other parts of their lives, but because by participating in the ongoing interpretation of the biblical story they come to know, actualize, and live out of that story. The challenge and opportunity before us is to invite our people to actual engagement of the *biblical* story in an age where all kinds of grand stories and metanarratives clamor for their attention and allegiance. Our goal, that is, is less to develop biblical *literacy* than it is to nurture biblical *imagination*, where intimate knowledge of and regular interaction with the biblical stories invites patterns of thinking, speaking, and doing that would otherwise be unavailable to us.

The homiletical roundtable suggested by McClure prior to the sermon and the discussion groups afterward alluded to by Rose are important possibilities to consider, but typically only a fraction of our worshiping communities take advantage of such opportunities. Moreover, recent studies in adult education reveal that adults derive most of their identity from their sources of greatest competence. That means, among other things, that adults

44. Even a cursory review of two studies in particular throw in relief the ascendancy of post-Christian culture in North American: (1) The Pew Research Center's Forum on Religion and Public Life's report "'Nones' on The Rise;" (2) The Hartford Institute for Religion Research's "A Decade of Change in American Congregations: 2000–2010."

45. Brueggemann, *The Practice of Prophetic Imagination*, 2–4.

46. As early as 1967, Peter Berger in *The Sacred Canopy*, 127ff, pointed to the "crisis of credibility" and "problem of plausibility" traditional religious faith was experiencing. More recently, scholars like Wade Clark Roof in *Community and Commitment*, Mark Chaves in *Congregations in America*, and Diana Butler Bass in *Christianity After Religion* have provided insights into the decline of North American Christianity.

are often very uncomfortable in situations of new learning, they often feel like "imposters," and are not likely to develop confidence in exercising new abilities apart from repeated practice.[47] Yet in a performative model of preaching, the preacher is the only one who actively "practices" the essential skills of connecting the biblical story to our own story and sharing our faith.

An Experiment:
The Sermon as Invitation to Participation

For these reasons, in recent years I have advocated experimenting with a more participatory style of preaching where hearers are invited to practice and gain competence—and in this way develop confidence—in their ability to use the biblical story to make sense of their lives. Such participation should certainly include attention to sermon preparation, language and form, and the authority of the preacher as advocated by those who view preaching as a provisional monologue, but at the same time it must move beyond such concerns. To capture and illustrate this distinction, it may be helpful to recall the recent shift in our use of technology and the internet that some describe as the advent of Web 2.0.[48]

First coined by Darcy DiNucci in 1999, the term Web 2.0 refers to software designed in such a way so that it is completed only by the intentional and creative use of the consumer. As DiNucci predicted, "The Web we know now, which loads into a window on our computer screens in essentially static screenfuls, is an embryo of the Web as we will know it in not so many years . . . [when] the Web will be understood, not as screenfuls of text and graphics but as a transport mechanism, the ether through which interactivity happens."[49]

My suggestion is that we imagine the sermon not primarily as "screenfuls" of religious text and speech—that is, as a finished message, an artful interpretation of the biblical text, or a dazzling connection between faith and life—but rather as "a transport mechanism, the ether through which interactivity happens." What if the sermon not only provided the *content* of the biblical narrative as a source for identity but also promoted lively *interaction* with that story so one might gain practice in living out of that identity?

Such an engagement might certainly include mechanisms like Pagitt's "implicatory progressional dialogue" (though hopefully named more

---

47. See Brookfield, *The Skillful Teacher*, esp. 76–81.

48. I first developed and used this analogy in "Preaching 2.0."

49. DiNucci, "Fragmented Future," 32.

simply), but it would also recognize and make room for a host of other ways by which the congregation can actively interact with the biblical story out of which the sermon arises. Inviting parishioners to read and consider the text in advance, to engage in various activities during the sermon, and to look for and report where they see the biblical story being played out in their own lives are only a sampling of possibilities by which to engage our hearers with the claims and confessions of the biblical story both in the sermon and throughout the week.[50] The explicit move is from performative to *formative* preaching and ministry, where the overarching concern is not so much that the preacher excels at reading and using the biblical story but that, over time, our people increase in their competence and confidence in doing the same.

Preacher as Coach, Conductor, Teacher, Encourager

From this point of view, the preacher plays the role neither of the expert witness on all matters religious nor of merely a conversational facilitator. Rather, the preacher plays the role of coach, conductor, teacher, and encourager, always deploying his or her expertise to help all members of the congregation know the story, share the story, and live the story better. In short, if preachers hope that over time their people will develop greater confidence that the biblical story offers a compelling narrative by which to make sense of their lives, then they must give their people opportunities to practice their own skills in reading and using the Bible on Sunday morning. Because, quite frankly, what we do repeatedly is not only what we develop competence in but it is also what we value most highly. Hence, if we never give people an opportunity to practice reading and interpreting the Bible, connecting faith and everyday life, and sharing their faith, not only do we rob them of the opportunity to develop confidence in their ability but we are also—consciously or subconsciously—declaring that these things are not really that important.

I should be clear at this point I am not saying the performative model of preaching is wrong, merely that it is no longer adequate on its own. Nor do I pretend to know the way forward. This is not how I was taught to preach nor has it been the way I have taught others to preach for most of my

50. For the past several years I have played with a variety of means by which to invite greater participation in the sermon in a weekly column I write on the online preaching website WorkingPreacher.org. Those interested may look at the following articles: "In God We Trust," "God Bless You," "Salt and Light," "Perfect," "Picture This," and "Beyond Our Wants." These provide a sampling of approaches to engaging in more participatory preaching.

career. But I am increasingly convinced that if we desire preaching to play an essential role in helping our people become conversant in the Christian faith and enter into the ongoing holy dialogue that God has with us not only on Sunday mornings but throughout the rest of the week, then we must find ways to use the precious moments of the sermon not only to talk but also to listen, not only to witness but also to be inspired, not only to teach but also to encourage our people to greater competency and confidence in the essential skills of the Christian life. In this way we can equip our people to continue the faithful conversation of which we are only the latest participants.

Some Possible Strengths and Weaknesses of Conversational Preaching

The various approaches to conversational preaching we have just surveyed are united in a commitment to extend the "holy dialogue" of worship into the daily lives of their people. Where they differ is in how they imagine the type and placement of conversation. It is imagined or real; before, during, or after the sermon; spoken, or involving other activities designed to give people a chance to practice their faith?

These differences are important and lead to distinct styles and methods of preaching. In recent years, I have become increasingly persuaded that we need to move from performative to formative preaching that more intentionally seeks to "equip the saints for the work of ministry" (Eph. 4:12). The great strength of this approach is that it invites Christians living in a world of multiple and competing narratives to develop competence and confidence in the story and language of the faith. If today's Christians and seekers will not simply go to church because their parents did, but seek to commit themselves to experiences and communities that help them make sense of their whole lives, then I believe a more participatory style of preaching holds great promise.

But there may be limitations, or certainly at least questions, to this approach as well. Two seem worth particular mention. First, will the community's participation and conversation lead to proclamation? If the preacher's primary responsibility is to preach the gospel, can she abdicate that authority for the sake of "genuine conversation"? When considering this question, it is helpful to recall that the sermon is not the only part of the worship service. Perhaps some of the freight for "proclamation" can be distributed throughout the service. Further, trusting the congregation to proclaim—and equipping them to do so—may multiply the actual impact of that proclamation over time. In such a scenario, the pastor is not only the proclaimer, but increasingly the steward of proclamation.

Second, will any one sermon style, form, or approach serve in this age of diverse and manifold media? I suspect that given the variety of expectations and learning styles present in any congregation, today's preacher would be well served to develop a variety of patterns of preaching and choose between them based on the expected outcome of the sermon, the text at hand and, not least, the experiences and history of both preacher and congregation. One of the great challenges of participatory preaching is, quite simply, that it is unfamiliar for many of our people. Our hearers have traditionally been just that—*hearers* used to being more like an "audience" at a musical performance than "participants" in an ongoing drama or conversation. But if we seek to develop the confidence of our people to make sense of the Bible and the faith themselves, then we must develop their competence in doing so.

In this venture, preachers of Anglo-American, mainline congregations in particular can learn much from African-American preaching traditions where participation, while often in service to a fairly performative style of preaching and worship, has effectively drawn hearers into that performance and thereby shaped the hearts and imaginations of generations of Christians.[51] And that, finally, is the goal of conversational preaching, however you might practice it: to draw our people into a story that began at the dawn of creation, closes only with the end of all things, and beckons them even now into its majestic drama to be witnesses of, and participants in, God's grand design to love, save, and redeem the whole world.

Questions for Discussion

1. If you are new to preaching, review your history of listening to sermons. On a spectrum from provisional monologue to conversational/ participatory preaching, characterize the preaching you have heard. In relationship to the monological and conversational approaches, when have you felt most and least connected to the sermon? Why?

2. If you have been preaching for a while, review your history of preaching. On the same spectrum as in no. 1, place your preaching on that spectrum and describe it in relationship to provisional monological and conversational/participatory preaching. In relationship to these

51. LaRue makes just such an invitation in his book, *I Believe I'll Testify*. See also, R. J. Allen, *Interpreting the Gospel*, 68.

categories, when do you feel most connected to the congregation? What are the signs of connection?

3. What are the most compelling reasons for you to move in the direction of conversational preaching? What are some significant reservations?

4. As a thought experiment, what would you need to do to become a participatory preacher?

5. When thinking about your own context for preaching, what needs to happen to create a climate that is hospitable to conversational preaching?

Further Reading

Allen, Ronald J. *Interpreting the Gospel: An Introduction to Preaching.* St. Louis: Chalice, 1998, esp. 65–95.

———. "Preaching as Mutual Critical Correlation through Conversation." In *Purposes of Preaching*, edited by Jana Childers, 1–22. St. Louis: Chalice, 2004.

Allen, O Wesley, Jr. *Preaching and Reading the Lectionary: A Three Dimensional Approach to the Liturgical Year.* St. Louis: Chalice, 2007.

———. *The Homiletic of All Believers: A Conversational Approach to Proclamation and Preaching.* Louisville: Westminster John Knox, 2005.

LaRue, Cleophus J. *I Believe I'll Testify: The Art of African American Preaching.* Louisville: Westminster John Knox, 2011.

Lose, David J. *Confessing Jesus Christ: Preaching in a Postmodern World.* Grand Rapids: Eerdmans, 2003.

———. *Preaching At the Crossroads: How the World—and Our Preaching—Is Changing.* Minneapolis: Fortress, 2013.

McClure, John S. *Otherwise Preaching: A Postmodern Ethic for Homiletics.* St. Louis: Chalice, 2001.

———. *The Roundtable Pulpit: Where Leadership & Preaching Meet.* Nashville: Abingdon, 1995.

Pagitt, Doug. *Preaching Re-Imagined: The Role of the Sermon in Communities of Faith.* Grand Rapids: Zondervan, 2005.

Rose, Lucy Atkinson. *Sharing the Word: Preaching in the Roundtable Church.* Louisville: Westminster John Knox, 1997.

Tisdale, Leonora Tubbs. *Preaching as Local Theology and Folk Art.* Fortress Resources for Preaching. Minneapolis: Fortress, 1997.

5

Worship as Conversation

O. Wesley Allen, Jr.

It may seem obvious to think of Christian worship in terms of conversation. After all, worship is primarily characterized by language spoken or sung in community. But in truth, there has been little consideration of the conversational nature of worship in the literature of liturgical theology and practice beyond the occasional passing note that worship has a dialogical character to it, such as Don Saliers's line, "Liturgy is an intentionally gathered community in mutual dialogue with God's self-communication."[1] Most theological attention given to the communicative aspect of worship has focused on communication in one of two directions signaled in Saliers's comment.

First is communication from God to the gathered worshipers. The Protestant Reformations shifted worship from being a visual experience as it was in the medieval church in which the laity in the nave watched what the clergy were doing at the altar to an aural experience emphasizing the sermon addressed to the laity. Reading the Scripture and preaching were considered the Word of God proclaimed and interpreted in worship. Certainly praise and prayers were offered as part of worship, but the primary role of the gathered Protestant community was to receive the communication proclaimed to them.

The second direction is communication offered by the worshipers to God. Søren Kierkegaard offered an important (and often quoted) correction to a corruption of the Protestant configuration of the congregation as

---

1. Don Saliers, *Worship as Theology*, 26; quoted in Furr and Price, *The Dialogue of Worship*, 1.

recipients in worship.[2] He argued that people had come to view worship in the same way they viewed the experience of the theater. In other words, they came to worship with the mindset of an audience. Those up front leading worship were the actors, prompted in what they were to say by God. Kierkegaard turned the image on its head, suggesting that the worship leaders were actually the prompters. This means the congregation is actually to be the actors performing for the true audience of worship: God. This shift represented by Kierkegaard is found in much of the liturgical literature today in that the core of Christian worship is characterized as praise or adoration (etymologically, "worship" = worth + ship) or as prayer. Susan J. White notes, for instance, "To say prayer is a component of Christian worship is almost a tautology. Indeed, many people define worship itself as 'the church at prayer,' as the prayerful conversation or discourses between the Christian community and the God who has called it into being."[3]

When pressed, of course, liturgical scholars would argue, as White does, that both the congregation and God have the dual roles of speaker and hearer in worship.[4] In other words, they would acknowledge that the combination of proclamation and prayer/praise implies an ongoing liturgical conversation between the community of the faithful and the Divine.[5]

But in the following essay, I explore more fully a conversational model for Christian worship that expands the view of what voices engage in the liturgical conversation and draws on the particular understanding of conversation emphasized in this book to examine the power dynamics of the liturgical conversation. I will then, in turn, propose ways this model can be used in the process of renewing Christian worship.

Theological Model of Worship as Conversation

Voices in the Liturgical Conversation

The introduction above makes clear that at the center of any model of worship as a liturgical conversation must be the give-and-take between God and

2. Kierkegaard, *Purity of Heart*.

3. White, *Foundations of Christian Worship*, 27.

4. Norm Shouten rejects Kierkegaard's model as presenting God as passive in worship and instead argues for a view of worship as a two-way dialogue in "Worship Is a Dialogical Region."

5. This is the model found in Rienstra and Rienstra, *Worship Words*, 43–59; as well as in Furr and Price, *The Dialogue of Worship*, 7–23.

the gathered community. If we represent our conversational model with a diagram, this element of the conversation can be configured as in Diagram 1.

GOD

congregation

God is represented in the diagram using the larger and bolder font and is placed at the top of the image because, theologically speaking, God is the initiator of all divine-human encounter. God spoke first by calling creation into being. Every human expression to God since has been response. Regardless of the stance one might take on the classic twentieth century debate concerning whether humans in our finite, fallen state of existence have a point of contact for knowing God,[6] the very claim underneath any interpretation of the doctrine of revelation is that God is the one doing the revealing. God makes Godself known to us. God engages us in relationship. The transcendent God becomes imminent in creating and providing for, redeeming, and sustaining the world (and the church).

The core liturgical structure of word followed by table, proclamation followed by response, acknowledges God's initiative in worship. God offers us God's good news and we respond. It is not the other way around. In the liturgy, God's self-revelatory voice, therefore, is and should be the most prominent.[7] This is evident in the simple fact that usually in worship the longest amount time given to any liturgical act is assigned to the proclamation portion of the service. In no other part of the service do those in the pews remain in a receptive (not passive) mode for nearly as long as they do during the reading of Scripture and the offering of the sermon. But the voice of God is, of course, not limited to those moments in worship. God's voice is represented as calling us into worship and sending us forth from it. At

6. See the classic, early twentieth-century debate between Brunner and Barth in *Natural Theology*.

7. See O. W. Allen, Jr., "Revelation," for a brief survey of different approaches to revelation in relation to the liturgical act of preaching.

times hymns are worded as if God is speaking to those gathered. And, most importantly, in sacramental traditions that view God as the primary actor/speaker in baptism and Eucharist, the mode of revelation is quite different, but God-in-Christ speaks as loudly and directly as during the sermon.

God reveals and the *congregation* responds. Yet while response is secondary in terms of theological order, as Kierkegaard has reminded us, the worship service is primarily an occasion in which the people gather to make an offering of their praise and thanksgiving to the self-revealing God. The whole of the liturgy is constructed as a response to the God who has initiated a conversation with us.[8] It is no coincidence that we label the worship experience a "service" that we offer to God. The very purpose of worship is to respond dutifully to God's creative, redeeming, and sustaining care. We pray an invocation not because we think God will not show up in worship unless we do so or because we experience God primarily as absent (although we certainly know times when we experience God as silent). We invoke God's presence precisely because we know God as present (Immanuel). We confess our sins not because we are trying to convince God to forgive us; but in response to having experienced God's grace, we recognize and are compelled to name our own sinfulness. We offer our petitions and supplications not in attempts to persuade God to care about the suffering and evil that infests our world, but because we have experienced God to be concerned about those very things. In other words, the whole of worship is response to God's prevenient (coming before) grace (including those elements in which God is the designated speaker).

In the *ordo* of Christian worship (i.e., its core pattern or "order"), the congregation responds to the particular element of the good news proclaimed within the liturgy on this particular occasion (because no single worship service can include the entirety of God's good news). More broadly speaking, however, the whole of the service (indeed the pattern and practice of gathering for worship repeatedly) is a response to the whole of God's good news—that named in this particular service; that which has been proclaimed, experienced and known on other occasions; and that of which we have yet to learn. Thus, while God is appropriately placed at the top of our diagram with a larger font, paradoxically the arrow flowing from the congregation to God is the larger arrow. Faithful response of the sacred community is not an afterthought—it is the very goal of Christian worship. Worship is liturgy, after all, with *leiturgia* meaning, "the work of the people."

---

8. As Hughes Oliphant Old puts it in *Worship*, 1, "We worship because God created us to worship him [sic]. Worship is at the center of our existence, at the heart of our reason for being."

This work of the people, however, requires that there be "a people." A key aspect of liturgy is forming a community in conversation, so the diagram includes a loop around congregation. In a very real sense in worship, anytime the congregation speaks (say, in prayer) or anyone from the congregation speaks to the congregation (say, in a sermon), the congregation is speaking to itself, growing as a people. Gary A. Furr and Milburn Price refer to this aspect of the liturgical conversation as the "horizontal dialogue" within the community that occurs as the same time the "vertical dialogue" with God occurs.[9]

In the liturgy, the congregation's voice is most evident in those elements of worship that are direct speech oriented toward God—acts of praise and prayer. In terms of the *ordo* then, the congregation's voice directed to God is most obviously represented in the gathering and response portions of the service, as well as any individual liturgical act that is prayerful. The congregation also speaks to itself most obviously in moments such as the sharing of announcements or prayer concerns or in the passing of the peace.

The congregation, however, does not speak *ex nihilo* (out of nothing). Concepts, forms, and expressions of our contemporary faith-talk—of our proclamation, adoration, petition, and sharing—have been shaped by the historic Church and continues to be shaped by the global Church. The individual congregation is but a single, local expression of the one, holy, apostolic, and universal *Church* (see Diagram 2).[10]

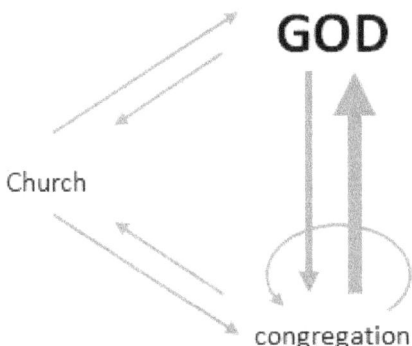

While there is much room for creativity in worship, the congregation speaks in line with or over against the way the Church has spoken liturgically and

9. Furr and Price, *The Dialogue of Worship*, 3–4, 25–40.

10. Although stylistic practices vary, in this essay I capitalize Church to indicate the historic, global church over against the local congregation so as to clearly distinguish the two voices in the liturgical conversation.

theologically for two millennia. The Sunday morning worship service, in other words, is a single moment in an ancient and ongoing (even eschatological) liturgical conversation that is an expression of the communion of saints across all times and places.

The broader voice of the Church that joins in the local liturgical conversation should be the universal, historic Church, the specific denominational tradition of the congregation, and the various expressions of the global Church today. Worship planners should be intentional about all these dialects being heard regularly in the liturgy.

The Church's voice is most prominent in liturgical elements that come from tradition, such as creeds and older hymns/global music. But biblical readings, sacraments/ordinances, traditional prayers, and even liturgical structures are moments when the communion of saints speaks within a specific gathering of the faithful. At times the voice of the Church resonates with the congregation's as it speaks prayerfully, and sometimes it resonates with God's as God reaches out to the congregation. This last note serves as a reminder that preachers especially have the responsibility to allow the historic church to speak in sermons by referring to and interpreting figures from the church's history and traditional doctrines that inform the church's theology.

As the congregation does not speak *ex nihilo*, neither does it speak in a vacuum. The church may strive not to be "of" the *world*, but it is certainly "in" it. For the liturgical conversation to be as full as it can and should be, the voice of the broader world needs to be heard regularly in congregational worship (see Diagram 3).

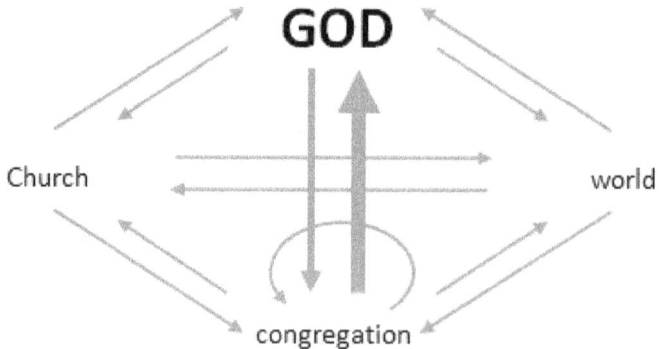

When the needs of the world are spoken in worship, the congregation's liturgical offering to God involves a commitment to bring justice, charity, service, and social transformation in society. When the strides made in human understanding in fields such as science and history are spoken, the congregation's faith is given the chance to remain faithful to contemporary worldviews.

The congregation's liturgy must be contextual to be relevant. Worship planners can consider local, national, and global issues, values, knowledge, and cultures in shaping the prayers of and proclamation for the congregation.[11] Then, liturgical faith-talk exhibits the recognition that, as creator, God cares for all of creation and all of creation is a gift to worship. To ignore the voice of the world in worship is paramount to distorting the character of God, diminishing the *missio Dei* (the mission of God) in which the church participates, and ignoring the importance of the achievements of human reason and culture for the life of the church.

The voice of the world is most prominent in liturgical elements that allow for variation week to week. While some hymns/music certainly call the congregation to engage in the world in broad fashion, the sermon is the place where the world most calls the congregation to its work outside the walls of the church building and the place where contemporary knowledge and experience is named as theologically formative. On the other hand, the congregation's concern and care for the world is most explicitly named in prayer where specific contemporary issues are lifted up to God in the form of petitions. The climactic moment of the world being given voice, however, is the Sending Forth, when the congregation is commissioned to leave worship and return to their lives and work in the world. Worship has not been an escape from the world but a liturgical conversation with it and preparation for living the Christian life in it. It is a shame that Sending Forth movement of worship is often the one that receives the least attention in the worship planning process.

An imprecise but perhaps helpful way to think about these different voices speaking in worship is to consider them in relation to the classical description of the *five primary functions of the Church* (see Diagram 4).

11. While not dealing with all of the issues being implied by including the "world" in the liturgical conversation in this essay, the "Nairobi Statement on Worship and Culture" produced by the World Lutheran Federation in 1996 is a helpful statement of the need for worship to be culturally contextual and the complications entailed with such a commitment.

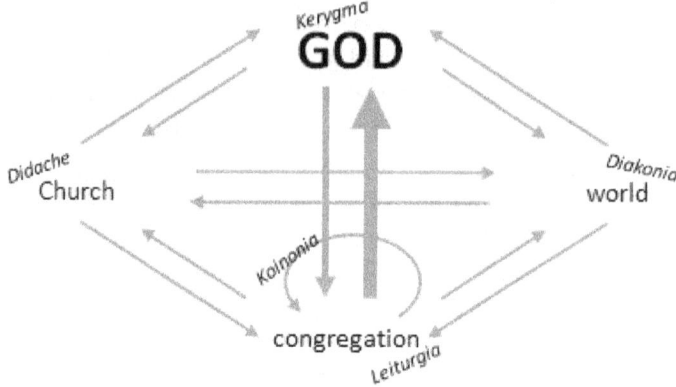

While these terms relate more to the whole of congregational life than is found only in worship, they all are found in worship as well. The voice of God speaking to the congregation, the wider Church, and the world, is *kerygma*, the Greek word meaning "proclamation." The voice of the congregation speaking to God, the wider Church, and the world is *leiturgia*. As noted earlier, this Greek word is the root of "liturgy" and refers to "the work of the people." Of course, in worship the congregation speaks to itself and builds community, so its voice also functions as *koinonia*, the Greek word for "fellowship." The voice of the wider, historic, and global Church speaking to the congregation, God, and the world is *didache*, the Greek word for "teaching." And, finally, the voice of the world speaking to the congregation, God, and the wider church, calls those gathered in worship to *diakonia*, the Greek word for "service."

Another helpful way to think about the different roles of these voices in the liturgical conversation is to see the conversation as mediated by *Jesus Christ* (see Diagram 5).

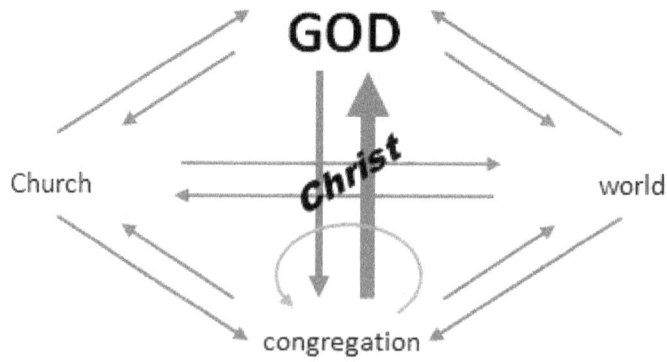

Visually this is suggested by the cruciform nature of the diagram. This mediation by Christ can be named differently in relation to each of the four conversation partners in worship. The person and works of Christ is the central revelation of *God*. The *congregation* gathers and prays in "the name of Christ." The *Church* is the body of Christ. And finally, Christ was born, ministered, died and was raised "once for all," for the redemption of the *world* (not just the Church).

The Nature of the Liturgical Conversation

To speak of Christian worship as a conversation is obviously to speak in metaphor. God does not literally speak in the liturgy. No voice comes from a candle that burns but is not consumed. And neither the words of Scripture nor the words of the preacher are synonymous with the Word of God. The historic and global Church does not literally speak in worship. The sacred assembly references, paraphrases, evokes, prays, or reads little bits and pieces of tradition here and there. Nor does the world literally speak in the congregation's gathering—the congregation speaks about or draws insight from the world of which it is a part. And even though the congregation speaks, the people in the pews do not really converse. Whether singing a song in four-part harmony, praying a responsive invocation or reciting a creed, most of the times the congregation speaks, their words have been scripted for them. Even when a formal passing of the peace gives way to informal greeting, it is small talk and not true conversation.

The metaphor of worship as conversation, therefore, is a heuristic model highlighting the diversity of voices that ought to be *represented* in the liturgy instead of only acknowledging the voices that literally speak. But it is also more than this. Not only does the metaphor help us expand our view of the range of voices to be evoked in worship, it also conveys something of the quality of the interaction of those represented voices that should be sought in planning, leading, and participating in the liturgy.

In other words, liturgy should be an expression of a collaborative, concern-filled, and open-ended dialogue between the four represented voices named above.[12] These conversational qualities are contrasted to the goals of debate or argumentation, which are, at best, attempts to persuade others to

---

12. The following discussion contrasting conversation and debate is a condensation of a fuller discussion found in Allen, *The Homiletic of All Believers*, 21ff. My description of the contrast is informed by calls for dialogue offered by The Study Circle Resource Center (http://www.infed.org/biblio/b-dialog.htm) and The Co-Intelligence Institute (http://www.co-intelligence.org/P-dialogue.html).

build consensus or at worst attempts to defeat one's opponent rhetorically. In conversation (or dialogue) mutual understanding and growth of all participants are the aims, and it is in this sense that worship is a conversation between God, the congregation, the Church, and the world.

Liturgical conversation is collaborative. As we have said, the very definition of worship implies community. Not all expressions of community, however, are collaborative. Look at the elected representatives and senators in the two-party system of the United States. Congress (sharing the same etymological root as "congregation") is properly described as a community, but can hardly (or rarely) be described as collaborative. Perhaps there has never been a "golden age" of American politics when the relationship between elected officials of different parties was not primarily defined by debate—trying to win enough votes to push through to law one person's or one party's stance over against the views of others. We, after all, rule by majority vote. But neither have all generations of politics been as vitriolic and uncompromising as we see today.

The Christian congregation, especially in worship, should and can do a better job at collaboration. In monologue a speaker works on the hearer. In debate a speaker works against another speaker. In collaborative conversation every person is both speaker and hearer, and all work together. We certainly hope to change others in worship but we also hope to be changed ourselves. In religious talk, this is another way of thinking of "conversion." This word is popularly used to denote the process of making a Christian out of a non-Christian (i.e., persuading them that our way is best and that they should join us). The literal etymologically meaning of "convert," however, is "turning" (from the Latin *vertere*) "together" (from *con*). As opposed to debate in which one hopes to turn another, in conversation the participants work toward mutual transformation through renewed enlightenment.

In Christian worship, then, the conversation should be constructed in a collaborative manner. It is not God over against the congregation or the Church over against the world. The congregation better serves God and the world both by listening to and learning from the broader Church and by challenging elements of tradition that do not fit with a contemporary worldview. God is more clearly heard when the congregation takes seriously challenges to the faith offered by scientific and historical reasoning and questions of theodicy that come from the world. Thus even though liturgy is mainly composed of monologic and scripted speech (speaking literally), it should have something of the give-and-take quality of collaboration to it.

Liturgical conversation is thus concern-filled. None of the voices in worship "attend" the liturgy only for their own sake. God as love speaks good news of mercy, repentance, judgment, and call to the congregation, the Church and the world. The congregation gathers to praise God, be faithful to the Church's gospel, and work for the transformation of the world. The Church universal serves God by passing on what it has learned of God in the past and around the globe so that the congregation might be faithful to the *missio Dei* today in its corner or the world. And the world speaks in worship as the whole of God's created (and fallen) order so that the tradition of the Church and the liturgy of the congregation will be relevant to the whole of life. There is no room, in other words, for isolationism in Christian worship. The concern-filled congregation welcomes all voices as others from whom we can learn, to whom we have much to offer, and with whom we dwell in peace and unity.[13]

This welcome of the other implies a liturgical conversation that is open-ended. In debate one side wins, the other loses, and the matter is concluded. Or one side persuades the other and the matter is concluded. In conversation, however, the participants are committed to one another but not necessarily committed to consensus. Recognizing a fellow conversation partner as an other allows room for an "I–Thou" relationship to be formed apart from seeing eye to eye on all matters.[14] Indeed, disagreement is valued as an opportunity to celebrate difference and to grow. Unity that grows out of being concern-filled need not be equated with uniformity.

The goal of worship, then, is ultimately not persuasion in which at the end of the hour all agree with the sermon or the choral anthem. The voices are committed to and concerned for one another but should not require or even hope for consent on all issues. The Church and world must not be made to say the same thing or agree. If that is a requirement they may never truly converse. There is no reciprocal, collaborative give-and-take when a certain type of outcome is prescribed ahead of time. The world must be allowed to challenge the Church's talk of "creation" based on natural selection, and the Church must be allowed to call the world to task over assuming the economic and political inequalities that lead to hardship and oppression are simply the natural order of things. God must be able to call the congregation

---

13. Although not dealing with the issue of liturgy more broadly, McClure in *Otherwise Preaching* and R. J. Allen in *Preaching and the Other* have dealt extensively with the concept of the other in preaching.

14. The language of "I-Thou" comes from Martin Buber's influential work, *I and Thou*. Buber condemns I-It relationships in which I objectifies the other ("It" is something for me to experience, to use, or to consume; i.e., something over which I have power). Instead he lifts up I-Thou relationships in which I recognize the other as subject instead of object—I don't experience a Thou, I relate to a Thou; I don't use a Thou, I enter into reciprocity with Thou; I don't consume a Thou, but a Thou demands something of me at the same time that it offers me something. I am changed by Thou—indeed we are both changed.

to struggle against injustice in the world and the congregation must be able to cry out in lament, "How long, O God?" The liturgical conversation leads to better understanding of the other, better self-understanding, and movement of all involved. The participants move toward each other in the sense of being filled with concern but may move in very different directions in terms of concepts, issues, values, and actions. The worship conversation is grounded on the Word of God. But no expression of God's news for humanity can be considered good if there is no freedom for partners in the conversation to say No (or "Let's keep working at it") to that expression.

Practical Implications of Worship as Conversation

Moderating the Liturgical Conversation

For Kierkegaard, those standing in the chancel serve as prompters, feeding the congregation their lines as they perform for their audience, God. In contrast, our conversational model holds the worship leader to be more like a person who moves around in a dialogue group, asks someone a question, holds the microphone while the person speaks to the others in the group, and then moves on to the next speaker. In other words, if Christ *mediates* the conversation between the four represented voices, the worship planners, musicians, liturgists, and preachers *moderate* it. These persons, to a great extent, decide who will speak, when they will speak, and what they will say.

Naming this fact explicitly makes clear that the nature of the liturgical conversation is not as simple a matter as the diagram and our discussion thus far would lead us to believe. Heuristic models are helpful in grasping and managing complex dynamics such as those involved in Christian worship, but they are also reductionistic. They are limited in their ability to fully name that complexity. In true conversation participants are both speakers and listeners. There is a reciprocal, spontaneous give-and-take that distinguishes conversation from the monological and scripted qualities of different elements of worship.

To moderate an extemporaneous conversation is to have considerable power. The moderator may be the one who sets the conversation agenda and gathers the participants in the first place. She can allow the conversation to move in some directions and keep it from going in others. She can give some participants the opportunity to speak unhindered and cut off the speech of other voices. By her tone and mannerisms, she can give credence to some ideas and be dismissive of others in ways other participants in the conversation cannot. The level of power of the liturgical conversation moderator is even more significant than this. Add to gathering the participants, set-ting the agenda, and lifting up certain voices over against others, the fact worship leaders script the conversation (for the most part) in advance and represent the different participants in the actual enactment of the scripted conversation. Let's consider the moderation of each liturgical conversation partner in turn.

In worship, something or someone speaks on behalf of *God*. They de-cide what God would say to these people on this particular liturgical occa-sion. While they may do so as thoughtfully, pastorally, and faithfully as their ability allows, this means that usually the senior pastor (or primary preacher in a congregation) represents God to the community in a way others in the community are not seen as doing. In a postmodern world, where authority from on high is viewed with significant suspicion, such localization of God's metaphorical voice is practically and theologically problematic. It should not be the minister who serves as God's mouthpiece, but as Rebecca S. Chopp puts it, "The *community* is the manifestation of the Word for the World."[15] Over against the Reformers' use of "Word of God" to refer to Christ, Scrip-ture, and preaching, the multitude of people and situations in the congrega-tion through which God can be heard needs to be valued (e.g., music, art, church school, committee meetings, social justice action, works of charity, fellowship meals, etc.). To reserve for the ordained preacher the right and responsibility to speak for God distorts a biblical view of the body of Christ as a community composed of baptized persons endowed with a plethora of spiritual gifts that are to be used for the building up of the Church and for ministry to the world (1 Cor 12). This applies not only broadly to the mission of the Church but specifically to the work of worship (1 Cor 14:26). Even if a pastor is ordained to Word and Sacrament, she should not be seen as holding a monopoly on God's voice in the congregation or even standing in the pulpit or lectern, at the table or the font. To represent the fullness of what God might have to say to a congregation, multiple representatives need to be, not simply allowed, but encouraged and equipped for various modes of proclamation in the liturgical life of a congregation.

A similar situation exists for the voice of the *congregation*. In most worship cultures, the congregation speaks more often in a unified voice than do individual members of the gathering speak their own thoughts and name their own emotions or concerns. A liturgist usually represents the congrega-tion in offering to God a prayer in a single voice; or when the congregation speaks in unison, a worship planner has composed or chosen the words those in the pew speak or sing. They decide what the congregation should

---

15. Chopp, *The Power to Speak*, 85, emphasis added.

say to God on this particular occasion—what adoration should sound like and what petitions should be offered on this day. While liturgists do these tasks as thoughtfully, pastorally, and faithfully as their ability allows, this means that these representatives and worship planners (again, often senior ministers or ministerial staff) have significant power and authority in defining the congregation's speech and experience in worship. In a postmodern age, it is inappropriate to assume that a monolithic experience is shared by all in the worshiping community. Care must be taken to expand the congregational voices that plan and speak publicly in worship. Making time in worship for the sharing of joys and concerns before a pastoral prayer or, better, using the form of a bidding prayer invites multiple voices to participate in a unified expression of adoration and petition. Moreover, using worship planning teams/committees composed of a group diverse in terms of age, gender, education, economic status, ethnicity, political orientation, sexual orientation, relationship status, and so on and so forth will lead to unison liturgical actions better representing the spectrum of perspectives in the community.[16]

This historic voice of the *Church* can be overbearing in congregations where nothing new ever seems to be uttered as if contemporary situations do not call for the reconsideration of historical elements and expressions of the Christian faith. Or it can be ignored with the hubris of modernity (or postmodernity) in congregations where the past (except perhaps for the past found in the biblical canon or in the particular congregation) is deemed irrelevant for contemporary faith.

Worship planners and preachers need to work to bring the voice of tradition into worship in a balanced manner—celebrating the congregation's inheritance and the faith passed down to us while being theologically critical of elements of hegemony in the Church's history. Worship leaders decide what the Church should say on this particular occasion—what theological, ritual elements from the universal Church are worth being heard in this local congregation and which ones are to be ignored or discarded. While they do so as thoughtfully, pastorally and faithfully as their ability allows, the worship leaders not only control speech "inside" the faith (i.e., the voices of God, the Church, and the local congregation), they also define the community's experience and liturgical encounter with the contemporary context in which they worship. Yet in a postmodern age, it is inappropriate for these clergy only to allow the Church to speak in ways that agree with

16. A powerful approach to this task would be a hybrid between the collaborative homiletic found in McClure, *The Roundtable Pulpit,* on the one hand and Norma de Waal Malefyt and Howard Vanderwell, *Designing Worship Together* or Barbara Day Miller, *Encounters With the Holy* on the other hand.

their theology. The body of Christ that stretches over 2000 years and reaches across the globe is not a monolithic institution and should not be represented as such. Clergy can present a myriad of traditional and historical issues, persons, doctrines, events, and movements from Sunday to Sunday, year to year, in the liturgical life of the congregation; model critical engagement with those voices; and empower the congregation to reflect existentially on them.

Finally, there is the voice of the *world* in worship. While the world is heard occasionally in hymns, traditional readings, etc., it primarily speaks in the sermon and in the prayers of the people. The worship leaders for the day decide whether and if so what social concerns of the world are to be lifted up on a given Sunday. They decide whose experiences in the world deserve to be named as valid and whose are ignored. They decide what aspects of secular, human reason are brought into liturgical expressions of the Christian faith and which ones are silenced. While hopefully they do so as thoughtfully, pastorally and faithfully, this means the worship leaders not only controls speech "inside" the faith (i.e., the voices of God, the Church, and the local congregation). They also have power over defining the community's experience and liturgical encounter with the contemporary context in which they worship. This is inappropriate given that worship leaders have no leg up in their knowledge of the world over the people in the pews. Ordained clergy may have legitimate claim to have higher levels of insight into Scripture and tradition given their specialized training, but they have no monopoly on reason that comes from the world or experience of the world whatsoever. Indeed, their narrow training may put them at a disadvantage in these areas. Means must be developed where those in the pew can bring their knowledge and experience of the world into the planning and enactment of the liturgy. But even the knowledge and experience of the whole of a congregation is limited. Worship leaders, preacher, and planning teams must intentionally seek out underrepresented knowledge and experience of the world that need to be voiced in the liturgical conversation. This is especially true for congregations that are composed primarily of those privileged in society in terms of economic status, political power, access to education, gender, sexual orientation, age, abilities, and so on and so forth.

Renewal of the Liturgical Conversation

For most of the twentieth century leading up to and then growing out of the Second Vatican Council, liturgical renewal in churches related to the historic denominations—such as the Roman Catholic Church, the Episcopal

Church, the Presbyterian Church, the United Church of Christ, United Methodist Church—focused on re-claiming liturgical structures and language from the past. This movement has had substantial ecumenical influence and resulted in the so-called "mainline" denominations and many of their congregations re-establishing a common fourfold *ordo* (gathering, proclamation, communion/response, and sending forth) in the worship service, reclaiming the liturgical year and developing an accompanying common lectionary, and reinvigorating sacramental rites.

In the late twentieth century another renewal movement, originating more in the evangelical end of the spectrum of the church but spreading to much of the mainline as well, focused its attention on a different liturgical style. Incorporating popular forms of music, modern technologies, and contemporary idiom—all taken from today's culture—this approach to worship renewal strives to have more appeal to the information and technology oriented populace, especially the younger generation.[17]

Regardless of which of these two streams a congregation is in (or wishes to be in), the conversational model of worship offers a congregation a different way to think about renewing its worship. Instead of assuming style is the key to renewal, a worship committee/team can use the conversational model to evaluate the theological, historical, existential fullness of worship in the congregation. There are two steps to using this model in renewing worship. The first is simpler than the second.

First, a worship committee needs to see which of the four voices are regularly represented in worship and which ones have been valued less than they should be. Almost every congregation will have gaps in the conversation. Usually the voices of God and the congregation are obviously evident, but those of the Church and/or the world might be muffled or even absent.

- How often are people, doctrines or events from Church history named in the sermon?

- What songs from other parts of the global Church are sung?

- How wide a range of and how often are social concerns lifted up in prayers of the people or the sending forth?

- When was the last time insights from science, sociology, economics, or psychology were brought to bear on a theological or ethical topic addressed in the liturgy?

17. Thomas G. Long describes these two options as "Hippolytus versus Willow Creek" in *Beyond the Worship Wars*, 1–9.

As the varying weights of the fonts and the arrows in our diagrams show, it is not that all the voices need be given equal weight. God's revelatory voice holds a primary place in the model, and the congregation gathering to make an offering of praise is presented as the loudest voice. But the world and the Church both deserve to be given *significant* weight in the liturgy.

A worship team can study a season of services and look for patterns that expose such gaps in the conversation. However, in truth, those most invested in planning, producing, and performing the liturgy may be the ones most likely to hear voices that are not really there. In my Introduction to Worship class, I sketch this conversational model for students and then have them do a very unscientific survey of a few members of their congregation. They simply ask those surveyed to complete the following sentence, "The purpose of Christian worship is _____." As a one-sentence, spur-of-the-moment response, the answers should not be expected to represent the full depth of what a respondent might say given more time for reflection and more space to expound their position. Nevertheless, the gut response may signal what is most important about worship for them. I instruct my students to gather the responses and analyze them collectively in terms of the conversational model. Over and over again, when I read the responses from students' congregations, I can immediately spot some patterns that signify gaps in the conversation. No one uses any language that connects the congregation to the wider Church. Or everyone speaks in individualistic terms so the voice of the "congregation" as a whole is missing. Or there are no hints of engagement of the world in worship. For the exercise (and for the sake of illustration here) it is not important that such observations are based on imprecise data. What is important is that students more often than not miss the gaps implied in the responses. In fact, in their analysis they name a congregation's commitment to tradition or to engaging society when none has been named in the responses whatsoever. Those responsible for worship assume *their* commitment to tradition or the world actually translates into liturgical practice when it may not. So it is important in a study of one's own worship practices for worship leaders to get other eyes and ears searching for gaps. These may be other persons within or outside the congregation.

Once gaps have been identified, the task then is to expand the liturgical conversation to include the muffled or absent voice(s). In some sense this is a statistical issue: raise the number of times the voice is represented in worship, both in terms of the individual worship service and across time. But simply referring to some issue, say, in the world is not the same thing as really giving it a weighty voice in worship. Multiple references are not enough. A sustained depth of expression, exploring the complexity of the issue as well as what it offers to and/or demands of the congregation is necessary. And this representation of the world's voice (but not necessarily of the specific issue) must occur repeatedly.

Interpretations in the liturgical conversation to include all of the voices in the diagram above is not enough. A second step of worship renewal that is required is to analyze and make adjustments to the ways all of the voices are represented in worship so that power is shared instead of collected into the worship leader. In other words, worship leaders must find ways to allow the multivalent nature of these voices be heard instead of turning the voices into puppets for the worship leaders as ventriloquists. As we have said, in a pluralistic age, the Christian community must be committed to shared conversation mediated by Christ; it must not be forced to share a single interpretation of any of the voices around the liturgical table. The biblical canon as one expression of God's voice is a helpful precedent for us. The canon includes the Yahwist, Deuteronomic, wisdom, prophetic, priestly, apocalyptic, synoptic, Johannine, and Pauline representations of God's voice (to name only a few). Add to the canon two thousand years of church teaching and experience as well as a plethora of contemporary Christian denominations and other religions, and God's voice takes on a much wider range of nuances than that which the worship leader's representation can offer. In truth, there is no way to represent the fullness of God voice (or for that matter the fullness of the voices of the Church, the world or even the congregation), but the representation can be broadened in ways that share the power of representing God (Church, world, and congregation) with many instead of localizing it in a senior pastor or even a worship team.

A congregation intent on renewing its worship practices in a way relevant to the current age can work to include in more significant ways all the voices of God, the congregation, the Church and world as mediated by Christ. But it must also find ways to share the responsibility for moderating the conversation and representing the voices with a broader range of people involved in and around the life of the community of faith. When a more collaborative, concern-filled, and open-ended liturgical conversation is created, worshipers will become more existentially engaged in it, and the liturgical conversation, in turn, will spark renewed theological and ethical conversations throughout and beyond the life of the community of faith.

Cautions for Employing
a Conversational Model to Worship

Leading and participating in worship are complicated activities. Things go awry with nearly every service. Add in the responsibility to get all voices heard appropriately and we may start to feel like a trained bear on a unicycle juggling wriggling fish. In closing, then, it is worth taking a moment to name some pitfalls to be avoided when applying the proposed conversational model to leading and renewing worship.

The first pitfall is to avoid the slippery slope of valuing multiple voices, perspectives and interpretations into the liturgical conversation to the point that "anything goes." Worship leaders have a responsibility to bring a critical eye to shaping the conversation for the sacred assembly. Hateful, unhealthy, or even just socially inappropriate speech can be filtered while still maintaining an ethic of conversation respect, reciprocity, and love for the other.

A second pitfall is similar to the first: the value of multiple voices can lead to a worship service that has little or no focus or intentional flow. It can become a conversation in which each speaker subsequently changes the agenda. Instead of a focused conversation, the liturgy moves along like a panel of speakers who do not really engage one another; a parade of ancient texts and contemporary issues, or a list of quotations from *Bartlett's* that share no more than a common key word. Above we warned against worship leaders moderating the liturgical conversation in ways that only supported their own viewpoints and goals. On the other hand, moderators must assert some control to focus the conversation and help it move along in a logical and even dramatic fashion.

A third pitfall is that the conversation of worship can be assumed to be enough conversation for the church to have with others. In truth, though, however skillful and faithful the worship leaders and worshiping community are at representing the voice of others in the liturgy, the voices are almost always *represented*. Those voices are filtered through our own voices. They take on our tone and timbre. Even while trying to represent the other, we represent ourselves. Especially in terms of the voices of the global, ecumenical church and the world, the church must seek out other opportunities for immediate face-to-face dialogue with those outside the congregation. The challenges experienced in such occasions will in turn enhance the representation of those voices in worship.

Finally, perhaps the most significant potential pitfall in the conversational model is one that is present in any approach to worship. It is the possibility of diminishing God. God is both the object and subject of Christian worship. Presenting God as one conversation partner among others (even one presented with a larger font and in bold type) hardly does justice to the distinction between the Creator and the created, between the Redeemer and the redeemed, between the Sustainer and the sustained. This is, of course, an inherent problem in the fact that God continues to reveal Godself through human activity such as worship. Nevertheless, worship leaders must be vigilant in making sure that all attempts to represent and moderate God's voice, to lead and renew worship of God, and to address God in prayer and praise do not result in making God in our own image. We must allow God to be God, or our liturgical conversation becomes just another means for idolatry.

Questions for Discussion

1. What aspects of worship as conversation do you find most theologically compelling and which ones less compelling?

2. In the worship service you lead or in which you participate, which of the four conversation partners speak most consistently and which voices are regularly muffled or absent? How might needed adjustments be made?

3. Christian theology has long spoken of Jesus Christ as a mediator, usually between God and humankind. The chapter presents a striking new dimension to the notion of Jesus Christ as mediator: Jesus mediates the congregational conversation during worship. How does this fresh image strike you? How does it expand your thinking about Jesus, and about Jesus's presence and role in worship?

4. In the worship service you lead or in which you participate is the mediating role of Christ evident throughout the liturgical conversation? In what ways?

5. In the liturgy you lead or in which you participate, who usually represents the voices of God, the congregation, the Church, and the world? Is this appropriate, or do adjustments need to be made and others be involved?

Further Reading

Furr, Gary A., and Milburn Price. *The Dialogue of Worship: Creating Space for Revelation and Response*. Macon, GA: Smyth & Helwys, 1998.

Miller, Barbara Day. *Encounters with the Holy: A Conversational Model for Worship Planning*. Herndon, VA: Alban Institute, 2010.

Schouten, Norm. "Worship is a Dialogical Region." *Perspectives* 18/3 (2003) 6–11.

6

Christian Education as Conversation

Nancy Lynne Westfield

❧ This chapter presents a slice of the ongoing conversation I have with the Master of Divinity students at Drew Theological Seminary in my Introduction to Educational Ministries course. The aim of the course is to persuade my students that faith formation occurs in the doing and being of Christian community, not simply in the classrooms of Sunday School. This formation is Christian education. I contend that local churches need to shift radically the approach to Christian education away from an antiquated system akin to public education and toward an approach that has as its foundation the concept of ubuntu.[1]

The Current State of Education in the Church

Unfortunately, the current paradigm of Christian Education is a crude duplication of the public educational system in the larger U.S. society and is so ineffective it is called obsolete by many scholars.[2] Established models of local church education encourage passivity to the status quo and benign memorization of data about Bible, tradition, and culture, while genuine concerns about oppression and suffering go unaddressed. While every

1. While teaching this material I have grown and become a better teacher, scholar, and minister. I write this chapter with humble gratitude to and for my students who have participated with me, a fifty-year-old, African American, straight, single, Christian, clergy, womanist scholar in exploring uncharted territories in liberative education.

2. I am particularly referring to the work of Kenneth Robinson when he speaks of schools killing creativity and calls for a shift in the paradigm of education in the United States. Dr. Robinson has several texts and YouTube videos with this central theme. Also see the work of such educationalists as: Stephen Brookfield, bell hooks, Parker Palmer.

major society, including the United States, is attempting to update and recast the educational system given that the world is rapidly changing in the process of globalization, the faith education system of the church has done little to grapple with or re-envision this needed shift. Christian education is reduced to or confined to that which occurs in the structured lessons of such programs as Sunday school, Bible study, vacation Bible school, youth fellowship, and such. Usually, this approach is a misinterpretation of developmental theory where learners are sorted by ages of years and stages of life.

The current paradigm relegates education to purchased, age-based curriculum, and contrived programs whose goals are to deposit biblical content into the students. Most learners are children (low percentages of adults participate in formal Christian education programming) who are sent through Sunday School programs in "batches," as if their age is the only factor determining their ability to learn faith and be church.

This system fails at its main goal of creating a biblically literate church membership. Moreover, if current seminary students can be taken as indicators, our people do not know our rituals, do not find substantive meaning in our rites of passage, and do not engage deeply in regular Christian practices in ways relevant to the rapidly changing world. Our system is not equipped to teach adults who are recent converts from other religions and/ or other nations living here in the United States. We have not considered the practices of faith or the nature of faith education, which will be needed for a society that is being globalized in significant ways. Our current system is flummoxed by the shifting expressions of family and the growing number of single and childless households. Worse yet, many church leaders are not alarmed with this antiquated system of Christian education, believing that Christian education has little significance in the life of the community. It is time to reimagine Christian education. One way to make the formative processes in the church more effective and relevant is to turn to conversation.

A Sketch of Conversation: Drawing Attention to Political & Spiritual Aspects

What happens in a space hallows it. Holy acts sanctify the ground and bless the people for generations. Conversation that teaches reconciliation, forgiveness, compassion, and love is a hallowing act that beckons justice. Conversely, acts of violence desecrate a space and splinter the soul. Violent classrooms are places of alienation, de-humanization, and hated. Conversation that teaches imperialism as truth, exploitation as love, and domination as "normal" putrefies a space. Conversation then, with the capacity to conjure the sacred as well as the profane, must be recognized for its power to liberate or dominate.[3] We must learn to harness the power of conversation for liberation.

There is spiritual power in dialogue—power to heal and inspire hope. Equally as important, there are volatile political aspects in the spiritual practice of conversation. Cornel West says, "Justice is what love looks like in the public."[4] Love in the public as a means to transform society requires communities of faith to discuss oppression, injustice, and domination. The Christian community has paid too little attention to the power of teaching as a prophetic act of the Holy, as a mystical act of healing, as a tool of transformation for all of society.

Some conversations are normalized and normalizing. As members of communities, churches, neighborhoods, and nations, we are quickly taught which conversations are accepted and which are taboo.[5] In our attempts to be good members of those contexts, we adhere to often unspoken, but rigid rules of speech. We must wonder, as thinking, curious people, what toll it takes on our community and our faith to keep conversations shallow and extraneous to the suffering of the people. We must yearn for and work for those conversations that inform and kindle our ability to reflect the radicality of the gospel in this era. The church must ask what critical conversations are ignored or forbidden in society as a way of maintaining the hegemonic structures of racism, sexism, classism, heterosexism—domination of every type and description—and dialogue about these very issues.[6]

By the end of the semester, students in my Introduction to Educational Ministries course often admit that they were overwhelmed at the beginning of our conversation. They report that their struggle was their discomfort and unfamiliarity with talking openly and unashamedly about issues of race and racism, gender and sexism, class and classism. During the course of our semester-long conversation, they discover that socially prescribed speech has established boundaries and borders between us that need to be re-thought and re-conceived for the work of justice to be transformative. By

---

3. The scholarly literature on liberative pedagogy and spirituality is wide. My teaching and this chapter is particularly influenced by Paulo Freire, bell hooks, Thich Nhat Hanh, Parker Palmer, and Howard Thurman.

4. Online: http://thejustlife.org/home/resources/quote-list/

5. For further discussion see, Thandeka, *Learning to Be White.*

6. Freire defines oppression as any situation characterized by the exploitation of one person by another. Freire says, "Such a situation in itself constitutes violence because it interferes with the individual's ontological and historical vocation to be more fully human" (*Pedagogy of the Oppressed*, 55).

the end of the course, students have acquired a wider vocabulary, expanded their word boundaries, and become more articulate about issues of justice.

Conversations have political agendas—both implicit and explicit. What we discuss shapes us. And of equal importance, what is rarely or never discussed shapes our individual and communal identity as well. Carter G. Woodson, author of *Mis-Education of the Negro*, says,

> If you control a [person's] thinking, you do not have to worry about his[/her] action. When you determine what a [person] shall think, you do not have to concern yourself about what he[/she] will do. If you make a [person] feel inferior status, you do not have to compel him[/her] to accept inferior status, for he[/she] will seek it for himself[/herself]. If you make a [person] think that he[/she] is justly an outcast, you do not have to order him[/her] to the back door. He[/she] will go without being told; and if there is no back door, his[/her] own nature will demand one.[7]

Whoever controls the conversation is likely to have control over the community and its hopeful or hopeless future. Conversations, then, are never politically neutral.[8] They may be deemed as benign, dull, or irrelevant, but the politic is powerful and often calculated.

Structures of domination, for their perpetuation, silence significant conversation about imperialism, particularly among those who are privileged in the oppressive structure. In my introductory course, it is typical to hear grown men say they have never in their lives had an in-depth talk about the subjugation of women and how they, as men, benefit from the structures of sexism. White students regularly report that rarely is there any serious conversation about their uncontested privilege and supposed superiority in their homes, churches, or clubs. Men and women who were born into the wealthy class rarely report conversing about the complicity of maintaining their lifestyle in keeping the poor, the under-employed, and the mis-educated disenfranchised and marginalized. My straight students who are unflinchingly against gay marriage have had few conversations about how their rationale serves to support their status in society. All this is to say, conversations that expose and re-imagine the structures of domination are kept silent and impotent by keeping communal speech focused on inconsequential ideas of sameness and the supposed "normality" of oppression.

The insidiousness of internalized oppression only adds to the complexity of the situation and the woundedness of the people. Internalized

7. Carter G. Woodson, *The Mis-Education of the Negro*, 84–85.

8. For further discussion see bell hooks, *Teaching to Transgress: Education as the Practice of Freedom*.

oppression is when oppressed folks come to believe and sustain their own labeling of inferiority, even teaching the lie to others. Internalized oppression thwarts conversations about and that result in justice, peace, and social change. In my classroom I have witnessed, women demoralizing other women; poor people idealizing the rich; and non-white people aspiring to the privilege and moral bankruptcy of white supremacy. There is no political neutrality in conversation when smart, capable people come to believe and practice their own inferiority. Participating in U.S. church culture has for too long meant being passive and inarticulate about issues of domination, and this passivity perpetuates societal structures that need to be dismantled and newly-constructed in the accordance with the gospel. Grant Shockley, scholar and pastor, offered these words of wisdom to the Black Church, which I would suggest pertains to all churches: "All education ultimately is for either domination or liberation, it cannot be for both. . . . Spirituality and personal salvation, not withstanding, a major and controlling responsibility of the black church has been, is, and will continue to be the humanization of the dehumanized and the liberation of the oppressed."[9]

Risk Taking in the Conversations of Christian Education

We do not lack fodder for conversations about structures of oppression. A cursory look at any reputable newspaper demonstrates the issues of violence, greed, racism, classism, sexism in our lives: the murder of Treyvon Martin, the wars in the Middle East, the growing conflict between Muslims and Christians, issues of immigration, the for-profit privatization of U.S. prisons, child sex-trade, modern slavery—the list goes on and on. The church and church people do not have the luxury of ignoring, spiritualizing, or avoiding the critical issues that drastically affect the brothers and sisters who sit in the pews each Sunday. My students have told me, when the notion of transformative conversations is surfaced in the course that they are aware of the need for deep conversations, but they are fearful of them.

The fear of intimate conversations in the church is not that an extremist might bully the conversation. My students do not fear that their conversation partners will tout neo-Nazi philosophies or suggest that women should wear burcas (although occasionally someone will oppose the ordination of women). No one fears open bigotry against gays or suggests that chattel slavery needs to be reinstated. Most students are too "politically correct" to cross those boundaries and most local churches have an ethos that requires non-hostile, "nice" interactions.

9. Nancy Lynne Westfield, et. al., *Black Church Studies*, 149.

The obstacle I have witnessed in the classroom and in the church instead is the experience of insensitivity by well-intended but narrow people. People will speak with insensitivity concerning highly sensitive issues of race, class, and gender not to reassert their own societal status or ideologies consciously, but because of their shallow life experience and lack of empathy. Transformative conversations require a kind of risk taking that most of us are not taught but must learn as we move into more diverse, globalized contexts. Well-intended people in conversations dealing with liberation and oppression will make blunders, social *faux pas*, and, in some cases, completely expose their own withered hearts. Surviving insensitive statements is a little like being pecked to death. Rev. William Sloane Coffin, former pastor of the Riverside Church, said it this way, "Regardless how you are stoned to death—jagged rocks or stale marshmallows—you are still dead."[10]

In the summer of 1984, while working as an intern with a group ministry in Philadelphia, I had a colleague who was a young, white woman attending an area seminary. While Susan (not her real name) and I were the same age, we came to the internship from different backgrounds. I grew up in Philadelphia and she grew up in the suburbs—I was comfortable in an urban environment and she was not. The group ministry was located in a lower/middle-class section of the city that struggled with crime, dilapidated housing, dwindling city services, and schools that needed drastic improvements. The mission of the ministry was to empower the poor and challenge racism. The structure of our internship made room for many frank conversations between Susan and me about the politic of race, the strangling presence of racism, and the nature of oppression in the city.

Susan was outgoing and eager for discussion, yet she struggled in such conversations because frank talk about race and class were new for her. In a few conversations, Susan would attempt to use a clichéd response to bolster her argument. As she spoke, she would realize the cliché trivialized her current summer experience and become embarrassed. We would find something to laugh about and keep the moment light and friendly.

One evening, Susan and I were riding in my car on the way to dinner. We were talking about North American chattel slavery and its impact on the current economic condition of African American people. Susan was making the case that the United States made opportunity for all people as long as they were willing to work hard. I was making the case that many poor, minoritized[11] people do not get the opportunities afforded white

10. From a personal conversation with Bill Coffin while he and I served on the staff of The Riverside Church.

11. I use the word "minoritized" rather than "minority" intentionally. No person or group of people is born a minority. The larger society must make this judgment

Americans. I went on to say that those people who had come to America as enslaved peoples continue to be discriminated against in systematic ways. Susan then said, ". . . as long as the slave masters were nice to the slaves, why was slavery so bad?"

I could give many, many other examples of insensitivity, cavalier statements of ignorance and brazen hostility cloaked in niceness that I have either witnessed, survived, or spoken myself, but the point is the church cannot let such moments derail our ability to fully participate in transformative conversations. Susan, even with her misstep, was making an honest attempt at dialogue. We must, as learners and teachers, raise our awareness, develop ego strength, deepen our spiritual reserve, and have patience with ourselves when we say foolish things or when foolish things are said to us.

I have come to learn that my job, as a teacher in the academy and in the church, is not to create a "safe" space for critical conversations. If I make the white men feel safe, I have likely disquieted the men of color. If the gay and lesbian folks feel safe, then some other group is likely to get defensive and suspicious. Rather than creating safety in a conversation, I encourage risk taking, respect, patience, forgiveness, and regard for dignity. I have learned to encourage my students to speak gently and act with kindness. I tell them, "Be on your best behavior—act like you've got home training." We have learned together not to be afraid to make mistakes . . . because we all will.

Why Should Christian Education Discuss Oppression?

While insensitive, Susan's question is important—what's so wrong with oppression if the oppressors are nice? Humanity has been exploiting, dominating, and lording over one another since the dawn of time. Why is it so terrible? What's at stake in oppression for the oppressed and oppressor? What is the communal harm with oppression? Why should Christian education be centrally concerned about the lack of liberty and the presence of domination, hatred, and violence? What's wrong with privileging one group with public policy while labeling another group as inferior? I want to give the three reasons for the necessity of liberative conversations in the church.

---

and construct public policies and procedures to enforce this labeling. Thus, groups of people, e.g., Blacks, gays, are minoritized. There is nothing minor about these people until they are victimized by systemic oppression.

Our Sacramental Tradition

First, we look to our sacramental tradition for guidance and insight. Baptism is a Christian sacrament that holds for us, in a cherished way, what is important, what beckons the sacred, what is expected. While there are many streams of Christian tradition and many differing rituals of baptism, most of the Protestant rituals have a section of the ritual that concerns justice and domination. There is a baptismal mandate against injustice and a call for each baptized person to work against oppression. The baptismal covenant puts the agenda of justice and liberation at the center of Christianity. For example, in the United Methodist rite of baptism, these two questions are asked of the baptizands or their parents:

> On behalf of the whole church, I ask you: Do you renounce the spiritual forces of wickedness, reject the evil powers of the world, and repent of your sin?
> Do you accept the freedom and power God gives you to resist evil, injustice, and oppression in whatever forms they present themselves?[12]

Working on dismantling structures of domination is a mandate to the baptized. At every baptism, we remind the entire community of the baptized of the power of oppression to wound and destroy and hold one another accountable to lives of service that intend on eradicating injustice.

Our Present Era

The second reason conversations about overcoming domination are central to Christian education is that we have never before had to be church or do church in a technological, hip-hop, globalizing world. We are, then, pioneers in the twenty-first century attempting to be faithful to the gospel of Jesus Christ in an uncharted territory of time. We must ask and answer the question of faith: What does it mean to *be* church in the twenty-first century knowing if we simply repeat our ancestor's answer the church will not survive?

Knowing we will be the first to respond to this question in this era should give us pause. No other generation of Christians has had to be church in an age of such liminality, ambiguity, disorientation, and uncertainty. We are the first Christians to practice and adapt Christianity in an age of globalized economics and social media explosion, yet little has changed in our

---

12. *United Methodist Hymnal,* 34

denominational structure, practice, and polity. We are the first generation to elect an African American man as president of the United States. And yet, race is rarely part of the conversation in the church because of the volatility and backlash unleashed by Blacks and non-Black alike. Consider that the children born in 2013 will retire in 2068 and most of us cannot imagine the kind of jobs these children will have, the kinds of families they will raise or the kinds of education that will support them. What kind of church will they need by the time they retire? What kind of faith will they practice by 2068? We are attempting to respond to this question, but the change is happening with such velocity that we feel overwhelmed. Grasping the perspective of pioneer is key to our survival. Liberative conversations recognize that people are grieving for a bygone lifestyle and fearful of the impending, never-before-seen reality.

God's Incarnation—Our Theology of Body

The third, and perhaps most critical reason Christian education needs to be a conversation concerned with justice is that God is Mystery. Mystery is not that about which we cannot know anything. Mystery is that about which we cannot know everything. We can know some of God. We will never, even in a million millennia, know all of God. What we do know of God comes, in part, from the miracle of the incarnation.

"The Word became flesh, and lived among us" (John 1:14, NRSV; or as it is put in the translation *The Message*, "The word became flesh and blood, and moved into the neighborhood"). There is probably no better description of the power and promise of human-to-human conversation than the gospel description of the incarnation of God through Jesus born of Mary. Before Jesus, Word was detached from the body, transcending human grasp. Now, Word enfleshed, embodied, is not only part of the human experience, but it is a most common, everyday experience of humanness. Jesus, the incarnate One, was fully human and fully divine. As such, he experienced humanity from the inside out. He experienced humanity as a human being. He experienced joy, pain, suffering, pleasure, delight, hunger, and fear—as we all do.

The human predilection to compete with, exploit, dominate, and subdue one another is antithetical to a theology of incarnation. God, creator and lover of humanity, inhabited the human body as Jesus. Rather than seeing the human body with reverence and respect, we create structures of domination that target the body for oppression and domination. We use the body to supply indicators for who should be targeted as inferior and who should be labeled as superior. As bell hooks says, "students are socially situated bodies in our classrooms."[13]

We have learned (contrary to scientific theory) to attribute certain bodily characteristics to determine race so that we might label each other and determine the others' social status and worth. In racism, we learn to observe and judge skin complexion, hair texture, facial features. Racism, the systemic oppression of non-white peoples could not be maintained without being able to determine, by sight, who is in which race. In our racist mind-set, we have determined that fine is better than course, light is preferred to dark, and thin is preferred to thick. Sexism, the systemic oppression of non-male peoples, is a societal structure that touts the inferiority of female to male. The system is upheld by identifying and judging gender character-istics of the body. In sexism, vaginas are subservient to penises, wombs are seen as menacing to men, softness and roundness and being penetrated is seen as inferior to hardness and penetration. The body is relevant in deter-mining the victims of classism as well. In classism, the body that performs menial tasks is perceived as dispensable and must struggle against the cul-tural values of greed, affluence, and materialism with little resources to gain worth in society.

Making the body present in the conversation allows participants to experience the irrefutable evidence of humanness. The power and possibil-ity of transformative conversations is in the eye-to-eye moments of conver-sation; in the ability to touch one another, we are changed when we gaze and when we are gazed upon. When we sit to talk, noticing the body of the other, our bodies have less of a chance of being objectified and rendered non-human. In face-to-face conversation we discover there is more to con-versation than words. The body, the body language, the gazing upon the body, the aesthetic of the body, the personality portrayed by the movements of the body—all play a significant role in transformative conversations. We are not dis-embodied, talking heads engaged in intellectual discourse and dispute. We are bodies, given life with the breath of God at creation. It is breath that connects body, mind, and soul. It is the same breath that we use in conversation for justice. We are passionate beings who think as much with our guts, hearts, and souls as we do with our minds. We are beings who teach and learn with our hearts and our hearts yearn for justice. No one wants to give up privilege, yet we do want to be faithful to the gospel of Jesus Christ. Ours is a gospel that gives an unrelenting call for justice. The work of justice is a lifelong calling.

13. hooks, *Teaching to Transgress*, 14–15.

From Scripted Conversations to Ubuntu

Having named the reasons why the church needs more conversation concerning issues of oppression, we turn now to describing the mode of conversation that allows justice to be envisioned and even created in dialogue. The current paradigm in Christian education described above utilizes *scripted* conversations. Scripted conversations squash creativity in a time when we need innovation, imagination, and wonder as practices of faith and freedom. Most of us have learned to answer questions while the person is still speaking—well before the question is fully constructed or posed. Many of us routinely argue with spouses, lovers, and friends as if following a rehearsed screen play—each says the same thing over and over with the other never listening but responding in-kind. Scripted conversations in educational settings are just as hollow and unsatisfying. They are dull and boring (for teacher and learner, alike) because everyone knows what is supposed to happen—the "correct" ending is always the same.

These scripts are designed to perpetuate the values of an individualistic and competitive view. They perpetuate the individualism expressed by Descartes: "*I* think, therefore *I* am." They reward students who are passive and compliant, who lack imagination, and who limit their curiosity to the agenda of the teacher. The teachers know at the beginning of the lesson what will occur, what is deemed right, and what the students will or will not say. It is a teacher-centered approach where the teacher is seen as all-knowing, the giver of the important information, the expert, and the judge. The teacher's task is to classify and sort students by contrived developmental stages and chronological age. It is assumed that any expert can teach or that the way to become a better teacher is to know more facts and data about the subject. The learner is seen as an empty, passive vessel in need of the teacher's data, information, and judgment. Knowledge is transferred from teacher to student. The primary way for students to demonstrate learning is to memorize and regurgitate the information back. The teacher has all power, control, and authority while the learner has none. The life experience of the learner has little significance for the experience of the classroom and little bearing on the assessment of learning.

The concept of ubuntu (pronounced oo-BOON-too), on the other hand, is a philosophical notion that gives us a new premise for the work of conversation in faith formation. If we are to shift the paradigm of Christian education to meet the needs of our people and to be faithful to our call to do justice for a time such as this, we need to rethink the philosophical assumptions that undergird the current scripted conversation. We must replace the individualistic, competitive approach with one that teaches community, cooperation, interdependence, and mutuality. Scripted conversations teach, "You're on your own—sink or swim." We want a philosophy that teaches "We are in this together."

"Ubuntu" is an ancient African concept of personhood. Its meaning is captured in the African Proverb, "I am because we are," as well as in the Caribbean adage, "All of we is one." The concept of ubuntu espouses that any one person's humanity depends upon any other person's humanity and the other person's humanity depends upon all of humanity. In other words, each person's identity or self-hood is formed interdependently through the community. The experience of ubuntu is the experience of mutuality, cooperation, and shared empathy. It is the experience of wholeness rendered through connectedness and belonging. Martin Luther King captured this concept when he said, "We are caught in an inescapable network of mutuality, tied in a single garment of destiny. Whatever affects one directly, affects all indirectly."[14] Simply put, "A person depends upon other persons to be a person."[15] The ubuntu philosophy teaches that there was Christ long before there was creation and there will be Christ forever. This is the teaching of John 1:1, "In the beginning was the Word, and the Word was with God, and the Word was God." Our communal conversation is our way of grappling with and seeking to understand the Mystery that is God. We seek "the Word" through learning to be just, gracious, and challenging in our exchange of words.

Sustaining community that has integrity and is life-affirming is the challenge for the twenty-first-century church. Christianity is inherently a communal religion, and by reaffirming the communal nature of our religion in a new day we are strengthening and deepening our own faith and commitment to God's liberating care for the world. We cannot wait to form deeper community and then be about the work of justice. The Christian community happens amidst the work of justice.

Community is enriched through the conflict and struggle of learning to be cooperative, of learning deeper understandings of mutuality and respect. When we develop the communal habits and practices of interdependence, we are strengthening and maturing our faith. Conversation is the means for experiencing, witnessing and practicing these communal values. When persons experience conversations relevant to the issues of society and those conversations happen within the matrix of church community, lives are changed and healing occurs. Praxis, i.e., belief put into action, becomes the way the community understands its roles and responsibilities. Belief is

14. Quote by Martin Luther King, Jr. in his "Letter from Birmingham Jail" found: http://mlk-kppo1.stanford.edu/index.php/resources/article/annotated_letter_from _birmingham/.

15. Michael Battle, *Ubuntu*, 3.

not meant to be stagnant or benign. Belief propels communities into action. Conversation guides those beliefs and actions for deep and meaningful engagement to construct a more just society.

Scripted conversations perpetuate self-serving individualism, while the ubuntu philosophy encourages community, mutuality, and cooperation. The two philosophies differ radically in their approach to education, as can be seen in the following chart:

Comparing Teaching Philosophies[16]

	Scripted Conversation	Ubuntu Conversation
Knowledge	Transferred from teacher to student; literature of dominant culture (white, male, straight, wealthy) considered "normal"; folk wisdom is excluded or tokenized; life experience and circumstance has little to no bearing upon curriculum	Jointly constructed by students and teacher; includes folk wisdom and literature from students' race, class, gender; life experience and circumstance has great bearing on curriculum
Teacher Role	Classify and sort students by ages and stages; demonstrate expertise; punish those who do not comply	Develop student competencies, creativities, and intelligences. Co-learner.
Student Role	Passive participant to be filled with teacher's knowledge; compliance and wide capacity of memory are key to success	Active participant in journey of life-long learning; discoverer, transformer of self and community; producer of knowledge
Primary Mode of Learning	Memorization; structured outcomes relevant to the past and the status quo	Impassioned discussion connected to problem solving, praxis, improvisation; connection of classroom and larger church and society through relevant events and relationships

16. I developed this chart by adapting the work of Dr. Iva Carruthers, General Secretary of the Samuel DeWitt Proctor Conference. This work is used with her express permission.

Student Goal	Complete requirements; achieve certification and high grades	Strive for life-long learning; solving of communal problems, furthering community and sense of connectedness with others
Relationships	Impersonal and individualistic	Relational and intimate; communal life includes family, extended family, responsibility stretches into community and beyond
Climate	Enforcing sense of domination, competition, individualism	Nurturing cooperative, collaborative, mutuality, creative climate
Context	Fear of stranger; xenophobia.	Welcoming of stranger; xenophilia.
Power	Teacher holds and exercises power	Students are empowered; authority is shared; practices of forgiveness, compassion and mutuality are expected
Ways of Knowing	Logical-scientific (often dated); reason; body seen as irrelevant to knowing	Narrative; imagination, body, faith, intuition, discernment; organic sense of wonder and awe
Teaching Assumption	Any expert can teach; does not require relevance to context or community; no experience necessary	Teaching is complex, relational and improves with experience; possess fluidity, imagination to connect multiple arenas and peoples for justice work
Implications of Body	Body is used to target those who are deemed inferior, lazy, or stupid; body is extraneous to learning	Body is welcomed and integrated into learning; spirit, heart, and hands are integral to learning

Practical Implications for Ministry

Once we are aware that we need to change from a philosophy of Christian education that touts individualism, xenophobia, and domination toward a more communal approach that teaches forgiveness, justice, xenophilia, and compassion, we must figure out how to effect the change. What works in one context may not be effective in another context. What worked "then" may not work "now." How one person or community of faith effects change might not be possible for another, even in the same context. Shifting the paradigm of Christian Education has many variables and cannot be recipe-ed, formula-ed, or contrived, but it must be attempted. How do we bring ubuntu to our local churches? I share with you habits and practices my students, over the years, have told me were particularly helpful while learning, internalizing, and instituting this pedagogy of transformation.

Practice #1: Taking Time for Conversation

Simply put, building community takes time. We must make time, in our busy-ness, to have transformative conversations. Being too busy to talk with each other is part of the strategy of structures of oppression to thwart societal transformation. Transformative conversations can be created in formal settings complete with lesson plan and a teacher. Such texts as Walter Wink's *Transforming Bible Study,* Anne Wimberly's *Soul Stories,* or Patricia Killen's *The Art of Theological Reflection* can assist with formalized conversations. Transformative conversations can also be in informal settings. Consider regular gatherings such as book clubs, at-home Bible studies, or theatre groups. Consider establishing intergenerational groups to strengthen the sense of belonging. In my experience, sharing a meal makes any conversation, formal or informal, more worthwhile and more edifying.

Practice #2: Asking Questions

In communities of learning, conversations are often sparked by questions. All of us, at one time or another, have survived tests that ask vague questions, trick questions, or questions designed to show what is not known or embarrass. All of us have answered a question with a question in an effort to seize power in the argument or debate. We are skilled at asking questions to change the subject of an uncomfortable conversation when we do not want to talk about the topic at hand. We ask questions to infer what others do not know or could not know. We use questions to conceal what we do not want revealed. Simply put, whoever asks the question has the power. But, authentic questions also have the power to inform, inspire, and transform. Questions can begin conversations that change perspectives and heal. We all, at some time, have felt the satisfaction of asking a powerful question that gets at the heart of important matters. Questions can generate needed conversations that challenge and mend. A well-articulated question can welcome truth telling and encourage risk taking.

There are numerous taxonomies of questions—many easily accessed through internet resources. The one I teach my seminary students is simple, elegant, and infinitely employable. It classifies questions by the degree to which the question is likely to spark and invite, rather than snuff-out, conversation. The intent is for the learners to ask the critical questions of one another. Then, the conversation is a shared, relevant journey. There are three kinds of questions in this taxonomy:[17]

1. First Order Questions: This kind of question asks the learner to use cognitive recall and rote memory. First order questions simply ask for specific facts gained from reading the book, observing a film, or hearing a lecture. They are usually simplistic and do not encourage dialogue, analysis, or wondering. They can be satisfied with a fact or data and squelch creativity, divergent thinking, or imagination. For example: Who did it? When did it happen? Where did it happen?

2. Second Order Questions: This kind of question asks the learner to begin to analyze data and make connections between facts. Second order questions utilize common information to prove a point or support a generalization. Oftentimes, these kinds of questions presume a standard or pre-thought answer, but are open to dialogue. They usually expect some kind of investigation, evaluation, or logic. They can also be questions that ask the student to use known information to reach some kind of value judgment. For example: What evidence is there that the Bible . . . ? Was the disciple right in telling Jesus that . . . ? What did the storyteller mean when she said . . . ?

3. Third Order Questions: These questions ask the learner to think divergently, independently, imaginatively, and analytically. They presume a complexity to the answer. They are questions that make use of some known information as a starting point, but the answer moves in some other direction, some new direction, some unexpected way. There is no prescribed answer to third order questions. The question is asked to spark and perpetuate dialogue. These questions are asked with the expectation of conversation, problem solving, and soul searching. For example: What does it mean if . . . ? In what ways might . . . ? How would Black women feel if . . . ? What would happen if . . . ?

17. I was introduced to this taxonomy by Dr. Archie Smith, currently Distinguished Professor Emeritus of Pastoral Psychology and Counseling at Pacific School of Religion when he taught the God-Talk with Black Thinkers course at Drew Theological Seminary.

First order questions have little significance in transformative conversations. Second order questions are necessary, at times, for clarification and orientation. Third order questions are the core for this approach. Encouraging new answers for old problems, new thoughts about un-charted situations, and improvisation by both questioner and respondent is the fodder for the kind of conversation we want to foster.

Practice #3: Rules of Engagement

My students have reported that one of their fears about having conversations concerning structures of oppression in their congregations is that arguments and fights will break out. As I noted above, creating a safe place is not the goal. Safety for some peoples means vulnerability for others. Instead, the goal is to create space in which people speak responsibly, considerately, and with open hearts and listening ears. A key component in setting the climate for transformative conversations is to have agreed-upon rules and responsibilities. The rules are intended to encourage conversation and disclosure. They are intended to mitigate conversations dissolving into arguments, fights, and bullying. Here is an example of the rules of engagement one class created after having studied the notion of ubuntu:

1. Respect differing worldviews, opinions, and perspectives.

2. Do not impose your meaning on my words—ask me to clarify.

3. Make sure you understand what I am saying before making your judgment; consider suspending your judgment until you have heard me out.

4. Listen to my entire thought; no interruptions; don't be dismissive.

5. Do not correct my pronunciation or grammar if you understand me; seek clarification if needed.

6. Do not define me by any of the categories to which you perceive that I belong; wait for me to name myself should I choose to; resist stereotyping.

7. Do not force me to respond. I can take time to consider my response before speaking. I can say "Pass," "No thank you," or "Come back to me later."

8. Define your terms and definitions. Don't assume we have the same definitions for the same words; our life experiences are likely to be very different.

9. All in the conversation must value the intrinsic worth of one another and show respect in tone of voice, body language, and words. Be courteous and kind even when you don't feel like it.

10. Don't try to debate, find fault, or trip me up with verbal sparring and argumentative tones. Don't try to be right. Don't bait me with hot-button words or phrases. Don't be sarcastic or belittling. Don't make your point at my expense. Don't poke fun. Don't make a joke of my situation or opinion.

11. Give examples, rationales, or tell why this is personally important to you. Help me get to know you and why you hold the values and perspective and worldview you do.

12. Don't recount my history if it is not your history—let me tell my history. Give me my dignity.

13. Be open-minded and willing to learn. Listen with your body, mind, and soul.

14. Privilege those who are minoritized in the conversation. Don't rely on assumed power; if I am minoritized in society or in this context, allow me to speak first and last. Those with power must listen to those with little power.

15. If I am perceived as a person who is a member of an oppressor group (e.g., white, male, straight), do not ambush me or punish me for the deeds of all oppressors.

16. Be aware that we are all learning as we talk. Be aware that we are all relying upon God's guidance as we talk.

17. Pray as we talk.

Cautions about this Approach

Transformative conversations are not for the faint of heart. Transformative conversations bring change—people have to be ready to change, be willing to take ownership of the change, and be willing and ready when the beckoned Holy Spirit shows up. I have two cautions.

First, change takes the ability to risk and the want to survive. Power is questioned and redistributed with this approach. My students have reported that when they have been about this kind of work in their churches, they no longer fit into their previous world and mindset. Their pastors are not glad when people begin to ask critical questions and begin to imagine new and relevant ways of being church with justice in mind. Few church leaders want to surrender authority to the laity. And, many laity refuse to claim the power and responsibility of their baptism. This approach brings as much chaos as it does creativity.

I had the privilege of taking my students to Maui, Hawaii, on a cross-cultural study. Xavier (not his real name) had taken several courses with me including my Introduction to Educational Ministries course. He was a conscientious student and, from my perspective, was going to be an excellent pastor. While in Hawaii, we were studying the demise of the Polynesian culture and the violence of tourism. On our last night in Maui, we splurged and I begrudgingly purchased tickets for the dinner theatre, which was the story of Hawaii. The show began, and after about twenty minutes of the Broadway-esque production, Xavier leaned over and said to me, "I hate Drew." I was stunned and confused—what was the problem. During intermission, he jokingly explained why he was upset: "Everybody else is enjoying this stupid show. You've taught me to see the exploitation and dehumanization not only depicted in the history of the people, but in the show as a production. I can't enjoy the show because I know it is elitist and is about the eradication of an entire people and their culture. You've made me see the world differently. I have a different conversation in my head now than I used to and this is not what I want. . . . I just want to be entertained!"

Xavier was being facetious, but he was also articulating some real pain and real fear of this new worldview. Once you begin the work of justice and liberation it permeates your thoughts, dreams, consciousness, sensitivities, and actions. My students—those who embrace this work—discover that the work is emotionally draining and taxes the soul. Many of my students leave my classroom empowered to do justice and healing but are met by congregations and pastors who do not want liberative conversation, who do not want to be healed nor transformed.

A second caution concerns what may happen when justice is successfully achieved. Transformative conversations are our shared narratives, which depend upon and summon the Holy Spirit. To participate in deep, meaningful conversations about love, forgiveness, equality, and hope is to raise consciousness concerning the blight of our society and the suffering of the people. But, conversation is more than political strategy or making people savvy about the ways of the world. The holiness invoked (evoked, provoked) by these kinds of conversations creates a mystical narrative that is splendor. A mystical narrative is what happens when you bring what you have and I bring what I have and together what is conceived is more than what either of us brought or previously knew. Mystical narrative brings into existence something that will not/cannot be created unless we are willing to talk and be vulnerable one to another.

Mystical narratives create new peoples, new communities, allow us to see new possibilities where previously there were only limitations and obstacles. The healing of people and the mending of broken communities makes the gospel message vivid and alive, refusing to relegate the activity of God to biblical times. Classrooms become places where people experience being born again. In transformation conversation, when hearts are opened, we discover we are not the same people, subject to the same rigid, life-stealing rules and structures. In these conversations, we are taken to the edge, we are given "ah-hah" moments where we see differently, know more clearly and become new and healed people.

Do not confuse the healing that occurs in the mystical narrative with therapeutic sessions. We are not trying to duplicate or substitute the work that occurs with a trained therapist. Therapeutic analysis should be done only by professionally trained, experienced persons. However, the church must not give over the responsibility of healing and transformative conversation exclusively to the therapeutic community. Our task, as Christian people in community, is to talk openly and honestly, waiting for the Holy Spirit to move within us binding us tighter together. We are to learn to speak the truth in love. Truth-telling is a daunting, risky undertaking.

Questions for Discussion[18]

1. In what ways do recent conversations hallow the space in which the community lives? Desecrate the space?

2. What is the pre-requisite for healing?

3. What is the pre-requisite for experiencing the sacred?

4. What is the pre-requisite for truth-telling?

5. What is needed for protection so that risk-taking might occur?

6. What would it mean to divest ourselves of privilege?

7. As we imagine transformative conversations what do they look like? Smell like? Taste like? Sound like? Feel like?

18. I developed this battery of questions from an un-published lecture by Dr. Iva Carruthers, General Secretary of the Samuel DeWitt Proctor Conference, during the God-Talk With Black Thinkers course, fall of 2011. This work is used with her express permission.

8. What would it take for the minoritized to speak and for the oppressor to listen?

9. What do you wish the teacher/pastor would take into consideration about your race, class, gender, sexual orientation so that you might contribute more fully in the conversation?

10. What would it take to bring the transformational conversations in our classrooms into the worship service, then take the experience of the worship service out beyond the church walls? What would it mean to create synergy between the classroom, the sanctuary and the town square?

Further Reading

Foster, Charles. *From Generation to Generation: The Adaptive Challenge of Mainline Protestant Education in Forming Faith*. Eugene, OR: Cascade, 2012.

———. "Communicating: Informal Conversation in the Congregation's Education." In *Congregations: Their Power to Form and Transform*, edited by C. Ellis Nelson, 218–37. Atlanta: John Knox, 1988.

Palmer, Parker. *Healing the Heart of Democracy: The Courage to Create a Politic Worth the Human Spirit*. San Francisco: Jossey-Bass, 2011.

Rapp, Anne. "Translating Critical Pedagogy into Action: Facilitating Adult Learning." *The CLR James Journal: A Publication of the Caribbean Philosophical Association* 17/1 (2011) 37–57.

Rasmus, Rudy. *Touch: Pressing against the Wounds of a Broken World*. Nashville: Thomas Nelson, 2007.

———. *Jesus Insurgency: The Church Revolution from the Edge*. Nashville: Abingdon, 2012.

Thurman, Howard. *Deep Is the Hunger*. 1951. Reprinted, Richmond, IN: Friends United, 2000.

Westfield, N. Lynne. *Dear Sisters: A Womanist Practice of Hospitality*. Cleveland: Pilgrim, 2001.

Wimberly, Anne Streaty. *Soul Stories: African American Christian Education*. Nashville: Abingdon, 1995.

Wink, Walter. *Engaging the Powers: Discernment and Resistance in a World of Domination*. Minneapolis: Fortress, 1992.

———. *Transforming Bible Study: A Leader's Guide*. Rev. ed. Eugene, OR: Wipf & Stock, 2009.

7

Evangelism as Conversation

Marjorie Hewitt Suchocki

🌼 EVANGELISM IS ONE of the most difficult expressions of ministry to relate to the idea of the church as a community of conversation. In this book, conversation includes listening to the other, especially for ways in which the other might have questions, insights, or perspectives that cause the church to reconsider aspects of its belief and practice. The church today usually uses the word "evangelism" to refer to efforts to offer the gospel to people who do not believe and to invite them to convert.[1] The church has often thought of evangelism from a non-conversational point of view: the church has the news the world needs to hear, and to embrace that news people from the world need to convert to the message of the church. In this evangelistic mode, the church listens to the world largely to discover ways in which the church can shape its evangelistic message to appeal to non-believers, and not for ways in which the world might prompt the church to rethink dimensions of its message and life.

This chapter asks, "What happens if we reconfigure evangelism in light of the all-important notion of the omnipresence of God?" Evangelism itself has an evolutionary history within the annals of Christian thinking, but so,

---

1. It is helpful to reflect on the relationship between new member recruitment and evangelism as churches use these notions today. New member recruitment refers to the church inviting people to become members of the congregation and includes both inviting people to transfer their membership and evangelism. Evangelism, in the strict sense, refers to offering the gospel to people who do not believe and inviting them to convert to Christianity. This chapter is concerned with evangelism and with how the church might enlarge its meaning in view of divine omnipresence.

of course, has the understanding of God. And the two concepts—evangelism and God—are intricately related.

Rethinking the centrality of divine omnipresence helps us think about evangelism in a way that is truly conversational with respect to both other people and God. Along the way, we discover a conversational way of engaging people who do not believe in the God of Christianity and we also discover an enlarged understanding of evangelism. Indeed, the word "evangelism" comes from the Greek meaning good (*eu-*) news (*angelion*). In the Bible and in parts of Christian tradition, it refers not only to converting people, but even more to announcing and enacting the multiple dimensions of God's good news.

We begin by with a brief history of evangelism. The heart of the chapter roughly traces the move from a dominance of omnipotence to a dominance of omnipresence in our thinking about God. The chapter then weaves together the implications for evangelism in the context of the omnipresent God and the church as a community of conversation.

A Brief History of Evangelism[2]

This survey reveals that while the church has often understood evangelism as inviting non-Christians to convert to Christianity, the larger understanding of evangelism as witnessing to God's good news in multiple arenas of life is also present. The divide between these efforts is most notable in the contemporary era, especially in connection with radio and television evangelism.

From the New Testament to the Middle Ages

Clearly the New Testament gives vivid testimony to spreading the gospel of Jesus Christ throughout the Mediterranean world through telling the story of Jesus. We read the great commission that culminates the Gospel of Matthew, enjoining Christians to make disciples of all nations; we read in the book of Acts the stories of how the early Christians told and retold the story of Jesus; we read Paul's letters to newly established churches in Greek and Roman cities. Indeed, the church often takes the call recorded in the book of Acts, "Come over to Macedonia and help us," (16:9) to be axiomatic as an evangelistic imperative to which the church has responded in every age.

2. Unless otherwise noted, references from history are drawn from Balge, "A Brief History of Evangelism in the Christian Church."

Late in the second century Celsus, a pagan critic of the church, complained that "wool workers, cobblers, laundry workers, and the most illiterate and bucolic yokels" were telling the story of Jesus.[3] Widespread throughout the Greco-Roman world was the idea that death was followed by punishment for one's misdeeds in life. The Christian message that through baptism sins could be remitted, enabling one to live pious lives now, was very effective—by becoming Christian, a person would escape eternal punishment and achieve paradise instead.[4] In the third century, the theologian Origen writes an answer to Celsus, arguing extensively for the rationality of Christianity, and its effectiveness in promoting virtuous living.[5] Origen also sent itinerant evangelists out to visit cities, villages, and villas, preaching a gospel of repentance for our former sinful ways, and conversion to a life of virtue and good works.

In the fourth century, with the establishment of Christianity as the official religion of Rome, all citizens were by definition Christian as well as Roman, and missionary efforts turned toward evangelization of Britain and Europe. This effort was later accompanied by translation of the liturgy and portions of the Bible into Slavonic texts.

The Middle Ages

The Middle Ages saw a crass form of evangelism undertaken in the form of the Crusades, ostensibly for military and monetary rather than spiritual reasons, although the rationale was couched in religious terms. Bloody and ruthless though the Crusades were, persons as eminently holy as Francis of Assisi participated in them.

3. Celsus cited by Origin in his *Contra Celsum*, 165.

4. See Justin Martyr, First and Second Apologies. The forerunners to Jesus are Socrates and certain philosophers; the function of the Hebrew Scriptures was to provide prophecies, which, in Jesus' fulfillment of them, proved him to be the Logos of God. The cross functions symbolically, representing in shape a ship's mast providing safety at sea, and a plow, providing nourishment for life. While Justin quotes extensively from Isaiah 53, his only direct use of crucifixion is to state that the Logos shares our suffering. Insofar as Justin represents second-century interpretations of the Christian message, Christ dying for our sins does not appear to have been a central issue.

5. See Origen, *Contra Celsum*, 165–66. Like Justin Martyr, he places Christianity within the Greek philosophical tradition, but also stresses its Judaic origins. Celsus had argued that Christians valued "foolishness." Origen answers that foolishness is a temporary device for those not yet learned enough to follow philosophical reasoning. Unlike Justin Martyr, Origen cannot conceive of an eternal hell, but develops a system of transmigration in which God successively educates souls, enabling them to live virtuously, and eventually to be able to contemplate God fully.

Meanwhile, the late Middle Ages in Europe saw the rise of many lay movements, such as the Beguines and the Beghards, each of which was a voluntary society that included a mission of good works among the poor. The Beguines were voluntary societies of women who valued work and simplicity of life, with a strong spiritual focus on the humanity of Jesus, especially his passion. The Eucharist was of particular importance to the Beguines, in an age when the church found it necessary to mandate participation in the Eucharist at least once a year.[6] Beghards were voluntary communities of lay men, most of whom either had been or were still associated with the craft guilds of the time. Like the Beguines, they engaged in charitable works, and many became lay preachers, preaching simplicity of life and holy living. They claimed that the Bible should be available in the language of the people and that only sacraments administered by priests who were holy were valid—indeed, God could call even lay persons of holy living to administer the Eucharist. The evangelistic message of these orders focused on what they viewed as apostolic simplicity and holiness of life.

In fourteenth-century England, Bible translator John Wycliffe trained itinerant lay persons to preach the gospel; these lay preachers were known as "Lollards." Wycliffe's teachings included the supremacy of the civil government over ecclesiastical government, particularly in regard to property. He advocated the Bible as the only valid source for doctrine, and held that all things are pre-known within God; salvation is by divine election from eternity. Preaching would awaken the called to their election. Like the Beguines and Beghards on the continent, Wycliffe advocated simplicity and holiness of life.

In fifteenth- and sixteenth-century Europe, the Hutterites taught that all authority comes from God, and that we are to live together in community according to the principles suggested in the second chapter of Acts. Temporal living outside the community leads to disobedience to the laws of God, especially by subjecting one to laws of the state that go against the gospel, such as military and police rule. Frequent persecutions against Hutterites were often based on their ardent pacifism. Hutterites also claimed that every believer has received the Great Commission, and should preach this gospel of communal living according to the laws of God.

The Reformation

In sixteenth-century Germany, Martin Luther taught that every Christian was an evangelist, with direct access to God through prayer and

6. See Knuth, "The Beguines," for further study on this interesting lay society.

responsibilities toward the neighbor. Like the Hutterites and Lollards before him, Luther strongly advocated reform of the church based on biblical principles. Justification is based on the free grace of God and not on works, regardless of whether or not those works are prescribed by the church of Rome.

The eighteenth century saw strong revival movements in Britain (Wesley, Whitefield), Europe (Zinzendorf), and America (Jonathan Edwards), each of which was an impetus to further missionary work. The gospel preached was of the grace of God for salvation from sin, based on Christ's death and resurrection. By participation in Christ we escape eternal punishment and receive a power for virtuous living. In Wesley and Whitefield, the personal experience of salvation becomes important.

In Austria, Zinzendorf taught that Christianity should be lived in community. Each Christian has a spiritual relationship with Christ, but the community as a whole has a special relationship through which the community can be guided. This included the sense that the relationship with Christ matured through life's stages, so that group houses were established according to one's stage in life. Assent to particular doctrine was less important than the living relationship to Christ in community, and the emotional aspects of life in Christ were stressed. Radical equality countered the social distinctions outside the community. Conflict with authorities in Austria led Zinzendorf to move throughout Europe and England, establishing communities. Soon missionaries went to the West Indies and America to establish communities in those lands, preaching essentially the same message belonging to the predecessor communities in Europe. Zinzendorf personally visited the missional communities in the West Indies and in Pennsylvania.

In North America

Nineteenth-century America developed a new focus on evangelism as the Puritanism of earlier America morphed into a revivalism culture. Methodism played a role as circuit riders took preaching—and the Eucharist—into the developing western edges of the nation. Subjective personal experiences of "rebirth" became increasingly important, along with exaltation of the Bible, and a sense of mission. Charles Finney, with the "Businessman's Revival" of 1857, and Dwight Moody following the civil war, were important figures.

Concomitant with many of these movements, Bible societies, rescue missions, and foreign missions flourished in America, and continue into our own time. The focus was usually more individually than communally oriented, stressing the importance of personal acceptance of Christ as savior from sin, and on subsequent holiness of life. The establishment of the National Association of Evangelicals in 1943 provided further strength to this evangelical message, along with mass preaching by evangelist Billy Graham beginning mid-century.

Radio and Television in Evangelism

The twentieth century's invention of radio and television added its own strange twist to the history of evangelism.[7] On January 2, 1921, Pittsburgh's Calvary Episcopal Church gave the first radio broadcast of the Christian message in history. This was soon followed by evangelists such as Billy Sunday and Aimee Semple McPherson, who also began broadcasting services and sermons. By 1927, there were sixty religious radio stations, each attempting to draw listeners to the broadcasters' understandings of the Christian message. The advent of the 1950's added television to the tools of public evangelism. When Billy Graham had one of his crusades televised, the TV station received over a million and a half letters of support. Clearly there was an audience for the evangelical message, and as the twentieth century progressed, televangelists proliferated.

The gospel preached usually centered on the dangers of hell and the importance of accepting Christ as one's personal savior, but the large audiences accrued through radio and television had a dangerous underside. This was not only the temptation to simplistic messages of personal salvation, with little input from historical or biblical studies, but also the very impersonalism of the media. The media gave the audience a sense of direct contact with the evangelist, but such contact was in fact illusory. The messages were addressed to mass audiences, and led easily to lucrative personality cults for the televangelists. Also, the vastness of the audience generated by this form of evangelism created an unparalleled opportunity for political manipulation of the audience toward ends only loosely or not at all connected with the gospel message, usually in the name of "Christian values" or "family values."

By the 1980s excesses and scandals began to plague televangelists, deflating some of the power of the personality cults. Many of those using television for evangelical purposes backed away from focusing on personalities,

---

7. For further information on the role of radio and television in evangelism, see "The Role of Evangelism in the History of the United States of America"; and Fore, "The Unknown History of Televangelism."

and turned instead to influencing programming itself. "Touched by an Angel," "Christie," and "Saving Grace" have been some of the results of this effort.

A major problem with the ways in which some Christian leaders have utilized mass media for evangelism is the distortion of the gospel that often results. The gospel preached is likely to be a simplified version of fundamentalist American Christianity that eschews biblical scholarship and Christian history alike. When such a message is identified too closely with evangelism, then those who do not follow the televised version of Christianity also shy away from evangelism itself. But the call to "make disciples of all nations" continues in every age, regardless of the variations of discipleship that find their way into the gospel message.

The Church Takes Account of Culture in Formulating its Evangelistic Message

This brief history of how the gospel has been preached in the various ages of the church suggests that the evangelistic witness of the church is always associated with the dominant issues of the age. The church must listen to the culture in order to identify what people perceive as needs and issues. The church then correlates its evangelistic approach to those needs and issues. Is there corruption in the church? Then the gospel advocates simplicity of life. Are the means of righteousness or acceptability to God arduous, involving acts of contrition impossible for common people? Salvation is freely offered by God through Jesus Christ by grace alone, operating through faith. Is there dissension among believers? Then the gospel advocates unity through community, where the personal relationship to Jesus Christ is supplemented by the communal relationship, guiding life and practice. Is there confusion concerning authority? Scripture alone, properly studied and properly believed, guides life and practice. Is there an underclass, with little hope of well-being in a world too often organized for the benefit of the well-to-do? Christ's love reaches the poorest soul, conferring dignity and opportunities for literacy, small classes, and a system of banding together for what common good is possible.

We have seen that evangelism involves much more than conversion. The gospel of John tells us that the Word *was* Christ (John 1:1–5). His entire life of compassion, simplicity, speaking truth to power, and caring for society's outcasts, is part of the evangelistic message. For much of the tradition, evangelism was less about converting people to Christianity, and more about ministering to people in the name of Christ. In the past two hundred years or so evangelism has become a more restricted concept, focused on converting persons to particular forms of Christianity.

From Omnipotence to Omnipresence

Without losing the converting element of the good news, this brief look at history suggests that we need to recover the wider breadth of the evangelistic task. Focusing on the omnipresence of God helps in that endeavor.

Omnipotence Held Sway for Centuries

Theology has taken a quiet turn in the past half century—so quiet as to be hardly noticed. For centuries of Christian history, the dominant category for understanding God was the notion of "omnipotence." Omniscience and omnipresence were supposedly of equal importance within the notion of God, and often, omnibenevolence as well. But as early as the formation of the Apostle's Creed, whose antecedents can be found already in the second century, we see the dominance of omnipotence. Twice in the brief creed, there is a reference to God's omnipotence: "*Credo in Deum Patrem omnipotenem,*" ("I believe in God the Father almighty") and again in "*Sedet ad dexterem Patris omnipotentis*" ("He sits at the right hand of the Father almighty"). But there is not a single reference to either omniscience or omnipresence within the creed, nor indeed, do these qualities play a strong role in theological developments in early Christian history. They were always viewed through the lens of omnipotence. Omniscience, for example, was important because an all-powerful God must know all things; otherwise the power of God would be diminished. Omnipresence, likewise, expressed the power of God, sometimes as a localized power, other times as a power of majesty spreading throughout the king's realm. Omnipresence and omniscience were functions of God's omnipotence.

As such, strange conundrums developed within Christian theology, particularly with regard to omniscience. The thorniest issue had to do with resolving the conflict between omniscience and human freedom: if God's power is absolute, how is there room for human freedom? And if there is no real human freedom, how is there justice in punishing people for doing that which they are predestined to do? Predestination and theodicy are the two major theological issues that evolved from conjoining omniscience to omnipotence.

With regard to omnipresence, the major problem had to do with reconciling the presence of God to the immateriality of God. How can something that does not have a body be, in any sense, "present," or contained in space? Anselm dealt with the issue in his eleventh-century treatise, *Monologium*. He made the distinction between being in space, which requires being circumscribed by place, and being. This suggests that God is present *to* space, but not *in* space. He also compares the presence of God in the world to the presence of a king's power throughout his realm. There is no place within the realm of a king that is not subject to the king's power; thus, the king is said to be present throughout the realm in and through his power. Hence omnipresence is fundamentally interpreted through omnipotence.

In the thirteenth century, Thomas Aquinas picks up a similar notion when he deals with omnipresence, holding that God's presence is to be understood through God's power. He writes, "God is in all things by his power, inasmuch as all things are subject to his power; he is by his presence in all things, inasmuch as all things are bare and open to his eyes; he is in all things by his essence, inasmuch as he is present to all as the cause of their being."[8]

Wesley and an Impulse toward the Priority of Omnipresence

John Wesley, writing in the eighteenth century, bases a sermon on the text in Jeremiah 23–24: "'Do I not fill heaven and earth?' saith the Lord."[9] Wesley bemoans the fact that so little has been written historically on the divine omnipresence—as well he should, given the overwhelming amount of material written on both omnipotence and omniscience, and relatively little on omnipresence. Omniscience, of course, raised the conflict between God's foreknowledge and human freedom, causing tomes of theology attempting to resolve this issue. But omnipresence was far less controversial, and consequently received less treatment.

Whereas both Anselm and Aquinas write of omnipresence in terms of the spatial presence of God, Wesley uses the Jeremiah text to deny the relevance of spatiality: "The presence or absence of any or all creatures makes no difference. . . . He is equally in all . . ." He also imagines the universe as a whole. Is God contained within the universe? Does the universe even have an "outside"? It matters not; "space exists beyond the bounds of creation . . . even that space cannot exclude him who fills the heaven and the earth."

Wesley makes omnipresence the basis of omnipotence, not the consequent of omnipotence. "If there were any space where God was not present, he would not be able to do anything there. Therefore, to deny the omnipresence of God implies, likewise, the denial of his omnipotence." But he does not go

8. Aquinas, *Summa Theologica* I, 8, 3 (1948 translation).

9. *The Works of John Wesley*, Sermon 111.

so far as to question whether or not God's omnipresence, as the foundation of God's power, in any way changes or shapes how we understand God's power.

In the twentieth century, two movements—liberation theologies and process theologies—not only make God's omnipresence central, but also begin to reshape the understanding of God's power, conceiving of it as the power of presence.

Liberation Theologies and Divine Omnipresence

Liberation theologies began in South America, receiving major theological formulation in 1971 by Peruvian priest Gustavo Gutierrez in *A Theology of Liberation*.[10] The focus is the poor, and the unjust social structures that make for poverty. In 1986, Brazilian theologian Leonardo Boff published *Ecclesiogenesis*. There were more parishes than there were priests within the Roman Catholic Church, and because a priest had to be present in order for the Eucharist to be celebrated, this meant that parishes in remote parts of Brazil were virtually without access to the Eucharist. Boff argues that God gives sacramental power through the Eucharist, and the priest is but a vehicle of God's power. Because God is present in and to the parish regardless of the presence of a priest, God can and does raise up a person from among the laity, whom God then empowers to offer the Eucharist, in which God in Christ is literally present. God's power is a power of presence.[11]

The awareness of divine presence is empowering. This fundamental key to all liberation theologies expanded from South American theologies—Protestant as well as Roman Catholic—into Black, Latino/a, and feminist liberation theologies of Central and North America, and also into the emerging "theologies of hope" in Europe. Empowerment had social as well as theological consequences, as can be noted in liberation theology's other mantra of "God's preferential option for the poor." Those without access to political, ecclesiastical, or social power are empowered by God to affect political, ecclesiastical, and social change that will lead to greater well-being among all people.

The empowering presence of God among the people received christological affirmation as the figure of Christ came to be represented in new ways. Suddenly the traditionally Anglo representations of Christ in paintings and sculpture gave way to many forms. The Black Christ and then the female Christ as Christa made their way into art; nativity scenes were no longer confined to white holy families, but showed families of all races and cultures.

10. Gutierrez, *A Theology of Liberation*.
11. Leonardo Boff, *Ecclesiogenesis*.

God's presence among us took on an identity with us that in turn empowered a new dignity, a new courage for what was often called "a place at the table."

Process Theologies and Divine Omnipresence

The other form of twentieth-century theology that turned toward the importance of God's presence was process theologies. Whereas liberation theologies emerged from social issues, process emerged from changes in the scientific understanding of the world. New findings in relativity physics led physicist/philosopher Alfred North Whitehead to ask questions about the basic structure of the universe, and his resulting philosophy suggested a somewhat radical reworking of the nature of God and of God's power.[12]

A process view of the world understands all things to be essentially dynamic, existing in and through relation at the most fundamental subatomic level. Whitehead coined the phrase "actual entity" to refer to the basic building block of existence. An actual entity is a momentary coming-into-being that emerges through its dynamic relation to a past and a future, integrating both influences into its own becoming, at which point it ceases to be except through its continuing influence in everything subsequent to itself. Also, each actual entity is unique, in that it always comes into existence through a particular past that is fully pertinent only to the point in time and space to be occupied by this particular entity. That is, since every entity has its own particular standpoint, no two entities have precisely the same standpoint; hence no two entities have precisely the same past.

It is relatively easy to understand an entity coming into being through the influence of its particular past, but one might question how the future, which does not yet exist, can participate in the formation of the present. Human experience gives an obvious answer, since so often what we do in the present is based not only on our past, but in our hopes for the future. Wanting to enter a particular profession influences a person to go to school and to study subjects that will prepare one for that profession: a possible future influences what we do in the present. But Whitehead takes this to a deeper level. If every actual entity must integrate the past it has received into itself, and if every actuality is unique, how does that entity "know" how to integrate the past in order to become what has never exactly existed before? What is the source of the possibility that the entity must grasp in order to become itself?

For Whitehead, that source is God. *All* possibilities, ordered in an infinite variety of modes of mutual relativity, form the primordial nature of

---

12. For a comprehensive introduction to the process worldview, see Whitehead, *Process and Reality*.

God, and this God is present to all things, whether spatial or nonspatial. God, present to all things, feels all things, so that God and only God shares every particular standpoint with every specific creature. From the fullness of God's relational knowledge, God feels the possibility best suited not only to the particular creature, but to the community of creatures subject to its sphere of influence, and offers this possibility to the becoming creature as its possible future. Thus the creature receives influences not only from its past, but also from God in the form of a possible future. What the creature does with these influences finally depends upon the creature itself. Within the constraints of past and future, it alone becomes what it will. Thus freedom is by definition an essential aspect of every creature whatsoever.

This very brief summary of what in fact is a quite complex system is sufficient to show that the presence of God is fundamental to both the power and wisdom of God. Often process philosophers and theologians speak of God's power as a persuasive rather than coercive force: God does not control all things, God persuades all things. Thus the issue of theodicy is considerably lessened: the world is responsible for what it does with what it has received. God has not foreordained it. The issue of divine knowledge is also addressed: God's knowledge is perfect because God knows all things as they are. God knows the past as the past—and, since in a process world every actuality receives as well as gives, God continuously receives each completed actuality into the divine self, knowing it there as it could have been and as it became One could say that God knows the past more fully than the past could ever have known itself. God knows the present as present, as becoming, as processing that which it has received. And based upon the fullness of God's knowledge of past and, to the extent that it can be known, the becoming entity, God knows all probabilities for the future. Given the presence of all possibility within the primordial nature of God, God knows all possibilities whatsoever, those that are relevant and irrelevant to any becoming world. In classical portrayals, God had to know everything as if it had already existed. In process forms of theology, God knows the actual as actual, the probable as probable, and the possible as possible. To know a thing as if it existed when in fact it has not existed would, in process terms, not be knowledge at all.

In many respects, process theologies make explicit that which is metaphysically implicit within liberations theologies, and, indeed, in the Wesleyan theology suggested in the cited sermon. When divine presence is the basis of God's power, then the old metaphor of earthly rulers as the exemplar of divine power must give way. God's power is a power with, not a power over; a power of persuasion, not a power of coercion; a power of empowerment, not a power of control. And when God's knowledge is based on God's omnipresence, then this knowledge is not a foreordaining power, neither to damnation, nor salvation, nor anything else. Rather, it is a fullness of knowledge that knows all things as they are and as they can be or as they could have been. It is knowledge *with* reality, and not over reality.

The Omnipresent God and Implications for Evangelism

We return now to a discussion of evangelism, and ask the question: what are the implications for contemporary modes of evangelism if we base evangelism on the omnipresence of God?

When the omnipotence of God is paramount there is often the assumption that God's efficacious presence is limited to Christianity. Thus only those who embrace Christianity find favor with God, and others are doomed to eternal death. In Reformation times this fate was theologically justified by the notion that the fullness of God's nature must be revealed: damnation for sin manifests the justice of God, whereas salvation for others manifests the mercy of God. The purpose of damnation and salvation, therefore, is to manifest the full nature of God. God's absolute power, along with a foreknowledge that is concomitant with that power, demands that there be both saved and damned. Evangelism for the sake of conversion is in the service of manifesting the mercy of God; the unevangelized and all who have refused conversion manifest, through their damnation, the justice of God. Thus God uses the preached word and other forms of evangelism to evoke converting responses in those who are elected to manifest the mercy of God.

What, then, if we approach the evangelistic task from a basic trust in the omnipresent power of God? Omnipresence is a power with, not a power over, and it is assumed to reflect the power we see in the Gospels, manifested in the compassionate Christ. Certain things would follow in our relation with persons within our own cultures as well as persons in cultures different from our own.

All Religions are Enculturated

We must understand that all forms of religion, including our own, partake of the cultures in which they evolve. There is no church unaffected by its time and place. To imagine we exist within a non-acculturated form of Christianity is to inhibit our knowledge of, and ability to communicate with, those in our towns and cities outside the church. All expressions of Christianity are encoded within the cultural sensitivities of its age, and cultural values are easily regarded as divinely sanctioned. For example, patriarchal assumptions about the role of women in society are woven into the theology and practice of the church, even though the gospel is as freeing for women as it is for men. Within both the Hebrew and Christian Scriptures, a functioning norm for discerning God's call to righteousness is the treatment of the least within society ("the widow, the orphan, the stranger with your gates"). This is a point at which conversation is especially important as the church engages in conversation within itself as well as with people outside the church to come to the best available understandings of where and how God is active in particular cultural expressions.

If enculturation is so for all forms of Christianity, it is likewise so for all other religions. Thus every religion we encounter is a reflection not only of the deepest etchings of its major figure or holy texts, but also of the society in which it exists. Insofar as we need guidance to discern the word of God among people in cultures not our own, the norm of the "wellbeing of the least" that is present in texts and nations provides an excellent starting place.

The Church Must Listen as Well as Speak

Evangelism within the context of the omnipresence of God has an innately conversational character as it calls upon the evangelist to be first of all a listener, studying the texts and culture of the other, listening respectfully to spiritual sensitivities. The Gospel of Luke gives an image of Mary encountering Elizabeth for the first time during their pregnancies. Elizabeth, we are told, felt the child within her leap for joy as they met (Luke 1:41). As we hear and see signs of God's presence in religions not our own, our own souls might leap for joy as we encounter God in and through the other.

We are speakers as well as listeners, sharing our own stories for the others to hear, and they, too, might experience that responsive recognition that knows itself in the presence of affinitive spiritualities. Evangelism honors the other, hears the other, speaking with, rather than to, the other.

The omnipresence of God means that true conversation is possible with those who are outside the Christian community. Indeed, they may have insights into the divine nature and purposes that the church does not have.

Evangelism and People outside the Church

If the work of such evangelism does not first of all seek to convert the other to one's own mode of religion, what is the point, and why in fact can it be called "evangelism"? On the one hand, God *may* convert some listeners to Christianity. No religion speaks to the perceived religious or spiritual needs of all persons within its culture. Sometimes the marginalized within a culture are the first to respond to an alternative message from outside the culture, but others, too, respond to the story of God's revelation in Jesus Christ. Christian churches grow and develop in many cultures. Sharing the story of Christ can indeed bring others into the church, where they are welcomed as brothers and sisters in Christ. But their entrance into Christianity is not because God was not present within their own cultures and religions, but because God's presence within Christianity spoke more clearly to their heart's needs.

What about evangelism within the context of God's efficacious and omnipresent work within one's own wider culture, when so many within that culture are unchurched? There are both internal and external responses. Internally, we must ask in what sense the church no longer meets the needs of persons within the wider culture in which the church is embedded. Here, as a part of its evangelistic work, the church needs to listen for how outsiders—others—perceive the church and its message.

Paradoxically, opposing reasons may be in play. For some, church doctrines, formulated long before we were able to understand so much about the immensity and structure of the universe and our evolving place within it, appear to be irrelevant. Or earlier ages in Western history assumed that some sort of hell awaited unconverted persons following death. That assumption is no longer wide spread. Why, then, should one become religious to escape a non-existent hell? Yet again, why should some churches be so adamantly opposed to evolution? Or, why are some churches so set against gay persons, let alone gay marriage?

For unchurched persons who view the church through lenses such as these, the church is simply out of touch with the way things really are. Yet for others, the problem is the opposite: why does the church—especially what were once called "mainline churches"—so strongly reflect the culture in which it exists and fail to offer the security and certainty of absolute knowledge? Where is the solid rock in the wild seas of so much change and confusion in the world? Persons within the church must prayerfully seek to understand how and why it no longer seems so easy an answer to problems all persons, certainly including the unchurched, face. The church may or may not be able to respond to any of the issues the unchurched may raise against it, but the church surely should attempt to understand those reasons. Conversation with the unchurched is essential in these regards: the church needs to hear how unchurched persons perceive the church and the world.

The Church Must Recognize Where God is Already at Work . . . Including among the Unchurched

We must assume that the omnipresent God has been active not only within the church, but also outside the church. If God is omnipresent, working incognito as well as in ways we recognize, then God is surely at work with all persons, churched or not. Indeed, the church works with the conviction that God is not only creatively at work throughout the universe, but that all things exist in and through the creative "withness" of God.

God is also present, whether recognized or not, in the lives of those who eschew organized religion. Perhaps, then, we in the church should attempt to discover what "spiritual" means in the "spiritual but not religious" formula so often cited by those who do not affiliate with the church.[13] Are there commonalities to what "spiritual" means in such cases—and could God, who surely works outside as well as inside the church, be involved in that process? Perhaps if the church honored what God does outside of its walls, friendships of respect could replace relations of opposition between the church and those who are not churched.

What the Church Offers

What does the church offer? It offers a witness to the "with-ness" of God; it offers the Name of the one who has been at work within us all. It offers a witness to the love and compassion of God through the love and compassion it shows not only to those who belong to the community of faith, but to those in the wider world, whether or not they join with us. It offers the story of Jesus, who revealed the nature of God in human history: a God who is with us in our sorrows and in our joys, a God who feels our pain, and the consequences of the evil we do to one another, a God whose resurrection power can transform us with new life, overcoming evil with good.

The church offers a family of faith, a testing ground for the power of love to take us beyond the concerns of our small circles of caring to a wider bonding. There is a joining together in worship, in study, in work together that strengthens our individual spirits as part of a communal spirit. In the process, we can grow in our capacity to participate in God's love, joining with God as we direct our love not only to one another but to the wider world. In these roles, God is like a cosmic conversation partner who is present in others to help us enlarge our sense of world community.

13. For more on this phenomenon, see Fuller, *Spiritual but Not Religious.*

Evangelism as Caring for the Well-Being of All

The fundamental purpose of evangelism is the glory of God, and the glory of God is the love of God spread abroad among all peoples. Love cares for the well-being of persons in community, and this is so in many cultures, many religions. As Christians share with persons of other faiths, ways of working together for wider forms of communal well-being may take shape. Initiatives for such communal work can also originate from other religions.

For example, the Japanese Buddhist group called Rissho Kosei-kai has focused on world peace, founding in 1970 the World Conference of Religions for Peace. This group seeks to involve persons from all religions in ministering to those affected by war, and to use religious influence in efforts to prevent wars. Christian examples of similar efforts to work across cultures abound: Bread for the World, The Heifer Project, Church World Service, and the Network of Christian Peace Organizations are but a few.

In addition to ecumenical and interreligious work, there is also the work carried out within each of the forms of Christianity, whether Protestant, Roman Catholic, Coptic, or Orthodox. Each form of the church of Jesus Christ engages in its own various forms of corporate acts of mercy, reaching beyond its borders to persons anywhere who are suffering. As persons work together across religious boundaries, mutual respect and mutual sharing occurs, and God is glorified. Working across such boundaries almost always has conversational elements. A gospel metaphor for such ministry comes from Christ's injunction that we "give a cup of cold water" (Matt 10:42). Christian evangelistic work involves working together and with other peoples to bring about greater good, and doing so in the name of Christ. In such efforts, Christians need to be open to the insights of others.

In the brief history of evangelism given above, the communal nature of church played a powerful role. Often the community itself was the drawing power. In and through community, lay people could gather together and minister to the needs of the society around them. And the very organizations mentioned in this section are powerful witnesses to the "much more" that the church can do through the strength of its communal nature, certainly much more than most individuals can do alone. The church today offers an avenue of service to its surrounding local communities and to increasingly wider circles of service to nations, peoples, and the world. There are, thank God, secular organizations of service as well. But a major component of evangelism in a world where God is known to be omnipresent would be an invitation to all—churched and unchurched, Christian or some other religion—to join one's heart and soul and body to the corporate and communal task of working with God toward the world's good.

Evangelism in the context of the omnipresent God does not assume we take God to others but that we look to find God in others, rejoicing in the wideness of God's mercy. We tell what we have learned and experienced of God through Jesus Christ, and listen to others as they return our sharing. We seek ways of working together, inside and outside the church, to increase compassion, kindness, and well-being among all peoples, and, indeed, to care for this good earth as well. We are called to give "the cup of cold water" in acts of friendship and mercy. And we are called to do this in Christ's name, in word as well as deed, as the embodied Christ, the church. In so doing, we glorify God and celebrate God's presence among us.

Critical Reflection

The broadly based understanding of evangelism derived from God's omnipresence offers the church several positive values. As noted already, the idea of God's power as power *with* rather than power *over* reframes theodicy and other issues in more compassionate and believable ways. Indeed, many people find it intellectually more credible to believe in a God who is ever at work through natural and historical processes than to believe in an omnipotent God who can control events at will but who allows innocent suffering to continue and who is expected to intervene in history in a giant apocalypse.

Furthermore, the foregoing qualities make it easier to evangelize, that is to talk with others about believing in God, becoming Christian, and to use the church as a venue through which to participate with God in enhancing the well-being of the world. It is more credible—and personally easier—to offer this understanding of God to others since we do not have to be as awkward about God's relationship to difficult situations. Indeed we do not have to apologize for God or ask people to accept things that test credibility.

The church does not have to agonize over the ultimate fate of non-Christians. The omnipresent God is unreservedly committed to working for the well-being of all. Christians under the influence of the idea of a God of controlling power often wonder, "Who is included in and excluded from salvation? On what grounds? On what basis do we think about such things?"

Evangelism in the context of the omnipresent God is genuinely meaningful to God. Because God feels everything we feel, what we do adds to the quality of God's life (and what we do not do diminishes the quality of God's life). Under the aegis of a God of controlling, omnipotent power, human activity has little meaning to God except that God will one day judge what we have done. Our evangelistic efforts do not make a real difference to God if God controls the outcome. However, the perspective on God set out in this chapter means that what we do (or do not do) makes a real difference to God because God feels everything that we feel.

At the same time, a church whose theological focus shifts from divine omnipotence to divine omnipresence does give up a certain sense of security. The omnipotent God was ultimately in complete charge of everything. Nothing happened without divine initiative or permission. No matter how bad things could get, a community could always take solace in the notion that God was in control. The omnipresent God pictured in this chapter does not have such absolute power, but works in partnership with others—human beings and elements of nature. When partners make poor choices, God cannot simply clean things up. We have to stand up and take responsibility for our part in the partnership.

The church of the omnipresent God must learn to live with a measure of ambiguity with respect to discerning God's purposes. While it is tremendously empowering to believe that God is already present and at work throughout the world, the church can sometimes find it difficult to identify where and how God is present in specific situations. These can include human-caused pain through the horrific evil we do to one another, or earth-caused pain through our tendency to live in places that are prone to earth's violent volcanoes and earthquakes due to plate tectonics, and other natural disasters.

The church finds it easy to motivate people to evangelize when the church believes in the omnipotent God who will one day judge all peoples, saving some and condemning others. God judges people both inside and outside of the church. One criterion of the judgment of the church is the degree to which church members have engaged in evangelism. If I think I am going to stand before God on the judgment day and give an account of my record of evangelism, I am motivated to evangelize. Since evangelism under the management of an omnipresent God lacks this impetus, the church needs to think afresh about how to encourage people to engage in evangelism in both narrower and wider perspectives.

Questions for Discussion

1. Think about your own history in relationship to the subject of evangelism. How have you and the congregations of which you have been part thought of—and practiced—evangelism? Have you been theologically comfortable with these motivations for evangelism and the way evangelism has been carried out?

2. Many Christians and congregations in the long-established churches today are uneasy with the idea of evangelism because they associate

evangelism with a kind of theological imperialism—telling other people what they need to believe and do. How might the perspectives articulated in this chapter speak to this concern, and to other reservations about evangelism you have heard?

3. What do you find most compelling about the idea at the heart of this chapter—evangelism as participating with God in places where God is already at work, offering possibilities for the world's good?

4. Think about your personal life and the life of your congregation from the perspective on evangelism in this chapter. What conversations could your congregation undertake with an eye towards identifying situations in which God is already at work and in which you could join God in seeking to manifest good news.

5. The church has often thought of evangelism as a one-way bridge from which the church tells unconverted people what they need to believe and do. In a conversational church, traffic runs both ways on the bridge. What might such a church learn about its message, its own life, and its possibilities for evangelism and mission by listening to the unconverted?

Further Reading

Abraham, William J. *The Logic of Evangelism.* Grand Rapids: Eerdmans, 1989.

Bell, Rob. *Love Wins: A Book about Heaven, Hell and Every Person who Ever Lived.* San Franciso: HarperOne, 2011.

Bosch, David J. *Transforming Mission: Paradigm Shifts in the Theology of Mission.* American Society of Missiology Series. Maryknoll, NY: Orbis, 1991.

Hartshorne, Charles. *Omnipotence and Other Theological Mistakes.* Albany: State University of New York Press, 1984.

Heath, Elaine A. *The Mystic Way of Evangelism: A Contemplative Vision for Christian Outreach.* Grand Rapids: Baker Academic, 2008.

Stone, Bryan P. *Evangelism after Christendom: The Theology and Practice of Christian Witness.* Grand Rapids: Brazos, 2007.

Suchocki, Marjorie Hewitt. *Divinity and Diversity: An Affirmation of Religious Pluralism.* Nashville: Abingdon, 2003.

———. *God, Christ, Church: A Practical Guide to Process Theology.* Rev. ed. New York: Crossroad, 1992.

Watson, David Lowes. *God Does Not Foreclose: The Universal Promise of Salvation.* Nashville: Abingdon, 1990.

Willimon, William H. *Who Will Be Saved?* Nashville: Abingdon, 2008.

8

Pastoral Care as Conversation

G. Lee Ramsey, Jr.

🌿 I currently serve as pastor of a United Methodist congregation located in a rural area about an hour north of Memphis, Tennessee. Recently I was standing outside the church talking with one of the members before the others arrived for worship. The conversation progressed from comments on the weather and the crops to family and then to matters of personal health, where the member shared his spiritual, emotional, and physical struggles with chronic illness. I had only been his minister for six weeks. That day out underneath the trees that shade the parking lot, I began to be his pastor.

How did this movement from official, ordained minister to pastor begin to happen? For starters, this otherwise unremarkable conversation was more relaxed than our previous introductory exchanges. There in the parking lot, with time to talk, the conversation slowly ebbed and flowed between us as we sought a deeper level. Second, the conversation took place outside but within sight of the sanctuary where interactions are more ritually circumscribed. The meanings of Christian congregation and worship framed our discussion but we were not ruled by them. Lastly, the conversation was mutual. Revealing at points and punctuated by humor, we opened ourselves to each other in that first tentative way that many pastoral relationships begin. We acknowledged our differences (he is 82, and I, 56; he was raised in the country and grows crops while I am an urban dweller and plow through books; he has great-grandchildren and my children are unmarried and still in school). We found common human ground (how it feels to be separated by distance from your family; the muscle aches and heartaches that come with age; our shared denominational commitments). We shared a central theological belief (God does not send suffering upon us). Where this beginning of a pastoral relationship will lead I do not know. I do know that a potentially fruitful pathway for pastoral care has opened up; it started in that most natural of human ways—through conversation.

This essay will explore the ministry of pastoral care as conversation. The pastoral moment described above will provide practical grounding and texture for the article. First, we will consider conversation and dialogue as essential to most forms of pastoral care. Next we will review the ways that Christian pastoral care and conversation have been understood and practiced within clinical (modern) and contemporary movements in pastoral care. Then we will turn to a fresh appraisal of how pastoral care as conversation can enrich Christian ministry in postmodernity given the increasing opportunities and challenges afforded the church by pluralism, the need for articulate public theology, and the re-embracing of communal and congregational contexts for pastoral care.

Pastoral Care and Conversation

Christian pastoral care is a continuation of Jesus Christ's ministry of shepherding care through the church and its representatives in the world. Pastoral care refers to the caring concern of the church towards persons, families, groups, and communities in times of joy and distress.[1] With this broad definition, pastoral care may occur in many ways. But of all the areas of Christian ministry, pastoral care (along with preaching) has been most associated with *conversation*. While pastoral care does happen in and through silence, symbolic action, and public worship, we most readily associate the mutual giving and receiving of pastoral care with interpersonal conversation. Whether that conversation is a dialogue between two persons, as occurred between me and the church member noted above, or within a larger group, for example a family or a sub-set of the congregation, when pastoral care occurs two or more persons are mutually communicating with one another regarding matters of life, death, belief, or faith within a Christian framework of meaning.

Conversation is central in pastoral care. This is true whether conversations occur under the oak tree in the church parking lot or interrupted by beeps and wheezes inside the intensive care unit of a hospital. Conversations, large and small, loud and whispered, dialogical or multivocal, go on at the heart of pastoral care. Indeed, pastoral care as conversation has been

1. Hiltner, *Preface to Pastoral Theology*; Clebsh and Jaekle, *Pastoral Care in Historical Perspective*.

around since the beginning of Christianity though it has taken different forms in different eras.

Approaches to Pastoral Care as Conversation

A quick review of recent history of pastoral care can outline how conversation has been central to pastoral practices in the church. From the classical approach to pastoral care as cure of souls to the modern approach to pastoral care as clinical pastoral conversation, conversation and dialogue have been vital to the practices of pastoral care within the Christian congregation and the wider community.[2] We will briefly review the evolving understandings of conversation in pastoral care. Then we will turn to emerging approaches to conversation by looking at communal contextual influences and intercultural understandings.[3] The issue is not whether pastoral care has incorporated conversation in its understanding and practice but how.

From Classical to Modern Approaches to Pastoral Care and Conversation

The first pastoral documents from the New Testament and early church suggest that pastoral care was directed towards the care of individuals and congregations through the function of pastoral guidance. The letters of Paul and the Pastoral Epistles are filled with pastoral direction from the writer to the recipients of the letters. As pastoral care evolved through the history of the church, especially in the West, the priest, and later the Protestant pastor, became the official provider of pastoral care, whether through the offering of the sacraments in pastoral situations and liturgies (confession, reconciliation, marriage, sickness, death, etc.) or through conversation between the pastor and a lay member who was seeking spiritual direction. Stylized approaches to pastoral conversation emerged in which the pastor or priest offered comfort and care within the framework of "cure of souls."[4] Here conversation became more mutual in pastoral care though not fully dialogical because the ordained leader remained firmly in control of spiritual support during pastoral care occasions.

2. McNeil, *A History of the Cure of Souls*; Faber and van der Schoot, *The Art of Pastoral Conversation*.

3. Patton, *Pastoral Care in Context*; Ramsay, *Pastoral Care and Counseling*; Lartey, *In Living Color*.

4. McNeill, *A History of the Cure of Souls*; Clebsh and Jaekle, *Pastoral Care in Historical Perspective*.

It would be hard to mistake the pastoral care conversations of these earlier eras of the church as truly mutual in the way that this study suggests. To think of the minister prior to the twentieth century as a "conversation partner," and ministry as "becoming ever-better conversation partners in service to the gospel" (McClure, chapter 2) would be a stretch. There was simply too much assurance of *the Truth* of the gospel to warrant mutually transformative dialogue among strangers or friends. Such mutuality could only emerge following the innovations of the clinical period in modern pastoral care.

Clinical Approaches to Pastoral Care and Conversation in the Modern Era

Pastoral care took a crucial turn during the first third of the twentieth century that reshaped our understanding of pastoral care as conversation. The pathfinder was Anton Boisen who, although he did not wholly intend it, shifted the spotlight of pastoral care away from concern for salvation of the believer within the context of the church to the clinical and psychological needs of the individual.[5] He did so through the innovative move of steering ministry students towards clinical settings for training in pastoral care. Ironically, this creative approach to training in pastoral care began to sever the roots of pastoral care from its Christian identity. Brooks Holifield documents the clinical turn in pastoral care in a historical study that bears the significant subtitle, "From Salvation to Self-Realization."[6]

Those ministers particularly interested in pastoral care and counseling began to look towards the burgeoning social science fields of psychology, sociology, and communications to orient themselves in pastoral care. Many counselors and pastors focused upon the non-directive and client-centered counseling techniques of Carl Rogers.[7] Newly established pastoral counseling centers emerged under the professional umbrella of the American Association of Pastoral Counselors.

Boisen and those who followed launched the Clinical Pastoral Education (CPE) movement during the middle decades of the twentieth century. Riding upon the wave of popular psychology that crested following World War II, the clinical settings (hospitals, mental health institutions, addiction clinics) began to dominate the training of pastoral care in most mainline and many evangelical seminaries. CPE's unique form of pastoral care training encouraged ministers to hold therapeutically styled conversations with a

5. Boisen, *Out of the Depths.*

6. Holifield, *A History of Pastoral Care in America.*

7. Rogers, *Client Centered Therapy.*

skilled supervisor while reflecting upon the real-life experiences of pastoral care in the clinic. The aim was to tease out the deeper questions of personal and vocational identity that have an impact on the giving and receiving of pastoral care.

Ministers could not help but see themselves through these therapeutic lenses offered in training, even if some of the leading instructors in the field—such as Wayne Oates, Seward Hiltner, and others—cautioned against the possible loss of theological identity and congregational grounding for pastoral care.[8] In the rush to embrace the exciting new possibilities that arose from aligning pastoral care training with the insights of the social sciences, pastoral care in both the classroom and within the congregation began to lose theological and ecclesial definition. Paul Pruyser, a prominent psychiatrist of the Menninger Clinic who worked with hospital chaplains, spotted the dangers of this drift within pastoral care, and he urged the pastoral care movement to recover its true theological identity.[9]

Despite these misgivings, the gains are significant when we consider pastoral care as conversation. The clinical movement in pastoral care fixed a laser beam upon what actually occurs in pastoral conversations. The tool was the clinical pastoral verbatim, a form of reporting and evaluating modeled upon the medical or psychological case review. This one tool has been the source of profound insight and transformation for many students and ministers who are committed to pastoral care. With the increased self-understanding that emerges in clinical pastoral education, the pastor is able to more authentically provide care for the other, even as he or she knows that such genuine pastoral conversations are mutually transformative.

The watchwords of this style of clinical pastoral care are *presence* and *relationship*. The goal: to be fully present to the other as a receptive human being and representative of Jesus Christ. The theological accent here is upon the incarnation. Such presence is not easy. It demands discipline and vulnerability on the part of the pastor. It requires effective listening skills, patience, and tolerance for ambiguity. Those pastors who are fully present to others surrender their own authority in the situation, trusting that God is fully present to both persons in the relationship through the incarnation of Jesus Christ. Within such a framework, pastors understand God's presence as hidden though nonetheless real.[10] Ministry begins from below within the givenness of the human situation where Christ the incarnate God is

8. Oates, *Protestant Pastoral Counseling*; Hiltner and Colston, *The Context of Pastoral Counseling*.

9. Pruyser, *The Minister as Diagnostician*.

10. Tillich, "The Theology of Pastoral Care"; Nouwen, *The Living Reminder*.

revealed. All parties—pastor and others—are open to wherever this incarnationally freighted relationship leads.

While this style of pastoral care sounds fuzzy and weak on actual content, it is much more challenging than it appears. Many theology students and pastors find clinical pastoral education daunting. The self-awareness that a good program exacts can be painful and discouraging. The challenge and rewards of authentic and mutually receptive listening are hard-won. Even more, it is difficult to transfer the self-knowledge and skills acquired in the clinical setting to congregational leadership. Other images for ministry crowd out the image of relational pastor. Pressures are great to provide authoritative leadership and solution-centered pastoral care as one goes about the business of managing the church organization. Pastors can lose patience and close themselves off to others even if occasionally attempting to "shift" into pastoral care listening mode when extreme moments arise. When this happens, the minister begins to lose sight of all that has been gained through modern approaches to pastoral care.

This clinical approach to the training and practice of pastoral care alters our understanding of conversation within ministry. The changes can be seen in the conversation that I mentioned at the beginning of this chapter. In an earlier era, that conversation would not likely have happened as it did. As the pastor, I would have been more intent upon interjecting overt theological content and pastoral guidance into the conversation. In the style of the Reformers or early church leaders, I would have assumed that I had something of spiritual value that needed to be communicated to the parishioner through conversation, prayer, exhortation, or reproof. Instead, influenced in part by my own experience in clinical pastoral education, the pastoral conversation was marked by a different set of concerns. The pastoral aim of the conversation, as I reflect upon it, was to simply invite a deepening relationship with the church member through the practicing of pastoral presence. That was an agenda, to be sure, but it was an agenda more inviting than driven. It required openness and a degree of vulnerability on my part as I offered parts of my own story, as appropriate, to the other person. The conversation moved towards mutuality as we each listened to one another without seeking some kind of fix to whatever concerns we shared. While my pastoral authority certainly influenced the tone and direction of the conversation, it was more a matter of context, role, and identity than of fixed content. My role and identity as the designated pastor, and the church context within which we met in the first place, made the conversation potentially pastoral. But there was no objective content that necessarily had to be communicated for this to be pastoral care.

Here we see the dialogical nature of conversation as it shapes modern approaches to pastoral care. In authentic dialogue, both partners can and usually are changed. The minister who understands him or herself as a conversation partner with others does not stand somewhere slightly outside of the conversation. He or she brings to the conversation as much of him or herself as possible and remains open spiritually, emotionally, and mentally to the unfolding conversation.

The particular nature of the dialogical pastoral conversation requires focus and discipline including careful attention to emotional and physical boundaries between the pastor and others. As the relationship deepens through conversation, and personal defenses lessen on both sides, the danger rises of violation of one's authority. The pastor enters the mutual relationship with awareness of this danger. As the responsible party, the pastor must maintain vigilance throughout the relationship.[11] But there is no way to avoid taking such risks in this modern approach to pastoral conversation. When as pastors we enter into mutually transformative relationships with others, misunderstanding, self-deception, and abuse of others is always a danger. It is the pastor's responsibility to make sure the danger does not become a reality while the relationship continues.

The clinical approach to pastoral care moved the needle of conversation in a positive direction. Nevertheless, critiques emerge within the modern approach. First, heavily influenced by Rogerian understandings of counseling and conversation, pastoral care in the clinical mode privileges the individual voice and self-direction of the care receiver to the extent that the Christian tradition begins to fade into the background. In many modern pastoral conversations, it is hard to name what is Christian about the dialogue, especially if the pastor suppresses his or her vocational identity in the name of mutuality. Theological liberalism contributes to this development as human relationship becomes the identified source of revelation.

Secondly, the *individual* within the pastoral care conversation is so highly valued that he or she appears to be free to do whatever seems appropriate for personal growth. Cut off from Christian community, engaged in intense one-to-one conversation, the individual has very little to ground him or herself other than personal experience. If the pastoral caregiver has anything of moral or spiritual guidance to offer to the isolated individual, it is usually understated or without communal support.[12] In this situation, the conversation is not really mutual since the pastor is withholding moral and theological judgments in the interest of maintaining relationship. The

11. Fortune, *Is Nothing Sacred?*

12. Browning, *The Moral Context of Pastoral Care.*

end result, however, is more a monologue than a true dialogue, this time weighted towards the parishioner rather than the pastor. One wonders if in extreme situations the one seeking pastoral care or counseling would be "free" to harm themselves or others if they thought it would lead to self-realization. Nevermind the paradoxical claims of the gospel that in order to find ourselves we must lose ourselves, and in order to gain our lives we must give our lives over for the sake of the gospel (Matt 10:39).

Thirdly, the modern approach to pastoral care can create confusion about pastoral authority that subtly affects conversation. Many modern practitioners of pastoral care are reluctant to claim their given authority based in ordination and the social role of the minister. Clergy are slow to acknowledge the authority of their ordination for fear that it would hinder mutuality in ministry. This is naïve if not duplicitous. Hiding one's ministerial identity is in itself an authoritative act. The well-trained, educated, and ordained pastor can pretend that he or she has no authority within the pastoral relationship as a matter of professional choice. This is either veiled condescension or vocational identity confusion that actually inhibits mutual conversation and relationship. It assumes that the clergy knows what is best in the relationship, in this case to obscure one's own vocational identity and all the meanings associated with it, even if the minister is not going to directly tell the other what he or she thinks is best. This is hardly the way to establish a pastoral relationship through genuine conversation.

Lastly, modern pastoral care practices emerged just as significant social, political, contextual, economic, and gender concerns arose throughout Western culture and particularly within training for ministry. Women's and minority concerns began to test the limits imposed by the clinical paradigm. The economic and cultural assumptions of the modern approach were unveiled and revealed to be largely Western, male, Caucasian, and middle class. Teachers and pastoral care practitioners began to question the psycho-social theoretical foundations of the modern turn in pastoral care. They began to wonder how social context figures into the giving and receiving of pastoral care; to ask what happened to the Christian congregation in pastoral care; to explore how religious pluralism and globalization would and could impact pastoral care and conversation.[13] Pastoral conversations are always contextualized, and without attention to these broader realities, how can we claim that pastoral conversation is authentic?

So, for all its contributions to pastoral care and conversation, the modern movement leaves us with some questions. While I may be overstating

---

13. Ramsey, *Care-full Preaching*; Ramsay, *Pastoral Care and Counseling.*

this set of reservations, the fact that the field has begun to turn over new ground in which to plant its work indicates that further change is needed.

New Directions in Pastoral Care as Conversation

Two cultural shifts are prompting new directions in pastoral care as conversation: postmodernity and pluralism. These new directions are already in progress and are beginning to make marks upon the teaching and practice of pastoral care. The kinds of conversations that are now occurring in pastoral care are distinctive from those of earlier eras. These conversations are happening in the seminary classroom, in the congregation, in the hospitals and clinics, and within the wider public. Significant texts register the changes as the discipline of pastoral care shifts from modern to postmodern cultural realities and from the clinical to the congregational and communal context.[14] Coupled with these shifts is the broader concern within pastoral care for care of the public. Pastoral theologians are researching, writing, and fostering creative conversations about pastoral care's responsibility for the social, environmental, and economic well-being of the public as pastoral care steps out of the clinic and engages the social world.[15] It is too early to see where the various new lines in pastoral care as conversation will converge, but we can discern fresh directions.

Postmodernity, Pluralism, and Pastoral Care as Conversation

With the slow erosion of a grand, western cultural and religious narrative, Christian ministry is in new territory. McClure cogently charts some of these changes in chapter 2 and suggests that within the ferment of postmodernity a popular new image of the minister has emerged as "counterculturalist." This minister, whether consciously or unconsciously, adopts a narrativist understanding of religious identity and practices within postmodernity, and within that identity finds direction to lead the church as a counter-cultural community of Christian believers. While I agree with McClure

14. Couture, *Child Poverty*; Doehring, *The Practice of Pastoral Care*; Gill-Austern and Miller-McLemore, *Feminist and Womanist Pastoral Theology*; Johnson, *Drinking from the Same Well*; Kim, *Bridge Makers and Cross Bearers*; Kujawa-Holbrook and Montagno, *Injustice and the Care of Souls*; Lartey, *In Living Color*; Patton, *Pastoral Care in Context*; Ramsay, *Pastoral Care and Counseling*; Ramsey, *Care-full Preaching*; Stevenson-Moessner and Snorton, *Women Out of Order*; Wimberly, *African American Pastoral Care*.

15. Browning and Clairmont, *American Religions and the Family*; Clinebell, *Eco-Therapy*; Couture, *Child Poverty*; Miller-McLemore, *Christian Theology in Practice*.

that the image of minister as counterculturalist has gained purchase within certain segments of the contemporary church, namely mainline Protestant and emergent church circles, the image is not dominant across the whole spectrum of the Western church. I do not see much evidence that those who gravitate towards this understanding of ministry are having much success establishing it within actual congregations. The culture in which the church is always located is strong and cannot be rinsed out of church and ministry like dirty laundry, nor should it be.

The cultural conditions of postmodernity, as McClure suggests, have opened up (others would say fragmented) *multiple* theologies of ministry that mitigate against a dominant metaphor. New, rich, and textured approaches to pastoral care are popping up all across the postmodern landscape. *One* of these can be fruitfully understood as conversation.

The very ground for pastoral care has shifted, so the discipline and practice is shifting as well. Charles Gerkin spotted some of these shifts in the mid-1980's and called for a "widening of the horizons" of pastoral care. As Gerkin says, "[In] the situation of radical pluralism in which we now find ourselves . . . pastors will need to widen the horizon of their pastoral interests from the concern with psychological and relational well-being that has been the focus of the recent past."[16] Neither the fixed (and crumbling) world of assumptive Christian meanings nor the clinical world of individualized care could engender the kind of pastoral care as conversation that is needed within postmodernity. What is needed is sustained *mutual* conversation(s) between church and public, Christian faith and other religious worldviews, and between pastor and congregational members.

The pastor as conversationalist within postmodernity approaches pastoral care with the awareness that conversation does not seek or establish fixed theological meanings. Pastoral conversations explore multiple meanings between two or more persons from within a Christian framework that is truly open to the other as a bearer of God's image. Conversation, whether from pulpit or pew, flows back and forth between the pastor and others guided by trust and respect that values "hospitality, mutuality, and compassion."[17]

This is the kind of conversation that occurred between the church member and me discussed at the beginning of this chapter. As the ordained pastor in such conversations, I claim my own vocational authority and identity while opening myself to the authority and identity of the other. Our differences of age, experience, morals, social locations, and human needs

---

16. Gerkin, *Widening the Horizons*, 19–20.
17. Ramsey, *Care-full Preaching*, 35, 86.

all add positive value to the conversation as we mutually guide and sustain one another in Christian ministry. The primary goal of such pastoral care is the deepening of a mutually edifying relationship within a Christian context that opens both parties to transformation.

Admittedly, such an understanding of pastoral care as conversation can seem alternately nebulous and complex. The nebulous nature of pastoral care as conversation is to be expected. Genuine conversation may strive for clarity but usually does not attain it. That is why it is called conversation. The back and forth nature of conversation is not for the purpose of winning or losing contested ground but for the purpose of hearing, seeing, knowing, and being in relationship with the other. This value has carried over from the modern pastoral care movement into postmodern approaches to pastoral care but with additional import. For now, the other may not be the congregational church member or the counselee but a member of another ethnic group, another religious body, or from another educational or social background. Such differences may drive us apart towards retrenchment, as seems to be happening in much of North American politics and economics, or it may draw us towards one another in mutual respect with a genuine longing to see the image of God within one another.

A powerful example of such postmodern influences upon pastoral care and conversation has emerged in my hometown of Memphis. Following September 11, 2001, the people from one of our local United Methodist Congregations, Heartsong UMC, began conversation with their neighboring congregation, a Muslim community center. The Christian congregation decided to share their building with the Muslim neighbors who were erecting a new building on the adjacent property. Over the course of a year, the members of both congregations became friends who enjoyed rich interfaith communication. Their next step, which is underway, is to cooperatively fund and construct a shared public park between their houses of worship. In the in-between spaces of place, faith, and time, members of both religious groups and the wider public will gather for rest, recreation, prayer, and conversation.

There is no way to avoid the complexity of this approach to pastoral care as conversation. While the metaphor of "conversation" sounds softly inviting, the reality is far different. Genuine conversations are truthful. They do not avoid disagreement. Pastoral care in the conversational mode moves carefully through conflict with the confidence that God desires wholeness for everyone. Pastoral care as conversation will not seek the lowest common denominator of agreement where this is real difference; instead, it will honor the differences that cause conflict and prayerfully discern how to move forward in relationship. While Christians can be clear about our own identity in Christ, there is no room for imperialism of belief.

Yet another challenge and opportunity for contemporary pastoral care as conversation comes along with the social fragmentation within postmodern culture. Mayberry does not exist anymore, if it ever did. We live in "multiple" worlds. Daily commutes to work, church, school, and entertainment venues carry us across and into multiple spaces and worlds that seem at odds with one another. The anonymity of the freeway challenges the intimacy of home. The faceless bureaucracy of the corporation undermines the camaraderie of the office team. The promise of leisurely learning at school is threatened by the demands to finish quickly, efficiently, and be off to the next place whether bank, church, or grocery store. All of this is now surrounded by circles within circles of cyber networks where we interact on a daily basis. How in postmodernity do we hold all of this together? What is the promise and responsibility of pastoral care?

Here is another arena in which pastoral care as conversation holds promise. We have already established that a therapeutic retreat to individual counseling or one to one clinical pastoral care, while sometimes necessary for healing and restoration, is no longer a fully viable approach. Pastoral care is more than an individual salvage operation after crisis occurs. Pastoral care as conversation can artfully sustain and guide ministers and congregations through the complexities of contemporary life because it is *real* conversation. This leads us to the congregational context for pastoral care as conversation.

Pastoral Conversation in Communal, Congregational Context

Pastoral care as conversation is grounded within a community of conversation known as a congregation. The communal context of Christian pastoral conversation helps make it potentially redemptive and transformative. Severed from the congregational context, pastoral conversations may reinforce isolation, a particular threat within postmodernity. We find our God-given selves in relationships within the Christian community. Created in the Trinitarian image of God, we are made for each other within community. A primary task of pastoral care, therefore, is to bind persons into life-giving (saving) communities where the redemptive grace of God is mutually shared among the members of the community and spills over into the wider world. Such communal belonging emerges where conversations are authentic, hospitable, and mutual between believers and pastoral leaders, and where conversations remain open to the gifts of others who are not directly connected to the congregation.

Pastoral care as conversation speaks the internal language of belonging for those who seek the centering of a congregation within a fragmented social world. But pastoral care as conversation also speaks an external language of hospitality to those of other faiths or no faith who seek dialogue with the church on their own terms. These conversations can only be real if the church is open to the possibility that conversation with the other may in fact alter our own self-understanding. Pastoral care can hold these two types of conversations in tension as we go about the day-to-day work of Christian ministry without retreating to the safety of a closed congregational identity or losing all Christian distinctiveness in the rush to embrace pluralism. Indeed, a Christian congregation that is clear about its own identity grounded in the servanthood of Jesus Christ and sustained through authentic pastoral conversation cannot help but be open to the wider world that God loves (John 3:16).

So while conversation remains at the center of the practice of pastoral care in contemporary church and culture, pastoral care is now ready to participate in a broader conversation that moves back and forth between church, community, and wider public with mutual conversation that both establishes and risks Christian identity for the sake of God, others, and self. As long as we remain rooted in Jesus Christ and connected to the Christian community, as conversationalists we have a much clearer understanding of how to care for others and self within postmodernity than the narrativist who draws a tight circle around the conversation for the purpose of securing Christian identity. There is something to be gained from the emphasis upon narrative and Christian practices within the postmodern landscape. But the dangers are easily recognized within pastoral care if we turn Christian practices into either contestations with others or into talking to ourselves. Pastoral care can stay grounded within the church as a community of conversation while embracing an ecclesiology that opens windows to the world where God's redemption is also at work.[18] So, while the image of pastoral care occurring under the oak tree may initially sound romantic, it is a theologically and spatially engaging metaphor. At its best, conversation is both leisurely and moves across various boundaries inside and outside of the church. Pastoral care occurs on the borders between gathering and departing where all are free to speak and to listen without fear of being attacked or dismissed.

18. Ramsey, *Care-full Preaching*, chap. 5.

Implications for the Ministry of Pastoral Care

Taking Time for Real Conversation

Pastoral care as conversation requires pastors to slow down and take time for authentic conversation. As in the conversation with the parishioner at the beginning of this chapter, there is no substitute for the natural, unhurried ebb and flow of real, face to face dialogue. Conversations do not occur while we rush from one appointment to the next while answering emails and responding to texts and tweets or frantically eating a hurried lunch while talking *at* one another. Pastors who are too rushed, distracted, or focused upon their own ministerial agendas to actually converse with others are too busy to be pastors. The tyranny of the "now" that has crept into contemporary culture has established a beachhead in the church as well. Pastors who understand the theological and emotional significance of mutual conversation will not only resist the maniacal speed of contemporary culture but will actively cultivate habits within self and congregation that yield the fruits of honest conversation—habits such as prayer, Sabbath keeping, deep listening, discipline in scheduling personal and congregational calendars, and exercise.[19]

Creating Space for Conversation

Somewhere to hold pastoral care conversations is better than anywhere. While it is true that pastoral care conversations can and do occur almost anywhere—sanctuary, fellowship hall, parking lot, under the tree, hospital, grocery story, coffee shop, home, automobile, office—it is also true that location matters. Pastors will want to pay attention to the actual spaces within the church building or the community where pastoral conversations occur. If they happen to occur on the parking lot of the church, then it will be a good thing to spend time in the parking lot speaking and listening rather than trying to force folks to "sit down and talk." While the art of pastoral conversation is portable, generally people open themselves to one another and to God when they feel comfortable in the surroundings or conversely disoriented by the surroundings, such as in a modern hospital. Either way, ministers will need to attend to how the environment shapes the conversation.

Attentiveness to space can lead to innovative approaches to pastoral care, especially when we move beyond the walls of the church, for example, the shared park that I referred to earlier that is being built by a Christian and

19. Peterson, *The Contemplative Pastor*; Dawn, *The Sense of the Call.*

Muslim congregation for the purpose of cultivating neighbor love and inter-faith relations. Another example of the importance of space in pastoral care and conversation is the way in which corporations are providing staff chaplains to assist employees with spiritual, emotional, and social development. These nontraditional chaplains must carve out real spaces within their host institutions to engage in mutual conversation with employees whether that space is an office, a cafeteria, or standing around the coffee pot. Where is pastoral conversation most likely to occur in the given setting for ministry, and how does the pastor enhance that space to maximize conversation? These are the questions we want to think through when asking about the settings for pastoral care?

Preaching and Pastoral Conversation

Preaching in postmodernity has entered into fruitful partnership with pastoral care. The fields of preaching and pastoral care were frequently separated in the modern clinical era (preaching as public, pastoral care as private) or too thoughtlessly joined by therapeutic approaches.[20] Conversational approaches to both disciplines, especially theologically grounded conversation, brings the two practices together on solid ground .[21] Understanding the sermon as ongoing theological conversation between preacher, congregation, culture, biblical text, and God aligns well with the understanding of pastoral care as a continuation of Christ's shepherding ministry in church and world through conversation. The two disciplines should not be collapsed into each other any more than they should be artificially separated in ministry. They are mutually informative and supportive just as real conversation is between persons.

One area of real promise in Christian pastoral preaching in postmodernity is to consider the ways that preaching attends to others. How are those of differing faiths, differing cultural or economic backgrounds, differing political and social values presented in the preaching conversation? Who is missing in our pastoral sermons? Who really are these others that we read about and see on television but do not really know? Pastoral preaching will aim to bring these others and their gifts into the view of the congregation through intentional use of story, cultural references, and careful interpretation of the "other" in key scriptural texts.[22] If we introduce

20. Ramsey, *Care-full Preaching*, 12ff.

21. O. W. Allen, Jr., *The Homiletic of All Believers*; McClure, *The Roundtable Pulpit*; Rose, *Sharing the Word*.

22. Allen, Ronald J., *Preaching and the Other*.

positively into the conversation of the sermon those who might threaten the congregation by their difference, then it is possible over time to change the conversation within the congregation. Values such as mutuality, hospitality, and compassion may emerge within congregations that were previously closed and distant from the wider culture.[23]

Conversation in Christian Community

It is a truism of late modernity and early postmodernity that people are hungry for community. Isolation threatens contemporary existence as we race through our days while withdrawing from one another into virtual worlds. We argue, contest, shout, and talk at each other but find it harder and harder to converse with one another in genuine community. We know what is missing but can't seem to plant ourselves among the same people long enough for community conversation to take root.

Pastoral care invites community conversation within the church. This will require letting go of some aspects of clinical approaches to pastoral care, namely the default to private, individualized counseling. Private pastoral conversations will certainly be necessary from time to time as individuals and families seek support for various problems in their lives. But the greater challenge is for the pastoral leader to foster redemptive conversations within the congregation as a whole. Within the conversational model, pastoral care shifts from focus upon the individual as the "living human document" to focus upon the congregation and the community as the "living web"[24]

Practically speaking, we encourage such communal conversation by inviting full participation of the laity in worship leadership, the prayer life of the church, and visitation of those who are sick and homebound. We make space in worship and in congregational meetings for genuine conversation by moving away from the scripts that govern worship and administration when needed. We tend the margins of formal church gatherings where much of real conversation takes place, for example the sanctuary *before and after* worship; the fellowship hall during clean-up after the meal; the parking lot after bible study; e-mails that arrive late and early in the day; the casual comment when someone is saying good-bye; the spontaneous meeting in the local coffee shop. Often in these marginal times and places, real pastoral conversation emerges within the Christian community.

23. Ramsey, *Care-full Preaching*.

24. Miller-McLemore, "The Human Web and the State of Pastoral Theology," 366–69.

We trust that in speaking and listening to one another openly and honestly within community that we offer and receive pastoral care. As Dietrich Bonhoeffer says in *Life Together,* "He who can no longer listen to his brother will soon no longer be listening to God."[25] Listening to God together, we speak honestly about God with one another in community. The pastor need not be the only or even the lead conversational voice within the community. He or she is more like a turnstile who keeps the community conversation moving through the seasons of birth, life, death, and resurrection.

This approach to pastoral care will resist those forms of communal self-identification that pit "us" against "them." Sure, there is always "insider" language within a congregation. But this should be the language of open belonging rather than exclusive membership. Congregations can enjoy healthy communal conversation without disparaging those who carry on other conversations. There is much to disorient the church in the wider culture, to be sure, but there is also much within the conversation of the wider culture to nourish community life. Jesus Christ speaks inside and outside of the church. He forms community wherever persons gather in his name (Matt 18: 20). As we speak pastorally within the church, it will avail us to also listen for the sounds of real conversation in the wider world.

Cautions about Pastoral Care as Conversation

Conversation is a broad term with multiple references of meaning depending upon the associated fields of interpretation. Our interest here has been in the pastoral and theological implications of conversation as a model for ministry. But meanings spill into this discussion from communication studies, psychology, sociology, linguistics, and philosophy. A danger with this approach to pastoral care as conversation is that the term is so broad that it loses Christian distinctiveness much in the way that pastoral counseling during the second half of the twentieth century lost Christian identification. We will need to pay attention to the theological and biblical norms that inform our understanding of conversation. For example, what makes a conversation within a church community a *Christian conversation*? Is the care that we express in conversation necessarily *pastoral*? What makes it so? Any model of pastoral care as conversation will have to address these fundamental concerns if we want it to be applicable within the Christian community.

More work, then, is needed to give shape and definition to pastoral care as conversation. What constitutes an authentic conversation within the

25. Bonhoeffer, *Life Together*, 98.

congregation, and how do we know one when we hear it? We will need to guard against superficial or romantic notions of conversation within community. For example, some folks are powerfully expressive within congregational settings, but they may not necessarily be contributors to community care and edification through conversation. Some conversations go in circles, some are shallow, and still others jump off track. Some conversations can degenerate into diatribes while silencing "others." And still other types of conversation can be evasive or pool ignorance. Clear definitions will help us steer clear of such false understandings of conversation.

Finally, this incarnationally grounded approach to pastoral care is both a strength and a weakness. Christ is revealed in and among Christians who gather to speak and listen to one another, to their neighbors, and to God. Openness to the other is paramount as we converse with honesty, integrity, respect, and appropriate transparency. Revelation occurs within the human situation as we listen and respond to one another. With all the strengths of theological liberalism supporting this approach, we do run the risk of blocking out God who is always among but more than us (the critique of neo-orthodoxy). While conversation holds great promise for pastoral care, it must surely be more than us talking to ourselves—at least if it is Christian pastoral care. We should ask, when does *our* conversation cease and God's Word interrupt and re-direct the community conversations that we so ardently pursue with one another? How will we know the difference?

These are some of the additional lines of thought that we will need to pursue to fill out the promising model of pastoral care as conversation that can contribute to the practice of Christian ministry today and in the years ahead.

Questions for Discussion

1. Since conversation has always been associated with the ministry of pastoral care, discuss what is distinctive about pastoral care and conversation in contemporary culture. What has changed and what difference do these changes make with respect to pastoral conversation?

2. What new opportunities for pastoral care as conversation are emerging today in light of the increasing pluralism within church and world?

3. What are the costs and benefits for pastoral care in which ministers attempt to utilize newer forms of technological communication (social media, e-mail, blogging) as a way of extending conversation?

Further Reading

Augsburger, David W. *Pastoral Counseling Across Cultures*. Philadelphia: Westminster, 1986.

Clebsh, William A., and Charles R. Jaekle. *Pastoral Care in Historical Perspective*. Northfield, NJ: Aronson, 1975.

Faber, Heije, and Ebel van der Schoot. *The Art of Pastoral Conversation*. Nashville: Abingdon, 1965.

Gerkin, Charles V. *Widening the Horizons: Pastoral Responses to a Fragmented Society*. Philadelphia: Westminster, 1986.

Kornfeld, Margaret. *Cultivating Wholeness: A Guide to Care and Counseling in Faith Communities*. New York: Continuum, 2005.

Kujawa-Holbrook, Sheryl A., and Karen B. Montagno, editors. *Injustice and the Care of Souls: Taking Oppression Seriously in Pastoral Care*. Minneapolis: Fortress, 2009.

Lartey, Emmanuel Y. *In Living Color: An Intercultural Approach to Pastoral Care and Counseling*. 2nd ed. London: Jessica Kingsley, 2003.

McNeill, John T. *A History of the Cure of Souls*. New York: Harper & Row, 1951.

Patton, John. *Pastoral Care in Context: An Introduction to Pastoral Care*. Louisville: Westminster John Knox, 1993.

Ramsay, Nancy, editor. *Pastoral Care and Counseling: Redefining the Paradigms*. Nashville: Abingdon, 2004.

Scharfenberg, Joachim. *Pastoral Care as Dialogue*. Philadelphia: Fortress, 1980.

Stevenson-Moessner, Jeanne, and Teresa Snorton, editors. *Women Out of Order: Risking Change and Creating Care in a Multicultural World*. Minneapolis: Fortress, 2010.

Wimberly, Edward P. *African American Pastoral Care*. Rev. ed. Nashville: Abingdon, 2008.

9

Mission and Ecumenism as Conversation

MARIAN MCCLURE TAYLOR

JESUS' PARABLE IN Matt 13:33 is about the reign of heaven being "like yeast that a woman took and mixed in with three measures of flour until all of it was leavened." In this one-sentence parable, we find the key components of a vision for mission and ecumenism. The reign God is bringing about is comprehensive in scope, and it requires diverse ingredients that can be moved and transformed into something new.

Practical implications of such a vision—diversity, cooperation, intentionality, vulnerability, to name a few—are best worked out in conversation. That is because conversations are the ingredients' metabolic process, to use the baking analogy again! In conversations, we develop the resilient strength we need to hold a new and expanded collective shape.

Congregations that are active in ecumenism and mission sometimes miss the key role of conversations. For instance, perhaps your congregation supports a community service ministry that is also supported by congregations of other Christian traditions. This is a very common vehicle for both ecumenism and local mission. Too often, these community ministries miss their opportunities for transformational learning through conversations. Busy-ness trumps the opportunity, as governance, fund-raising, and volunteer coordination absorb all the energy available. We forget to marvel at and explore what could make our togetherness more transformative. We do not talk at length and as an equal with the people who seek the organization's services. We do not delve into the theology or the piety of fellow volunteers or study together our traditions' approaches to advocacy concerning the social issues that bring people to need the organization's services.

Even if your situation is exceptional and these kinds of transformative conversations are being held, how are the persons most involved in this work sharing this process with your congregation as a whole? Have you mastered the art of making mission and ecumenism conversations become collective experiences?

In short, you may be addressing needs, but are you being kneaded? God's reign needs to knead you so that a new creation will emerge from learning experiences of many kinds. And so in this chapter we will explore the crucial role of conversation in mission and ecumenism, and we will address the distinctive challenges faced by congregations and their leaders in fostering such conversations well.

A Century that is Affecting Your Congregation

Each congregation[1] has a distinctive history and set of commitments. And yet all are affected by conversations swirling in the larger world of thinking about mission and ecumenism. It may help for your congregation to enter more intentionally into those conversations, some of which are highlighted in this section. Each topical subsection therefore concludes with a possible starting question for a conversation your congregation might wish to have.

Doctrine, and the Harmony/Disagreement Conversation

"We just won't talk about it." A major missionary conference in Edinburgh, Scotland, in 1910 set a precedent by banning discussions of doctrine. The idea was that doctrinal debates that had already proven to be divisive among the various Christian families might keep the churches from seizing the historical moment for cooperation in mission. And so the 1910 mission conference launched the modern ecumenical movement in a way that highlighted the need for additional efforts to address the doctrinal issues that had been banned.

Since 1910, theological discussions have greatly enriched mission thinking and action, but the relationship continues to be ambivalent. One reason is that the spirit of urgency is strong in mission circles, as people ask, "How can we let our ability to deliver a cup of water and a cup of the Living Water be slowed by these debates?!"

1. Not every local worshiping community calls itself a "congregation." I will use that term, with apologies to those who are more familiar with "parish" or "meeting" or some other term.

In congregations there is an additional reason why people leading mission efforts avoid the doctrinal issues that undergird the division of the Christian world into denominations and factions. Today a major reason people are involved in a church at all is for the sense of community they find there. Potentially divisive topics can be seen as threatening the prized fabric of relationships.

A conversation starter: When do we avoid talking about theology
in order to smooth the way for something else we value?

Mutuality and the Boss/Friend Conversation

One of the most quoted speeches from the Edinburgh conference helped move the world's churches to explore the issue of inequality and its effects on mutuality. V. S. Azariah was a Christian from India who later became a bishop in the Church of South India. In a controversial speech about relations between mission workers from abroad and their indigenous counterparts, he said: "Co-operation is assured when the personal, official and spiritual relationships are right, and is hindered when these relationships are wrong." He said personal relationships are right when modeled on Jesus as a friend to his disciples, coming alongside them; official relationships are right when one party is neither paymaster nor employer to the other and instead shows joy when one decreases so that the other can increase; and spiritual relationships are right when the foreign workers cultivate the forms of spirituality that are natural in a place. Concluding with now famous words, he said, "You have given your goods to feed the poor. You have given your bodies to be burned. We also ask for love. Give us friends!"[2]

The history of the past century has had us re-visiting these same issues in mission and ecumenism. De-colonization, the changing patterns of super-power domination, the rise of corporations larger than many modern states, and efforts to face racism and genocide, all contribute to the inequalities and the feelings and behaviors that accompany them. The quests for respect and mutuality in mission and ecclesial relations have led to much soul-searching and many innovations.

These patterns often emerge in congregations' involvements in mission. Though the challenges are particularly strong in trans-national relationships, they also crop up locally. As the pastor of an urban Methodist congregation said to me, "The suburban congregations that want to do urban ministry through us sometimes forget that the money they bring to the partnership

2. Azariah, "The Problem of Co-operation between Foreign and Native Workers."

doesn't make them the commanding partner. They cannot do this ministry without us, and they have a lot to learn about wise ways to be truly helpful to the kinds of people who come off the streets into these halls."

A conversation starter: In what ways are our congregation's relationships with other congregations and with mission partners affected by inequality, real or perceived?

Sentness, and the Evangelism/Justice Conversation

The sending of Jesus and his sending of us are at the heart of the understandings of both ecumenism and mission that have evolved in the past century. John 17:21 relates Christian unity to the witness of Christ in that Jesus' hope for the unity of his disciples is "so that the world may believe that you have sent me." Later, in John 20:21, Jesus says to those disciples, "As the Father has sent me, so I send you." These biblical quotations and related ideas appear frequently in circles active in mission and ecumenism in support of the widely held belief that sending and sent-ness are part of God's very nature and of what it means to imitate Christ.

As a result, a bridge is slowly forming over a chasm that greatly affected both mission and ecumenism after the evangelical social reform consensus of the nineteenth century broke down under the weight of fundamentalism and the rise of communism in the first decades of the twentieth century. Evangelism and social justice priorities began to be pitted against each other, and ecumenism came to be associated with the justice part of the debate.

A cornerstone of the bridge was laid at the 1966 World Congress on Evangelism, when John R. W. Stott, pastor of All Souls Church in London, England, led a meditation on John 20:19–23, in which the risen Lord appears to the disciples who are in a closed room and tells them (as cited above), "As the Father has sent me, so I send you."

After a rich reflection on the model of sent-ness Jesus provided us, Stott gently but incisively credits each side of the evangelism-justice divide with its distinctive strengths before chiding both sides for imitating Jesus' sent-ness only partially, either proclaiming a message but from a safe distance, or identifying deeply with another's needs to the point of not bringing a message at all. Stott succeeded in drawing a Jesus-shaped circumference around both evangelism and justice.[3]

3. This speech is available in the audio archives of Wheaton College, online: http://www.wheaton.edu/bgc/archives/docs/Berlin66/audio.htm.

A conversation starter: How are evangelism and justice emphases both embodied in the life and ministry of Jesus and his disciples?

Place, and the Local/Global Conversation

The most often used definition of ecumenism was issued by the Third Assembly of the World Council of Churches in New Delhi in 1961:

> We believe that the unity which is both God's will and his gift to the Church is being made visible as all in each place who are baptized into Jesus Christ and confess him as Lord and Savior are brought by the Holy Spirit into one fully-committed fellowship, holding the one apostolic faith, preaching the one Gospel, breaking the one bread, joining in common prayer, and having a corporate life reaching out in witness and service to all and who at the same time are united with the whole Christian fellowship in all places and ages, in such wise that ministry and members are accepted by all, and that all can act and speak together as occasion requires for the tasks to which God calls his people.[4]

This definition connects "all in each place" with "the whole Christian fellowship in all places and ages" and with acting and speaking together as God calls us. This has implications for congregations. The "world church" is first a world of local churches. The principle of subsidiarity puts congregations in a lead post in all the work God gives to the church, including mission and ecumenism.

In our current era's celebration of the leading role of congregations, two large points can be missed: 1) the theological point about the connectedness of the church in time and space, and 2) the sociological point that what happens in each place today can have reverberations in every place. As Sherron Kay George has written, "The cutting edge today is the *hyphen* in local-global mission."[5]

A "hyphen" story will illustrate this reality affecting both mission and ecumenism. A group of Presbyterians visiting Christians in Alexandria, Egypt, were present during the celebration of a recent surprise decision by (Muslim) town authorities to allow renovations and construction at a church site. Such permissions are rare. The municipal official who gave this authorization explained that he wanted to do something for Christians

---

4. "Report of the Section on Unity: Third Assembly of the World Council of Churches, New Delhi, 1961," 88.

5. George, *Better Together*, 45.

in recognition of the fact that when he had done university studies in a Midwestern college town in the United States, a local Christian couple had shown him good hospitality during school holidays when he couldn't afford to return to Egypt.

> *A conversation starter: In thinking about the congregation's work and priorities, when does it help to divide local and global, and when does it not? Why?*

Spirit, and the Hearts/Experts Conversation

In recent years ecumenical thought has given less emphasis than previously to visible unity, and more emphasis to practical and spiritual intermediate measures that allow us to grow into full communion for the sake of the fullness of Christ. Now-retired Catholic Cardinal Walter Kasper's book, *A Handbook of Spiritual Ecumenism*, influenced and illustrates this tendency. He wrote:

> The way toward reconciliation and communion unfolds when Christians feel the painful wound of division in their hearts, in their minds and in their prayers. . . . Only in the context of conversion and renewal of mind can the wounded bonds of communion be healed. . . . The work of ecumenism, therefore, is rooted in the foundations of Christian spirituality, requiring more than ecclesial diplomacy, academic dialogue, social involvement and pastoral cooperation. It presupposes a real appreciation of the many elements of sanctification and truth wrought by the Holy Spirit both within and beyond the visible boundaries of the Catholic Church.[6]

This elegant last sentence can be restated in a more colloquial way as, "We can all find something of real spiritual value in a tradition other than our own, thanks to the unfettered work of the Holy Spirit." The conversation to which Kasper called all the churches was one in which mission and ecumenism might be grounded in our awe of God's Holy Spirit, and "owned" by every Christian, rather than delegated to diplomats, scholars, reformers, and clergy.

An excellent aid for any congregation in this regard is Steven R. Harmon's *Ecumenism Means You, Too: Ordinary Christians and the Quest for Christian Unity*. In a chapter listing ten regular practices for Christians, he imparts this wisdom as helpful for mission relationships as well as for ecumenical ones: "Both parties in a relationship have to contribute something

---

6. Kasper, *A Handbook of Spiritual Ecumenism*, 11–12.

to the deepening of the relationship as an intentional, ongoing practice; otherwise the relationship's already on its way to dissolution."[7]

Starting in the 1990s, the field of mission outreach went through an analogous conversation about who "owns" the vocation and the value of congregations' involvements. Networks of "mission pastors" grew exponentially. And most denominational web sites now post resources that support the role of congregations. The "missional church" movement perhaps coincidentally also uses "broken heart" language to center and guide people in this calling, as Cardinal Kasper did about Christian unity.

> *A conversation starter: When are the wounds of division most painful between Christians and between mission partners, and why?*

Conclusion:

Given the great increase in relationships forged through both ecumenism and mission endeavors, and given the more holistic ways of thinking that prevail in the larger conversational environment, the time for a conversational approach in congregation-based ministry is ripe. Ecumenism and mission both pose some particular conversational challenges and pitfalls. Congregations can be better prepared by knowing about those, and they will be flagged in this chapter's next sections. In addition, there is a special challenge for congregations, as compared to individuals and specialized agencies. It is the challenge of how to have a collectively owned conversation. We will also explore this special challenge of congregations involved in mission and ecumenism.

What "Good" Looks Like—A Conversational Approach

Our culture has become highly polarized, and riling up specific "segments" of the population is a make-or-break art form in political campaigns. Church leaders have become very concerned and are looking for models that show how to be open to people who disagree. It has become countercultural to show what a good conversation is.

Some of those models will be of help as we now explore answers to the question, What does 'good' look like? Proverbs 29:18 says that without vision the people perish. In business circles where project management teams get trained, they say that a successful endeavor will begin with a statement

---

7. Harmon, *Ecumenism Means You, Too*, 56.

of what a "good" outcome would look like. So we must begin to envision for ourselves what a conversational approach to mission and ecumenism can look like for congregations. Up to this point, we've outlined the larger themes of conversation in the environment that affects churches' conduct of both ecumenism and mission. In this section we will address them separately because the concrete activities pursued in each kind of ministry tend to be distinct. In each example is a glimpse of what "good" may look like.

Ecumenism

One pressing reason for intentional efforts to explore ecumenical topics conversationally is the fact that very few congregations are made up entirely of persons who grew up in the same tradition. Before guest preaching at a Presbyterian church in central Pennsylvania, I asked the senior pastor about the congregation. His terse reply: "Half of them are divorced and re-married Catholics." Notice that he did not say, "former Catholics." I wish I had asked if there had been any intentional conversations about that in the congregation. It is usual for new members to be given an orientation to their new congregation's tradition. But how often are they also engaged in a conversation about what they have left behind, how they feel about it, and what gifts they bring from their past? And how often is that conversation shared with the whole congregation?

There are many other pressing reasons to pursue ecumenical conversations. Families and work places are made up of people from diverse traditions. Public debates on topics like whether health insurance reforms impinge on religious liberties are deeply rooted in the perspectives of distinctive Christian traditions. It has become a requirement for good citizenship to gain some perspective on alternative perspectives. And the best time to find out about these perspectives is before you have to, before a crisis, and in relationships formed by respectful conversations.

Two examples of good ecumenical conversations at the local level will help to set the stage for a detailing of some of the challenges involved. The first example involves a cluster of congregations in Lexington, Kentucky, that collaborates every year for a worship service marking the Week of Prayer for Christian Unity. Eight Christian traditions are involved. They obtain basic materials from the Graymoor Ecumenical and InterReligious Institute.[8] Ecumenical worship services for special occasions are not uncommon. The Lexington cluster's intentionality about observing the Week of Prayer for Christian Unity is less common, however. What is most special about this

8. Online: http://www.geii.org/.

example of what "good" looks like is notable in the two innovations this cluster has introduced. Both pertain to conversational approaches.

The first innovation is to invite the cluster's pastors to take turns leading a conversation to which all are invited, on the assigned biblical text and theme for that year's Week of Prayer. In this way, theological nuances that can pertain to the distinctive aspects of each tradition can be aired and explored in the weeks leading up to the ecumenical worship service.

A second innovation is that the different congregations of the cluster invite their top regional officers and leaders of the Kentucky Council of Churches to attend the worship service. The Lutheran bishop drives the longest way to get there—188 miles. These judicatory officers and ecumenical leaders are served a relaxed meal in a private room before the worship service. Teenaged members of confirmation classes serve the meal and are treated to the sight and sounds of diverse Christian leaders enjoying company and conversation.

Then, during the worship service, each of these leaders is given a few minutes to preach using the main Scripture text. The worshipers see and hear the Word being discerned and shared by leaders representing a broad array of traditions. Placed side by side in this way, these brief homilies open a kind of conversation with all who are present, because a question is implied, Were we fed by people of other traditions?

The second example of good ecumenical conversation at the local level involves the itinerant work of a Catholic priest. The Rev. Paul Ryan, who is skilled in fomenting ecumenical dialogue, leads a workshop that shows the power of conversation when it focuses on apt questions. In this easily replicated workshop, participants from various traditions sit at round tables in groups of five to seven each. All present are reminded that each tradition has brought at least one distinctive gift to the body of Christ. Then the table groups are asked to discuss three questions:

1. What is one gift you truly cherish in your own tradition, a gift you would not want to lose?

2. What is a gift you have noticed in another tradition, a gift that gives you "holy envy?"

3. What could you do to avail yourself of that gift?

The first time I participated in such a conversation, two Baptists at my table both had the same answer to the first question: they cherished the Baptist gift of emphasizing the individual's conscience before God. When it was their turn to talk about their "holy envy," they also had the same answer. However, the gift they coveted in other traditions was the under-side of the very gift they cherished in their own. They admired other traditions' stronger sense of pull to "stay at the table" during disagreements. The cherished focus on the individual's conscience before God meant that Baptists like themselves experienced less of that pull to stay. They wanted more of the gift of committing to stay together with other Christians and wrestle with conscience together. It was clear that they would not have shared this admiration for another tradition without first having an opportunity to say what they loved about being Baptist. The order of topics in a conversation can greatly affect participants' willingness to grow in understanding and to change.

Mission

Until recent years, congregations typically assigned the topic of mission to a committee where it became a catch-all for everything that does not directly serve the needs of congregation itself, such as its education or worship life. To this mission committee flocked individuals who had a particular passion, whether it was support for a missionary, or addressing homelessness, or something else.

Increasingly, however, congregations are coming to see mission as the very reason for the church's existence. Mission is our primary vocation, and programs through which we take care of ourselves are in place to help us grow in our ability to be in mission. Two examples of helpful conversational approaches to this transition will help introduce a review of some conversational practices and considerations.

The first example involves a traditionally white and English speaking Presbyterian congregation that had become somewhat diverse, but mostly by accident. Marriage was one of the reasons. Another reason for the diversity was proximity to a seminary. The seminary students from other countries did not have cars and could get to this congregation easily without them.

People thought this diversity was good. Since it was not increasing, however, they grew concerned they might be overlooking ways they could more positively promote diversity in the congregation. The Evangelism Committee was asked to lead a discussion concerning multiculturalism and growth in diversity for the congregation. The chair of the Evangelism Committee looked at her almost entirely white group of native English speakers, however, and said, "Let's wait to discuss this topic until our committee is diverse. Let's not talk about people; let's talk with people." It took months to recruit Ghanaian and Guatemalan seminary students to increase the committee's diversity.

When it came time to talk about diversity, the conversation was entirely different than it would have been without this delay. Here is a sample of it:

A longtime member of the church asked in the committee, "The women who sit with the Ghanaian students—do they speak English?"

One of the seminary students answered, "Yes."

"Oh. They don't talk with people after the service, so I wondered why."

"They don't know what to talk about, since they haven't seen anyone all week in their homes. In Ghana, we visit each other informally during the week."

"Oh, so would it help if the women got involved in the current round-robin of cottage suppers?"

"That is too intimidating. Scheduling a meal like that is so formal, and it comes with all sorts of unwritten expectations. They wouldn't know what to serve."

The learning curve was steep and fast, but it was true because it was not guesswork. Caring hearts and well-informed minds came together in a conversation marked by genuine questions asked with enough preparation and sensitivity not to alienate the persons who needed a chance to talk. What does this have to do with mission? Learning how to learn about differences through face-to-face conversations is a key skill in mission. In addition, a congregation that can present a diverse face as it reaches out beyond its walls has also taken a big step forward in signaling openness to those kinds of conversations.

A second example of a conversational approach to a church making the transition from focusing on programs for members to mission involves a congregation in Michigan that had for many years been in the mode of delegating mission to a committee. And what a committee this one was! Its budget was as large as the whole budget of the diversifying congregation described above. Congregation members' involvement in specific mission projects in the US and around the world had been successfully cultivated to the point that passionate reports from each project dominated the committee meetings. Each group wanted to convey the worth of their own work through their spokesperson on the committee—for one thing, their share of the budget was at stake.

When the associate pastor staffing this committee left, the senior pastor and the committee co-chairs decided to create a retreat experience for the whole group with the help of a consultant. In small groups and in plenary they engaged in extensive conversation. They were asked: "What do you find yourself praying about most?" They interviewed each other with this question: "Would you please tell me about how the evolution of your faith has been connected to what you have discovered along the way about the church's mission in the world?" They split into groups to talk about global, national, and local situations, and conversed about "What in this sphere is heart-breaking to God? How is God moving in this situation?" Worship sessions and substantive presentations were interspersed with additional conversations that focused on the congregation's connectedness to other churches, on what connects service and evangelism for the sake of the whole person, and on what words like "structure and focus" mean in mission endeavors.

The notes from the last session of the retreat show no trace of the parallel but disconnected meeting conversations of before, "our Philippines group this" or "the ESL program that." Instead, the notes quote statements like:

- "We are a teaching church and this can be tied to our 'sent-ness' and our identity."

- "Improving relationships is important by caring for each other, all the task force members."

- "We need diverse options for a diverse membership. How do we go to the next level and involve more than just the 50–100 who are currently involved?"

- "We confuse the meeting with the mission."

- "Justice has been a powerful motivation."

- "Children need a fair start in life."

- "Our 'silo effect' is an obstacle to starting new ventures."

- "We learn from those with whom we are in partnership. We go (instead of just sending money) in order to establish friendships and relationships."

Moving the conversations to a higher level, to uniting themes and personal journeys, had revealed the common threads running through their mission endeavors. It had also moved the calling of the whole congregation to the forefront.

What Can these Conversational Directions Mean for Daily Ministry?

Anecdotes can inspire and illustrate. What can these glimpses of "what good looks like" add up to, in practical terms, for the ministry of leaders of congregations?

Modes: A Meeting or a Conversation?

One practical implication is that leaders need to be attuned to when a group needs a conversation, and when it needs a meeting. The art of meetings and the art of conversation are not always the same. In conversations, we are more likely to learn, we delve deeper, we are surprised by a new insight, and we re-orient our goals. A good meeting presupposes that kind of conversation has taken place. It can also make room for such conversations. Sometimes you may need to stop a meeting and shift it to the conversation mode. But a meeting can also simply be about implementing a vision that has already emerged.

Questions: Open and Honest, or "Leading"?

Leaders also need to grow in the art of asking good questions, and helping others turn their questions in better directions. An excellent resource on this art is Parker Palmer's book, *A Hidden Wholeness*, and the materials he has allowed to be posted on the internet about "circles of trust."[9] One of Palmer's insights is into the nature and form of "open, honest questions." Reflecting deeply on his insights may lead you to join me in suspecting that many—perhaps most—of the questions asked in conversations emerge from something we want to hear or experience, not from a true openness to being surprised and learning. It takes a courageous leader to let go of defining leadership in terms of what courts of law call "leading questions," that is, getting people to articulate the answers we want them to give.[10]

9. Online: http://www.couragerenewal.org/.

10. Westfield shares this concern as seen in her description of "scripted conversations" on 123–26 above.

Inclusion: Whose Conversation Is It?

The greatest challenge for a congregation's leaders may be that of turning the insights and new directions emerging within dyadic or small group conversations into conversations that belong to the whole congregation. This is more important for the church than for any other social group, because we are asked to be "one body" that has "the mind of Christ."

Consider the challenge faced by the apostle Peter after his huge learning experience in the home of Cornelius (Acts 10). This experience had opened his mind about the scope of God's action, the inclusion of Gentiles, and the importance of not letting purity concerns prevent the spread of the Gospel. It would have been far easier to form a group of like-minded persons and not return to Jerusalem. But Peter had to turn his learning into learning for his faith community in Jerusalem. His speech before the Jerusalem Council eventually inspired much conversation (Acts 11:1–18).

Congregations often do not know what to do with members who "got religion" through some mission or faith experience and then keep trying to talk about it. In fact, specialized mission organizations and specialized ecumenical agencies are full of people who have had that experience in their congregation or denomination. Moreover, some pastors and denominational executives send enthused individuals to such agencies as a strategy for reducing the potential for conflict.

Methods are needed for helping individuals' and groups' fresh infusions of God (enthusiasms) become part of a larger conversation, for the common good. How can these new ingredients be kneaded together with the other ingredients? How do conversations play a role? Three practical measures that have been known to help are listed here as "Send groups and plan for a report-back", "Develop job descriptions for liaisons," and "Articulate a philosophy of affirmation and adoption."

Send pairs or groups and plan for a report-back: When a church member may need to process a big new experience, it can help to be accompanied by a conversation partner. This is true whether one is being sent as a delegate to a denominational gathering, or volunteering for a service project. Leaders of congregations can be sensitive to this in two ways. One is to look for ways that members can have someone with them when going somewhere where the experience may be new or challenging. The other is to plan for report-back opportunities. A personal debriefing time may be needed in order to help make the report-back the best it can be.

Develop job descriptions for liaisons: The mediatory role can be elevated in its importance by providing job descriptions. It is possible to make it clear that making certain experiences part of a larger group's conversation is someone's special role. The following is an example of a job description that one congregation's "Outreach Council" developed so they could recruit someone in the congregation to take on the role of liaison to the denominational mission personnel the congregation was supporting.

Reporting to the Outreach Council at least quarterly, this volunteer will:

- Stay up-to-date about needs and desires for support and involvement as expressed by each co-worker and, when relevant, by his/her family members.

- Seek ways that individuals and groups in the congregation can help meet the needs and desires that are expressed.

- Facilitate two-way flows of communication, to co-workers about the life of the congregation, and to the congregation about the lives and work of the co-workers.

Some methods we commend to the liaison:

- reading the letters from co-workers;

- noting family members' birthdays and special dates to commemorate;

- interviewing each co-worker about practical needs and about how we can grow through deeper engagement with his/her calling, partners, and daily work.

Here is another example of a similar a job description, this time developed for an ecumenical liaison role:

- Help the congregation give an award from time to time for members who are engaged in ecumenical ministries or activism.

- Sponsor an essay contest as a way to give an award to younger people for ecumenical spirit, and help the Christian Education classes teach children about Christian unity.

- Suggest ways for the congregation to mark the yearly Week of Prayer for Christian Unity.

- Keep concerns of the world church before the congregation/parish during spoken prayers of intercession.

- Alert us to opportunities to connect with other Christian traditions in the community.

- Relate to the state council of churches by subscribing to their legislative alerts, attending the annual assembly and then report back about something especially meaningful and providing two-way communications.

Articulate a philosophy of affirmation and adoption: Individuals' passions can be affirmed without becoming equally shared or "adopted" by the whole congregation. After giving a fair hearing to what is making individual members excited, it may turn out that it is more important to affirm them as individuals than to adopt their specific passion into the life of a larger group. There are many ways to affirm without adopting their proposals, for instance, inclusion in an event when volunteers are honored, references in pastoral prayers or space on a bulletin board or at a mission fair.

Cautions

If congregational leaders choose to foster an environment of mutual transformation through conversation and to cultivate that environment specifically in the areas of mission and ecumenism, there are some cautions to keep in mind. Just as you might drive by a sign that says "Caution: Men Working" you may need to post one in your church building saying "Caution: Bubbles Bursting." We all have ideas that we hold onto with varying degrees of tightness. Some of those ideas are ones we do not even know we have until they are challenged. Others are ones we are known for, that are part of our public identity. These may have to change, in an environment of kneading, of combining ingredients in a combustible way for the sake of growth and transformation.

What follows are some examples of the kinds of discoveries for which you may need to prepare the way in your own heart and mind, in pastoral approaches and in preaching. To make these kinds of discoveries acceptable in your community of faith, you will need to cultivate in yourself a determination that God's transformation of you is more important than your "standing" or "being right." You will need to foster, and model, a sense of humor and even enjoyment of those moments in life when prejudices are burst like bubbles and then float away from us. You will need to cultivate a willingness in yourself and others to live with ambiguity, to suspend choosing until greater clarity has come, and to accept that even people you don't admire for one reason or another may nevertheless have a truth you need to hear.

Some of the influences that work against good communication through conversation include cultural differences, power differentials, strong feelings of repugnance or previous injury, and some bad habits such as universalizing oneself, imputing motives, and swapping parallel anecdotes while failing to connect at the level of ideas. The following paragraphs may remind you of experiences of conversation you have had. If so, jot them down; they may be useful when you catalyze a congregation's exploration of conversational approaches in mission and ecumenism.

It is important to be aware of conversational habits we may have picked up and that are not helpful. A few of those follow before we explore the larger topic of cultural influences, power, and repugnance.

Learned Habits of Conversation

Much of what passes for good conversation, is not. Unlearning poor habits and acquiring new ones will not be restful. Here are some examples:

Universalizing one's own viewpoint: Parker Palmer's work on the kinds of questions and tenets that build conversational "circles of trust" is worth studying in depth if only to unmask and unlearn some of the most common bad conversational habits most of us pick up. His work on "open honest questions" helps us re-examine the kinds of questions we ask to keep a conversation moving in a direction we want it to go rather than in a direction that might allow the souls that are present to find truth together. One of those habits is to think what we would be feeling if we were in the other person's situation and then ask a question that makes our own feelings a standard, such as "Are you feeling angry about that?"[11]

Imputing and questioning motives: Another common habit is to impute motives rather than deal in a straightforward manner with what another person is saying. A document entitled "Guidelines for Presbyterians in Times of Disagreement" available on the Presbyterian Church (USA) web site includes this advice: "Focus on ideas and suggestions instead of questioning people's motives, intelligence or integrity; we will not engage in name-calling or labeling of others prior to, during, or following the discussion." In a congregation, the labels and motives imputed are varied—Charismatic! Revivalist! High Church! Proselytizer!—but the effects on learning are the same, a failure to be kneaded and transformed.

Stringing anecdotes without exploring ideas: In a stream of consciousness sort of way, we often swap stories that seem to us similar to ones already offered in a conversation. This habit can divert us from the in-depth exploration that is possible when someone has offered a story of some significance to him or her. This is not the same as finding out what one soul

11. Palmer, *A Hidden Wholeness*, especially chapter 8, "Living the Questions: Experiments with Truth," 129–49.

is offering to another in the way of learning. The Michigan congregation's outreach council moved beyond serial swapping of stories from its project-focused "silos" and found fruitful and profound topics to address for the sake of learning more, involving more, discerning more.

Cultural Influences on Conversation

Eric Law has done a service by laying out some of the cultural determinants of conversation that must be watched for if the many thresholds of mission and ecumenism are to be crossed.[12] Some cultures have values and childhood training that put their people at the microphone first, and others that put their people there last if at all. Some are more comfortable with plenary debate and others with consulting experts and then coming back through someone who is more authorized to speak. If these differences are not accounted for in the format and process of gatherings, it is likely that the results will be skewed.

An example of this insight occurred at an international meeting of the World Alliance of Reformed Churches in 2004. A new policy statement was being reviewed in a large plenary setting, a statement challenging the way the global "free market economy" was affecting countries disadvantaged in that marketplace. The document reflected many insights gleaned from consultations held in many parts of the globe. Now it was either going to be accepted or rejected. Nearly an hour went by during which Western European and North American voices dominated the microphones, mostly in opposition to this document. The meeting lasted a whole week and this particular session of it was several hours long. Otherwise we would never have heard from people from South Pacific, Native American, and Asian cultures who mostly spoke in favor of the document and whose insights had already shaped it due to the previous consultations. Without a process that accounted for cultural differences, the world church, like it or not, would not have received "The Accra Confession: Covenant for Justice in the Economy and the Earth."[13]

Cultural influences are not only manifest in how meetings transpire. Many people born and raised in the United States have a strong tendency to see ourselves as "quick studies" who can size up a situation pretty quickly and generate some good ideas about what needs fixing first and how to do it. We like to be the "know-how" people. For many reasons like our size, our having

12. Law, *The Wolf Shall Dwell with the Lamb*, sensitized many white Americans to the dynamics in conversations where multiple cultures are present.

13. Online: http://warc.jalb.de/warcajsp/side.jsp?news_id=1157&navi=45.

only two national borders, and the global dominance of the English language, our life experiences tend to protect us from the kinds of life moments that reveal we are clueless. And this issue is exacerbated by the fact that many of our mission involvements are in countries where people highly value "saving face" and therefore are loath to ever contradict, correct, or say No to us.

I liked to tease my father about a time when he exhibited the American tendency to "know best." I had been in rural Haiti for a year. I said something to him about the poverty I had seen. He scarcely lowered his newspaper before saying simply "Send them tractors." After all, that helped the farmers with whom he had grown up in Ohio. But it was a stunningly inappropriate solution for rural Haiti, where farm plots are tiny and steep and often not contiguous, and where supply lines for parts and repairs are undependable in the extreme.

Even months in another's place can be insufficient, however. Having told on my father, now I'll tell a story on myself. I stayed six months in one rural Haitian village where a coffee cooperative had been built on the Catholic parish property. I attended a meeting of the coop's officers where the conversation centered on inviting the president to stand for another year in office. After some time of this, I gave a little "democracy 101" speech about "listening to the will of the people." Immediately the president agreed to serve and I was pleased with myself. An hour later I learned in no uncertain terms that I had misunderstood the situation. No one had wanted the president for another term, but they had to appear to want that. He had yielded to my speech because, as a guest of the priest of the parish that owned the land for the coop, it was assumed I spoke for the priest.

Because of these issues built into cross-cultural communications, some denominations have encouraged congregations in cross-cultural mission to go through long and slow processes of conversation and mutual acquaintance leading toward a partnering agreement that spells out what gifts *each* will offer to the other and what needs *both* parties are willing to articulate. Some congregations are impatient with such processes, but sooner or later they learn what others have learned before them.

Anger and Repugnance

We do not always really want to hear what someone else has to say because we are already too turned off by what we think it is. Two examples, one from ecumenism and one from mission, will illustrate the need for self-discipline, self-understanding, and a regular practice of the art of conversation.

Ecumenical Dialogue and the Dangerous Topic of Reproduction: There is a long-standing dialogue group in one city in which leaders of the Roman Catholic churches get together with leaders from the Christian Church Disciples of Christ churches. There is great stability of membership in the group and a warm sense of a shared and long journey. And so it seemed right at a certain point to try having a conversation about an area of considerable difference between the two traditions, the area of human reproduction and beliefs about birth control. It exploded. Only with some difficulty did it become possible to give an adequate hearing to the different points of view, and at subsequent meetings it was necessary to debrief and talk the group's way back to the good relations they had always enjoyed.

Haiti and Meeting a Real Duvalierist: During a research trip for my doctoral dissertation years ago, I made a visit to the Cap-Haitian headquarters of a Catholic missionary order. I was introduced to a fellow guest who also had a habit of stopping in to visit. It quickly became apparent that he grieved the end of the era of Papa Doc Duvalier and "Duvalierism," which was rooted in part in a kind of black pride movement called "noirism." I was face-to-face with someone who actually embraced an era I did not think anyone could defend. I could have asked an open, honest question: "What did you value about Duvalierism?" But I really wanted to manage a smooth exit. So I said something about what I was admiring in Haiti, especially the vibrant spirituality of many of its people. He exploded. "You come here and think you can pronounce upon what is good and imply what isn't. Why don't you Americans acknowledge our right and ability to self-govern?!" I had been patronizing, and my thought that it might fall to me to make global observations about Haiti was just another manifestation of the cultural pattern described above. My doctoral dissertation might have benefited from really listening to an aging Duvalierist, but I missed the opportunity, and it never came back.

Power Differentials

Power differentials undergird many of the other conversational snares described in this section, for instance in the question of who owned the coffee coop land. Some power differentials are felt because of one's identity as American, white, male, having more money than others, or speaking a particular language with a particular self-presentation. Others emerge from more surprising or secondary sources. In ecumenical circles, some of the most salient differences are in how power and authority are exercised in the various Christian traditions. When mission involvements have to do with cross-denominational partnerships, the opportunities for working harder at good communication simply multiply.

Questions for Discussion:

Composing your own open, honest questions is the most important next step as you think about these pages you have read. Some "conversation starters" were suggested in the first major section. What "conversation starters" would you craft in relation to the remaining sections?

Conclusion

"The [reign] of heaven is like the yeast that a woman took and mixed in with three measures of flour until all of it was leavened." (Matt 13:33) What God is bringing about in the world through mission and ecumenism is comprehensive in scope, and it requires diverse ingredients that can be moved and transformed into a new creation. If real conversations are taking place at the congregation level, the ingredients will be moved, metabolize into something new, and create the resilience that the new shape will need.

Congregations that are kneaded in this way will find themselves entering intentionally into some global Church conversations that have been underway for a hundred years. These include conversations about doctrine, mutuality, sent-ness, place and Spirit. Congregations willing to be transformed through conversations will look at glimpses of "what good looks like" as they search for models that have been tested and refined as well as invent their own models. They will master new ways to connect individual conversations to the life of larger groups, to affirm most members' commitments and adopt many of those commitments collectively, to navigate the influences of culture and power, to ask open and honest questions and discern when to have a meeting and when to have a conversation. Perhaps most of all, they and their leaders will trust the Baker and enjoy the vocation of being ingredients in a surprising process of change in which conversations play a major role.

Further Reading

Bonk, Jonathan J. *Missions and Money: Affluence as a Missionary Problem*. Maryknoll, NY: Orbis, 2006.

George, Sherron Kay. *Better Together: The Future of Presbyterian Mission*. Louisville: Geneva, 2010.

Part 2: The Tasks of Ministry

Harmon, Steven R. *Ecumenism Means You, Too: Ordinary Christians and the Quest for Christian Unity*. Eugene, OR: Cascade, 2010.

Huertz, Christopher L., and Christine D. Pohl. *Friendship at the Margins: Discovering Mutuality in Service and Mission*. Downers Grove, IL: InterVarsity, 2010.

Law, Eric. *The Wolf Shall Dwell with the Lamb: A Spirituality for Leadership in a Multicultural Community*. St. Louis: Chalice, 1993.

Palmer, Parker. *A Hidden Wholeness: The Journey Toward an Undivided Life*. San Francisco: Jossey-Bass, 2004.

10

Social Witness as Conversation

Pamela D. Couture

In conversation with Heather Weaver-Orosz, Chencho Alas, Bishop Ntambo Nkulu Ntanda, Susan Beaver, and James Glass

On September 19, 2012 Bishop Ntambo Nkulu Ntanda, United Methodist from the Democratic Republic of Congo (DRC), testified to the United States Congressional Foreign Affairs Subcommittee on Africa, Human Rights, and Global Health. He, along with Mark Schneider of the International Crisis Group and Jason Stearns of the Rift Valley Institute, sought international support for restraining Rwanda in a new conflict perpetrated by the rebel group M23 at the border of the DRC and Rwanda. His witness resulted from a series of conversations beginning among religious and civil leaders and their constituents in the DRC, continuing at the United Nations, and expanding into church and government in the US, Canada, Belgium, Italy, and Spain. Bishop Ntambo sought to bring leaders responsible for US foreign policy face-to-face with the human suffering that would either be reduced or multiplied by their decisions.

This hour in the US Congress represented thousands of hours of conversation with a wide range of people, most of whom do not know one another, many of whom would not identify themselves as social activists, but all of whom care about peace in the DRC and Rwanda. Bishop Ntambo's testimony embodied a previously frequent but now increasingly rare form of social witness—direct encounter with government leaders to advocate a change. These testimonies differ from those of religious leaders who are brought to Congress to buttress specific partisan political positions.

I watched the proceedings from the Congressional gallery packed with many friends and a few foes of the witnesses. I felt that I was watching an ironic, postcolonial version of modern Christendom: ironic, because this interchange occurred in an era in which many believe religion is a private matter and should not speak to public, political issues; postcolonial, because a Congolese bishop spoke for himself; modern, because the committee chair, Rep. Chris Smith, cared about the religious leader's perspective and invited the delegation to converse in his office afterwards.

How have Christians made known their understanding of faith to the society that surrounds them, how have they justified their actions, and what kind of future exists for social witness as a Christian practice? Social witness, broadly defined, is any practice by ecclesial bodies or persons of faith giving public voice to particular ways of bringing about an eschatological vision of society: peace, justice, virtue, love, mercy, abundance, or other qualities of what people variously call the kingdom, kin-dom, reign or realm of God. The justifications for social witness are biblical, theological, cultural, mystical and experiential. In every era, social witness creates controversy, as it asks for change. Social witness is a transforming practice whose future manifestations might be as surprising as the invitation for Bishop Ntambo to testify in Congress.

Social Witness in Christian History

Social witness is as old as Christianity itself and has transformed itself depending upon the relationship between Christianity and political authorities. The oldest Christian social witness came from early Christian martyrs executed by Rome for being unwilling to pledge their faith to Roman gods.[1] At the beginning of the twentieth century in the United States, religious social witness addressed many issues, especially racial discrimination, women's suffrage and other enfranchisements, and poverty. The social gospel movement, emerging from nineteenth-century evangelicalism, developed in an era of social optimism, and, when the First World War dashed such hopes, evolved into post-war theological realism.[2] In the early twentieth century denominations developed social principles as common statements in social witness.[3] Notables such as the Roman Catholic Dorothy Day, the Anglican

1. Cooper-White notes in "Suffering," 23, that the word *witness* in English is the translation of the Greek word *martyr.*

2. Airhart, *Serving the Present Age*; Evans, *The Kingdom Is Always but Coming*; Young, *Bearing Witness against Sin.*

3. Online: http://www.ncccusa.org/centennial/maymoment.html.

William Temple, and Baptist Howard Thurman articulated the relationship among their faith, ecclesiology, and political positions.[4]

Two world wars, the civil rights movement, the nuclear arms race, worldwide movements for independence from colonialism, the war in Viet Nam, the War on Poverty, the fight among capitalism, socialism, and European style welfare states, and ecumenism, radically changed the context of Christian social witness in the West. Protestant denominational statements, Roman Catholic social teaching, and the World Council of Churches promoted the conviction that society exploited the vulnerable and might be organized more justly. Many were confrontational, in the manner of Saul Alinsky, trying to surface latent conflict.[5] Others followed the nonviolent resistance tactics of Mohandas Ghandi and Martin Luther King, Jr. They articulated the religious grounds for their ideas.[6] Ironically, in the last decade of the century, increasing secularism in Europe and the privatization of mainline religion in North America reduced the visibility of social witness, even as conservative Christians and politicians joined together to strengthen their voice and power.

Context shapes social witness. Social witness derives from how religious practices such as prayer, study of Scripture and Christian tradition, discernment, and ecclesial conversation lead the community to interpret particular societal issues of a given time. Such interaction pervaded social movements led by persons such as Dorothy Day, Martin Luther King, Jr. and Howard Thurman. Social witness is rarely the prophetic speech of a lone individual; rather, it is birthed by conversations within community. It may develop the momentum of a social movement.

The context of social witness in early twenty-first century is postmodern—marked by the prominence of local narratives, social media and technology—and postcolonial, notably identified by the emergence of strong voices from the global south. The cultural conditions noted by postmodern and postcolonial criticism are developing in the context of advanced economic globalization, the changing authority of nation-states, deep religiosity in interfaith contexts in the global south, and a peculiar secularization in North America that purports the decline of the religious voice at the same time that religious and political conservatism become public. However, the

---

4. Coy, *A Revolution of the Heart*; Pollard, *Mysticism and Social Change*; Temple, *Social Witness and Evangelism*; Thurman, *The Creative Encounter*.

5. See Alinsky, *Reveille for Radicals*; and Alinsky, *Rules for Radicals*.

6. Birch, *What Does the Lord Require?*; Gooch, *John Wesley for the Twenty-First Century*; Heyer, *Prophetic and Public*; Lewis, *Christian Social Witness*; Marquardt, *John Wesley's Social Ethics*; Runyon, *The New Creation*.

concern for the relationship between social witness and spirituality remains constant in the literature.[7]

A recent book, Jennifer R. Ayres' *Waiting for a Glacier to Move: Practicing Social Witness*, makes helpful distinctions from which to consider the relationship between social witness and conversation. Following Alistair MacIntyre on practices, Ayres explores the relationship between the "internal and external goods" of social witness. They seek a particular social change—an "external good." Success may be measured by whether such social change occurs through changes in law, different cultural norms, or new individual understandings. But "internal goods" may be even more shaping —as activists clarify and solidify commitments, find or question the meaning in activism, and meet supportive people. While seeking social change, activists themselves are transformed.[8] Ayres' categories help us understand the relationship between spiritual formation and social activism—spiritual formation is an internal good by which the activism can be evaluated, regardless of the social change that occurs.

Ayres highlights the theological themes of sin and hope as places for theological reflection.[9] She avoids individual definitions of sin, choosing instead to define sin as systems of exploitation that inevitably entangle people. Activism provides hope because it challenges sin, recognizing that we are all part of it, avoiding the "burden of perfection."[10] Social activism offers the opportunity to resist sin, even as we are embedded in sin. She concludes that theological reflection as an explicit part of social witness sustains activists' endurance.

In the last half of the twentieth century much social witness was synonymous with "protesting," as it is for Ayres. Yet more communal understandings of activism than Ayres' suggest that people seeking social change assume different roles at different times within an activist community. Some are "out front" publicizing a desired change; others are working through "backdoor diplomacy;" others write as scholar-activists; still others provide hospitality. Even within confrontational-style activism people take different positions at different times.

From this survey of Christian social witness we can determine criteria for Christian social witness: it seeks the peace and justice of society and the freedom, liberty, or self-determination of individuals for whom flourishing

---

7. Nangelimalil, *The Relationship between the Eucharistic Liturgy, the Interior Life, and the Social Witness of the Church*; Townes, *In a Blaze of Glory*.

8. Ayres, *Waiting for a Glacier to Move*, 28–37, 49–57.

9. Ibid., 129–33; cf. 133–41.

10. Serene Jones as quoted in ibid., 126.

has been diminished. It challenges systems that reduce the flourishing of vulnerable people to move toward alternative social arrangements. It seeks to rearrange power by undergirding that of vulnerable persons and circumscribing that of persons or groups who benefit from social arrangements that lessen life for others. Theologically, it addresses sin and evil; it promotes hope, community, and shalom.

Social Witness and Conversation

Conversation as central to social witness has a deep history, and it is foundational for new methods of social witness. For example, conversation for "clarification of values" was important in Dorothy Day's Catholic Worker movement. The Society of Friends has always used the conversational "clearness committee" to determine its interpretation of the will of God. The social witness resulting from conversation in the Friends' tradition resulted in their 1947 Nobel Peace Prize. Recently, many ecclesial meetings have moved away from parliamentary procedure and toward more conversational, consensual "discernment" models. Language such as "holy conferencing" (United Methodist) and "holy manners" (United Church of Canada) describes the respectful conversation churches seek to promote, even as protesters or lobbyists encircle the gathering.

An important question: do conversations, including "discernment" models of church life, sustain the status quo, while lobbying and protest create social change? Or is conversation a constitutive part of social witness, one aspect in the larger communal activity that is social witness? Two different forms of social witness, one hearkening to the more confrontational style, the other more collaborative, demonstrate that conversation is central to both.

Conversation in a "Protest Model" of Social Witness

At the United Church of Canada General Council 41 (GC41) in August, 2012 two significant acts of social witness occurred: the approval of a resolution recommending church action in relationship to Israel/Palestine, and the adoption of a revised United Church crest with First Nations' signing the Basis of Union. The former occurred through a process similar to many acts of ecclesial social witness; the latter was unique, reflecting recent developments in social witness process.

United Church of Canada members brought to several General Councils Palestinian Christians' request for support from other Christians for ending Israel's occupation of Palestinian territories. United Church members had long been divided over how to respond to this request. GC 40 commissioned a study to bring recommendations for action to GC 41. The draft of the study produced much controversy in Canada. Toronto newspapers ran articles ranging from "who cares what the United Church of Canada thinks" to condemning the United Church for contemplating a boycott of products from the settlements.

At GC41 lobbyists for both sides were provided with space for booths immediately outside the council meeting, "the court." They distributed literature and engaged commissioners in conversation for the first week of council before the final vote. After the study group made its presentation, a representative of the Canadian Jewish committee who opposed the boycott and the head of the Palestinian refugee relief society that sought it were invited to address the court.

Moderator Mardi Tindal presided, reminding the commissioners of "Holy Manners" and the consensus process of decision-making that was designed to foster civil conversation under intense pressure. For some, the process unnecessarily restrained the passion of the court in a conflict-avoidant way; for others, the process demonstrated that the church could respectfully deliberate about a divisive topic. Conversation in "circles" and careful listening resulted in amendments to the original resolution. In the end the United Church voted that its policy toward actions in the Middle East be consistent with eleven principles, of which one item recommends economic action.[11]

It became clear that the media, and, therefore, the general public were not interested in careful listening or painstaking conversation among people who held divergent and passionate views. Despite the fact that the deliberations at General Council were live-streamed so anyone could watch, no media gave the United Church credit for careful, faithful deliberations or the amendments making clear that the United Church saw responsibility on both sides. Rather, news reports focused on the breakdown of Christian and Jewish relations in Canada as a result of the court's vote for possible economic sanctions.

Conversation in a "Conflict Transformational" Model of Social Witness

In contrast to this highly publicized action of social witness that aroused public controversy, the first event of GC 41 changed the United Church in a

---

11. United Church of Canada; online: http://www.gc41.ca/.

more profound and permanent way. This social witness culminated decades of conversations.

In 1981 an indigenous woman, Alberta Billy, told the church, "It's time for you to apologize."[12] In 1986 the United Church formally apologized for excluding aboriginal spirituality and civilization and for imposing European traditions, values, and social organization on First Peoples. The apology was received but not accepted. Marilyn Legge, social ethicist in the United Church of Canada, notes that the aboriginal elders responded, "We must go back and talk to the people" and writes that "Reconciliation involves, therefore, not only listening to the suffering caused but evidence that it has been heard, the wrong-doing acknowledged, and steps of repentance and redress being taken."[13] Reconciliation, so defined, sets the stage for engaging *conflict transformational* aspects of social witness.

In 1987, after genuine conversation with indigenous congregations and in response to their request, the church established the All Native Circle Conference (ANCC) to create a permanent aboriginal presence in the ministry and decision making of the church. According to Susan Beaver, an indigenous clergywoman,

> The ANCC was meant to model that culturally-appropriate circle style of relationship, decision-making and conversation that would enable our people to have a more comfortable place in the church as well as more control over decisions and structures that directly affect us and to influence the way the wider church operates. It hasn't always worked out that way but we're not done yet. The ANCC's true relevance is that it helps us in the First Nations pastoral charges to do the work we need to do, which involves deepening our faith and witness to the teachings of Christ, making space for the spirit of life in our lives in the context of a murderous society, and generally undoing some of the damage wrought by the church and Christian-informed government policy. For the first time since Columbus stumbled into our territories, people feel like they can be authentically Cree, Mohawk, Anishnawbe and authentically Christian. We can see a certain reconciliation taking place within individuals who grew up in a context of dissonance and duality. We can also see healing in terms of valuing our own ways.[14]

12. In conversation with indigenous persons I learned that this portion of the story is frequently omitted.

13. Legge, "Negotiating Mission," 125.

14. Susan Beaver, personal correspondence, October 24, 2012.

Social Changes, through an Institution, as a Result of Social Witness

In the next two decades Canada began to acknowledge the horrendous history of child abuse in residential schools for native children, funded by the government and run by churches. The conversations did not always go smoothly, as Legge notes. In 2002 she commended three kinds of actions within the church toward strengthening right relations between aboriginals and non-aboriginals: relationship building to foster awareness between aboriginals and non-aboriginals; advocacy and agency that made space for marginalized voices; and creating healing communities of reflective solidarity.[15]

In 2008 Canada established a Truth and Reconciliation Commission (TRC), which currently hears the stories of survivors of the schools, identifies children who died or went missing, and negotiates reparations with individuals, families and communities. The United Church participates financially in such reparations. Years of conversation around native and Christian identity occurred in native Canadian "learning circles."

In 2009 GC39 commissioned a study of potential changes to the United Church's statement of formation in *The Manual*, its book of law, and to its crest. The working group was made up of three aboriginal (First Nations, Metis, and/or Inuit) and three non-aboriginal persons. They recommended adding to the official history of the denomination the 1986 apology and statements recognizing the attitude of cultural superiority inherent in the actions of Eurocentric Canadian Christians. The history notes that aboriginal congregations had been largely incorporated in the United Church through the Methodist Board of Home Missions without the congregations taking a part in the decision making process. The working group suggested a process through which these congregations could choose to sign the Basis of Union.

GC41 voted, with little resistance and much celebration, to change the denomination's crest and to modify the Introduction, Declaration, and Formation sections of *The Manual*. The crest now includes the Mohawk words "Akwe Nia'Tetewá:neren" ("all my relations") opposite the pre-existing Latin words *ut omnes unum sint* ("That all may be one"). The four colors of the medicine wheel—white, black, yellow, and red—have replaced the blue background upon which X, the Greek letter for Christ, is superimposed. These symbols recognize the contribution of the spirituality of the First Nations, Métis, and Inuit peoples to the United Church of Canada—especially the circle in which all people are equal and listen: to one another, to the land and to the four-legged creatures. The court was organized in circular

---

15. Legge, "Seeking 'Right Relations.'"

tables with tablecloths of the four colors. From an elevated level participants saw a giant medicine wheel, reminding them that indigenous spirituality involves, among other things, conversation in the search for wisdom. For people who consider theological reflection to be an embodied practice, this reimaging of the crest and reformation of the church documents constitutes a form of theological reflection. Furthermore, the configuration of the room contributed to the dialogical aspects of the deliberations during the Israel/Palestine discussion.

When the United Church apologized to its aboriginal congregations it entered conversations that even now have not been concluded. Yet the witness of 2012 reflects significant social change in the life of the church. The church's formative work, and the conversation, continues.[16]

The Emergence of Conflict Transformational Models of Social Witness

Beyond specific actions like those of GC41, something in the larger cultural milieu of social witness has shifted. A general recognition of the power of relationship inherent in conversation and collaboration has brought into the church methods of social witness that provide an alternative to confrontation. Such methods are reflected in the work of Rev. Tom Porter, J.D., and his colleagues at JustPeace (Boston University) where Porter integrates new methods of conflict transformation, including Appreciative Inquiry, interest-based mediation, and restorative justice, informed by his training in Navaho circle processes.[17]

For Porter, as for persons who adhere to confrontational social witness techniques, conflict is the basis for social change. However, conflict need not become hostile, nor should it be avoided; rather, rightly embraced, conflict, with collaboration and consensus, can yield permanent social transformation. These methods share the same eschatological aim as confrontational methods of social witness but their proponents believe they result in a more sustained social change.

- "Appreciative Inquiry" is one of a variety of strengths-based, positive reinforcement methods that emerged in human relations understanding at the end of the twentieth century. It belongs to that group of

16. The concerns voiced at GC41, especially around personnel policies, echoed those raised in Susan Beaver's unpublished article, "Right-ish Relations: Wesley in the United Church."

17. Porter, *The Spirit and Art of Conflict Transformation.*

techniques that promote change by underlining what individuals, families, and organizations are doing right, rather than focusing on their weaknesses or pathologies. It incorporates deep listening and recognition.

- "Interest-based mediation" is centered on the idea that each party in a dispute has genuine needs that should be recognized and satisfied in any settlement of the dispute. It focuses on "win-win" solutions.

- "Restorative justice," or victim-offender reconciliation, surfaces deep trauma. The victim faces the offender as a human being rather than as an object of violence. If offenders are capable of recognizing the harm they have done, forgiveness and reconciliation may occur.

These methods arise from western studies in human relations and are resonant with values and practices deep in aboriginal and global south cultures. The insights of conflict transformation and reconciliation are also acted upon by people from a variety of cultures who conceive of human beings with great empathy and who know how deep listening, recognizing needs, and responding to trauma reconciles their societies.

Appreciative Inquiry in El Salvador

The El Salvadoran liberation theologian and community organizer Jose Inocencio Alas Gomez, known as "Chencho" Alas incorporates Appreciative Inquiry and the spirituality of the Mayas into education for peace. As a young Roman Catholic priest, "Chencho" led Bible studies that formed the first "base Christian communities" in El Salvador, the embodiment of liberation theology with its "preferential option for the poor."[18] This helped peasants see how grossly unequal land distribution enabled the wealthy to keep them in poverty. As peasants experienced their God-given dignity and worth, they sought land reform.

Theological reflection was central to the growth of basic Christian communities and to sustaining Chencho's social witness. While attending a land reform gathering in 1977, he was kidnapped by death squads and tortured. Chencho "loved his enemy," believing they had something to learn from him. He survived the attack and continued to work on behalf of Latin Americans from exile in the U.S. After the revolution in 1992, he returned to El Salvador to practice peace building.

18. Tanenbaum Center for Religious Understanding; https://www.tanenbaum.org/programs/peace/peacemaker-awardees/jos%C3%A9-chencho-alas-el-saltabuvador.

Chencho announces his eschatological vision for peace: "Peace is the constant recreation of harmony between the body and soul, at the personal and community level, within an environment that is earthly, socially, economically, and politically good and beautiful."[19] He holds seminars in peace building in El Salvador and throughout Central America.

Over the years Chencho's theological methods changed, from those arising from liberation theology to those consistent with Appreciative Inquiry. Liberation theology begins with the problem, sin, moves to Bible study, and then determines what to do. In contrast, appreciative inquiry and the Mayas begin with the blessings that are already ours, culture, faith, skills, and the richness in creation. Indigenous people start with cosmology—the animals waking at dawn, the trees dancing in the wind, the meaning in the river, the sacred corn, all given by God. Mother earth is the foundation of the Maya sense of the sacred. So one begins with gratitude for mother earth.

> It is like the story of the anointing of Jesus. Some who were there indignantly started looking for the problem: 'Why this waste of expensive ointment by this woman?' Jesus reacted and told them: 'Leave her alone. What she has done for me is good work.' If you find the blessing first, you discover that she has come to anoint Jesus' body, just before his death that same week.[20]

As a western Christian, he now starts his theology and his Bible study with the first two chapters of Genesis, the original blessing. "I have a Hegelian method in Bible study. The thesis: creation is a rich blessing of which we are one part. The antithesis is sin, and the synthesis begins with Abraham."[21]

He has adapted Appreciative Inquiry for particular use in communities in Latin America. "We teach them to discover the *vivencias*—powerful moments in life when values are formed, when you are inspired to do good for others. We have an Appreciative Inquiry methodology that begins in gratitude and helps the participants identify those moments when those values were formed."[22]

The curriculum that launches from this theological foundation covers seven themes: earth and ecology; self-and-other richness, capacity, and beauty; gender; human rights and obligations; conflict transformation and reconciliation; economics; and politics.

---

19. The quotation here is from http://discover-peace.org/Projects.html.

20. Alas, conversation, October 22, 2012.

21. Ibid.

22. Ibid.

Interest-Based Mediation in the Democratic Republic of Congo

Bishop Ntambo, whose Congressional witness began this chapter, was elected to the episcopacy at the same time as the Mobutu regime was overthrown by Laurent Desire Kabila who was militarily backed by Rwanda. When the relationship between Kabila and Rwanda deteriorated in 1998, Rwanda invaded the DRC and war eventually terrorized two-thirds of the country. As the Congolese army could not be trusted to defend the country's inhabitants, the government encouraged the reemergence of Mayi-Mayi militias. The plan backfired, and the Mayi-Mayi, too, turned on civilians. The formal peace process had only included armed political groups, not the Mayi-Mayi. As combatants retreated after the peace accords of 2002, large portions of the countryside remained under Mayi-Mayi control.

In September, 2004, in preparation for the country's first democratic election, the government sought to engage the Mayi-Mayi in peace negotiations, open the roads they controlled, and reintegrate them into Congolese civilian or military society. After government emissaries were killed attempting to negotiate with local war lords, officials turned to Bishop Ntambo to organize a peace conference with government leaders, religious leaders of all faiths, traditional chiefs, military and civic leaders, and the warlords. By gathering these people in Kamina, the episcopal center, this town of 100,000, which had previously held the war at its doorstep, was put at risk. The religious leaders believed that God provided for the conference and guided it. This conviction combined with the seriousness of the threat, called forth unusual courage from ordinary women, men, and children.

These methods depended upon indigenous customs: the population's belief in the spiritual authority of the religious leaders and an appeal by kin of the warlords to participate. The religious leaders dignified the warlords by using military titles to which they were accustomed and respecting rituals for eating that were appropriate to traditional chiefs.

The most feared warlord, Chinja-Chinja, did not originally respond to the invitation, and the leaders determined that the conference could not succeed without him. Rev. Boniface Kabongo, the United Methodist District Superintendent in Kamina, who attended elementary school with Chinja-Chinja, rode by motorbike over several hundred kilometers of dirt trails to appeal to Chinja-Chinja to participate. His approach combined a display of his own courage, respect for the Mayi-Mayi, and articulating Chinja-Chinja's self-interest.

As Rev. Kabongo worked his way through the military barriers protecting the warlord, he was arrested by the militia guards and he thought he would be killed. Then he was recognized by Chinja-Chinja's brother as one from their original village and allowed to proceed. But first he was required to declare the names of his wife, children, extended family, and people in his current village, pledging them as collateral for the safety of Chinja-Chinja: "If something happens to Chinja-Chinja, you and your family will be killed and your village will be burnt."

In the actual conversation in which he persuaded Chinja-Chinja to attend the conference, Rev. Kabongo appealed to the warlord's self-regard: "everyone is waiting for you—government leaders, religious leaders, traditional chiefs." This argument reduced the warlord's resistance. Then Rev. Kabongo engaged Chinja-Chinja's self-interest: "You have been fighting for all of these years with no salary. This is your chance to ask the government to pay you for your efforts."[23]

The success of the conference also depended upon methods consistent with interest-based mediation—"all the methods of diplomacy," according to Bishop Ntambo. Bishop Ntambo had credibility with the various participants because he had built relationships—had conversations—with all segments of society.

> You know, there were steps to come to that successful meeting. One was good relationships. I have very good relationship with governor and all his staff. Very good relationship with military. Good trusted by the sides of enemies of opposition. So by good relationship I was open to everybody. I was loyal to everybody. And I didn't play games. It was truth from the beginning until the end.[24]

Another key component was empathy and a willingness to hear grievances on all sides.

> I was honest with them, and I showed love and concern and understanding when they were reporting to me. I became a private advisor, it means most of the meeting was taken one side. Not in public. You call like, the chief, you stay with them, you talk, discuss, give direction. You call the Mayi-Mayi people, stay with them, talk, discuss. I go to the governor, I talk, discuss. You can hear why this one is angry, this one why they are angry, and you don't report everything to them. You need to choose what to report to them that can bring the reconciliation.[25]

23. Interview with Rev. Boniface Kabongo conducted under the auspices of my research project, "Where's the Peace to Keep?" January 11, 2008.

24. Direct quotations from interview with Bishop Ntambo conducted under the auspices of my research project.

25. Ibid.

Bishop Ntambo reflects on his own role.

> A mediator. That was my role. Doing mediation between. So that was tough. And most of the meeting was at night. You need to bring them together at night. And when we get to the big open session, most of the decisions were already taken, and then it was just approval of things. Because, my strategy, you can't allow this open discussion among the enemies in confrontation in a big open session, like a plenary. . . . They conflict and once they made decision it's very hard to bring them, very hard. So we use small small small groups for discussion.[26]

Finally, the Bishop brought the warring parties together by appealing to their common interest and aim—the peace and safety of the country.[27] The conference succeeded, the warlords traded their weapons for bicycles, and the roads were opened for economic activity and elections.

Bishop Ntambo's theology supporting this social witness is one of love in which he emulates Jesus who lays down his life for his friends.

> You may have strategies, you may have skill and wisdom. . . . You need someone you meet to refer as example. . . . Whatever I share with you, it is the love to my people . . . for me that love reached the high rank when I looked at Jesus. And not fanaticism, not to please people . . . or how to gain confidence or money, without the treasures. When I look at the cross and see, why did he die? Just he wanted to save human being, he didn't account suffering, he didn't account the loss of his own dignity, the goal was clear to him: to serve human beings as a savior. When you look at Martin Luther King, Jr., that extremism, is that fanaticism? No. If I don't accomplish, I can't sleep, I can't eat . . . and when people look at you and found such kind of passion and love to them . . . they will accept, they will follow you, they will commit to do whatever you need. And this is what happened to Kamina.[28]

In this social witness, a combination of personal and communal courage, borne out of love, combined with tactics familiar in mediation, provided a turning point for peace.

26. Ibid.

27. "Where's the Peace to Keep?," Indianapolis, Indiana, May 17, 2007; interpretation further corroborated in interviews with the Tanenbaum Center for Interreligious Understanding, New York, New York, November 10–11, 2010, and May 10, 2011.

28. From interview with Bishop Ntambo, per note 24.

Truth Commissions

Truth commissions originally emerged in Uganda and have been used in Bolivia, Argentina, Uruguay, Chile, El Salvador, Chad, and Zimbabwe.[29] They became famous when Archbishop Desmond Tutu led the South African Truth and Reconciliation Commission after the apartheid government relinquished power in 1993. The South African commission heard graphic testimony concerning human rights violations, paved the way for the granting of amnesty, and determined reparations. Archbishop Tutu states the eschatological aim of the South African commission:

> Having looked the beast of the past in the eye, having asked and received forgiveness and having made amends, let us shut the door on the past—not in order to forget it but in order not to allow it to imprison us. Let us move into the glorious future of a new kind of society where people count, not because of biological irrelevancies or other extraneous attributes, but because they are persons of infinite worth created in the image of God.[30]

The truth and reconciliation commission (TRC), a form of restorative justice, has primarily been used by societies with histories of gross violations of human rights during their transitions to democracy. In contrast, Canada's TRC[31] is the first to occur where democracy is well established. Kim Pamela Stanton argues that TRC is a form of public inquiry that has been used effectively in other situations in Canada, such as the Mackenzie Valley Pipeline Inquiry (the Berger Inquiry). By relating it to other forms of public inquiry, she hopes the method will be more widely used.

TRCs differ from usual public inquiries in their focus on restorative justice. They are predicated on "their symbolic acknowledgment of historic injustices, and their explicit 'social function' to educate the public about those injustices in order to prevent their reoccurrence."[32] Canada's TRC was established in the context of the failure of other legal systems—criminal prosecution, civil litigation, *and* alternative dispute resolution—to resolve the backlog of lawsuits resulting from harm caused by the residential schools. After many failed attempts to deal with such harm, indigenous

---

29. Stanton, "Truth Commissions and Public Inquiries," 28. Online: https://tspace. library.utoronto.ca/bitstream/1807/24886/1/Stanton_Kim_P_201006_SJD_thesis.pdf.

30. Truth and Reconciliation Commission of South Africa: The TRC Report, Summary and Guide to Contents; online: http://www.justice.gov.za/trc/report/index.htm.

31. Truth and Reconciliation Commission of Canada: http://www.trc.ca/websites/trcinstitution/index.php?p=26.

32. Stanton, "Truth Commissions and Public Inquiries," ii.

leaders sought a TRC to achieve the goals of "symbolism, a focus on victims, public education, and the goal of reconciliation."[33]

The Canadian TRC is not finished, but the effect on public education is already apparent. Survivors of residential schools who were encouraged to tell their stories to the TRC have begun to tell their stories elsewhere.

On October 21, 2012 Metropolitan United Church of Canada in Toronto introduced the changes made at GC41 to the United Church crest and the Basis of Union. Rev. Andrew Wesley, an Anglican priest and counselor at the Toronto Council Fire Native Centre, preached on "The Power of Forgiveness." He told of his experience during ten years in the residential schools beginning at from age six or seven.

Abuse initiated the experience. He had been taken from his home in rural, Northern Ontario, where aboriginal ways were practiced, to a school sixteen hours away where he was fed unfamiliar food. He vomited. A teacher beat him for retching and required him to lick the vomit off the floor. It happened twice. At the school, he says, he learned "four demons: shame, humiliation, dehumanization and degradation."

As an adult he met the now elderly woman who had beat him and saw her hands, now wizened with arthritis. He said to her, "Do you remember me?" She did. "I forgive you," he said.

Practicing forgiveness is part of indigenous and Christian spiritualities and grounds Rev. Wesley's life. Forgiveness is personal; it cannot be coerced. Its primary effect is on the *wounded*. "From my perspective and understanding, *'forgiveness'* empowers the wounded above and beyond the victimizer. Forgiveness does not make a person holy, nor does it elevate the person in the divine sense. Forgiveness does not further humiliate or hurt the wounded. Rather it makes the wounded strong through his/her courageous act of forgiving."[34]

Rev. Wesley reminds us that indigenous Canadians, like the Mayas, turned first to creation as the source of the sacred and saw themselves as one component of creation.

> Mother Earth plays the most important role in Creation, for without the soil and water there would be no plant realm. Without the plants there would be no animal realm, and without soil, water, plants and animals, there would be no human. Within this belief system, human is understood to be the least essential

33. Ibid., 81.

34. Andrew Wesley: http://www.arapacisinitiative.org/en/forgiveness-and-reconciliation/264-rev-andrew-wesley.

and the most dependent. Thus, human is not the master of creation, but a humble servant to the creation.[35]

Colonization, and a version of Christianity that put the human first, destroyed this sensibility. The willful destruction of indigenous spirituality by Christians in Canada opened the door for Native Canadian struggles with disease, addiction, and violence—all virtually unknown in Native communities.

Forgiveness is rooted in the First Nations' creation story and in the everyday practice of hunting and gathering. The hunter "asked the animal spirit and the Creator for forgiveness for the life he must take. After he makes his kill, he prays and makes an offering to the Creator and the spirit."

Rev. Wesley further understands his ability to forgive his abuser as a gift of God. "If it wasn't for the grace of God in my life, I might still be living with anger. . . . Forgiveness is not simply the letting go of resentment, but rather it is spiritual awakening of the soul to new vision and remembering the ancient knowledge and understanding of the Creator."[36]

Such forgiveness is an act of victim-offender reconciliation and requires empathy for the offender.

> In order to forgive, one must seriously consider and understand the value of other people. One must be willing to accept the invitation to go and listen and hear the offender's story, if an opportunity should present itself. One must be go with a truly open heart, and not with a preconceived idea that the other party will offer an apology or ask for forgiveness. Forgiveness is a personal act that begins with love, compassion and truth. And love is the ultimate and the highest goal to which human can aspire. One's salvation is through love. Therefore, love is stronger than hate and forgiveness is stronger than revenge.[37]

Only a small part of Rev. Wesley's spiritual witness consists of telling settler Canadians about his experience in residential schools. He works primarily among aboriginal persons. And on Saturdays Rev. Wesley walks streets of Toronto, listening to homeless people talk about their demons.

Postcolonial Social Witness and Mission

Questions of partnership and conversation in mission weigh heavily on the agenda of right relations between colonial settlers and indigenous persons

35. Ibid.
36. Ibid.
37. Ibid.

and between the global south and north. World Christianity has been created because of mission. For some, mission has been a central part of Christian social witness. Famously, those with an active interest in mission use the phrase, "The church does not have a mission; rather, God's mission has a church." For some, mission has been a handmaiden of the military, the government, and colonial powers; indeed, the word "mission" is so tainted it should be abandoned. For others, mission, despite human error in enacting it, has contributed to human flourishing in desperate situations, such as building enduring institutions providing education, medical services, and relief in war zones. These institutions have often provided leadership development for indigenous persons. Appropriate partnership depends upon ongoing, long term, honest conversations as we grow spiritually with one another.

Social Witness and Conversation in Summary

These powerful examples demonstrate that Christian social witness is an organic, improvised process that responds to a given context. Christian social witness has an eschatological vision toward which it seeks social change toward shalom—its "external good"—but the methods differ from setting to setting. Some efforts may be confrontational, heightening the tension where there are differences, and others collaborative, seeking common ground among persons at odds with one another. Just as these methods emerged from local cultures, social witnesses may occur through indigenous methods appropriate to the culture in which witness occurs.

Social witness calls upon theological resources from the Christian tradition, even while it critiques and challenges other aspects of Christian theology. In indigenous contexts it draws upon local practices shedding new light on Christian theology and practice. The examples here suggest that the social witness of persons in indigenous communities or the global south does not begin with sin but with creation, blessing, gratitude, and love. People in the dominant culture can learn from these foundational perspectives.

Regardless of the method, social witness honestly confronts sin, evil, folly, and trauma and the inhumanity of humans toward one another. Yet, sin is not just systemic; for that reason, as a feminist, Wesleyan theologian I distinguish between sin as individual wrong, and evil as systemic exploitation with a life of its own. Those who have known bloodshed have a deeper knowledge of the horrors of sin and evil than we who have not.[38] Those who have known the sin and evil of bloodshed may experience trauma, or the human capacity to survive horrific violation by dissociating from it. And

38. Couture, "The Blood that Tells (Knows) the Truth."

one of the sad realities is that trauma, unhealed, and may lead to further victimization, sin, and perpetuation of evil. Those who benefit from ignoring the sin and evil perpetrated by their religious organizations, communities or nations, are guilty of what Dietrich Bonhoeffer called "folly," or blindness to the way that we acquiesce to wrongdoing.[39]

Christian social witness needs a strong and nuanced understanding of sin, evil, trauma, and folly. However, the witnesses cited here, all of whom have offered social witness where bloodshed is known, teach the wisdom that sin does not begin the story. Rather, the knowledge of our rootedness in creation, blessing, gratitude, and love strengthens those who have been subject to inhumanity and those who are ashamed because their cultures have perpetrated it.

Social witness always engages the "internal good" of spiritual formation. For the witnesses cited here, spiritual formation is relational—it depends upon a series of conversations within a wide spectrum of society, those who are exploited and those with relatively more power. Conversation contributes to spiritual witness in many ways—in theological reflection, in Bible study, in determining action. In these stories, spiritual formation cultivates human virtue—courage, love, and absolute dependence on God. These stories free social witnesses from the burden of perfection, understood as perfectionism. However, they invite social witnesses to be free for perfection, understood in the Wesleyan way: "being made perfect in love" and "growing in the image and likeness of God."

Wesleyan perfection, being made perfect in love, is a relational process. While theological reflection is important to the self-expression of the social witnesses quoted here, it is not the only thing that inspires them. While their theologies may undergird their courage, they are also personally sustained by relationships within their communities that reflect the Great Spirit and Christ in their midst—relationships with mother earth, with four-legged creatures, with human beings who are not perfect but are open to change. They are buoyed, in part, by human conversation. I, as one who has no firsthand experience of bloodshed, hear their witness with humility and inspiration for the part I play as a writer and scholar/activist in partnership with them.

Practical Implications for Ministry

We can focus our conversation on four kinds of social witness: from one part of the ecclesia to another, not defined by geography; between church partners

39. See Couture., *Child Poverty*, 128–44.

of the global south and the global north; from the church of the global south to its own society; and from the church of the global south, in partnership with the global north, to North Atlantic governments and societies.

Intra-ecclesial Social Witness

The church needs social witness within itself. Different sides of the church need to bear witness within the church, to call it to repentance over ways it contributes to exploitation; in some cases, to break through the folly of its ignorance, and in all cases, to uphold the dignity and self-determination of suffering, vulnerable people. It calls for trust-building, especially between indigenous and settler descendants.

Social Witness as Partnership between Global South and North

Despite the negative North American involvement in El Salvador and the DRC, Chencho Alas and Bishop Ntambo believe that partnership in social witness requires that persons from the global north travel to the global south. (Travel between dominant societies and communities of indigenous Canadians is more cautious, as so much engagement in indigenous communities in Canada has been exploitive.) Travel, under the guidance of people from the global south, can provide a foundation for a habitus of ongoing, committed relationship. Within the context of conversation in this relationship, communities can sort out issues concerning money, self-determination, support for projects, appropriate use of local stories, the logic of different cultures, and practices from southern cultures that commend themselves in the global north.

Witness of the Church in the Global South to Global South Society

Bishop Ntambo and Chencho Alas lead peace-building actions of social witness to their society. For example, in El Salvador this witness includes resistance to the exploitation of the environment; in DRC it includes the transparent financing of projects and challenging the system of commissions and kickbacks. Projects in the church serve as models for other sectors of society—for example, agricultural training developed by the church was adopted at the Kamina Military Base.

Witness of the Church of the Global South to North Atlantic Governments

Social transformation requires that the global south speaks to power. War is a mischievous devil who knows the power of doing its work in inconvenient times—during the opening weeks of school, during the United States political conventions, after GC41 when all national staff of the United Church of Canada take a needed vacation, and when Canadian Parliament is recessed. To enable the Congolese delegation to speak to North American governments, the Congolese drew upon long-established relations with the United Methodist Board of Church and Society and the Churches Center for the United Nations. Furthermore, the United Church of Canada and its partner KAIROS expended great energy making conversations possible. The newly elected United Church Moderator, Rev. Gary Paterson, received his first ecumenical visitor, Bishop Ntambo, and heard Ntambo's plea for the assistance of the United Church as a partner in peace.

This particular social witness could be mapped as a web of conversations, some in the context of long term relationships, some in newly forming relationships, some in church and some in politics, toward the eschatological purposes of peace, justice, virtue, and the realm of God.

A Caution about Conversation and Social Witness

Conversation has long been part of Christian social witness and is, more than ever, essential to it. Conversation has roots in the organic communities out of which social witness arises, whether the methods are confrontational or collaborative. However, conversation in and of itself is not social witness—rather, it is a means that seeks an end in the eschatological vision of "shalom."

Questions for Discussion

1. How do you describe the eschatological vision toward which social change should aim?

2. For what internal and external richness and blessings do you give gratitude?

3. What are the moments in your life when values solidified allowing you to take risks for people who are more vulnerable than you?

4. When have you felt heard, and when have you listened and heard something new?

5. Who are the people in your life from whose differences you have learned?

Further Reading

Ayres, Jennifer R. *Waiting for a Glacier to Move: Practicing Christian Social Witness.* Princeton Theological Monograph Series 170. Eugene, OR: Pickwick, 2011.

Birch, Bruce C. *What Does the Lord Require?: The Old Testament Call to Social Witness.* Philadelphia: Westminster, 1985.

Coy, Patrick G. *A Revolution of the Heart: Essays on the Catholic Worker.* Philadelphia: Temple University Press, 1988.

Pollard, Alton B. *Mysticism and Social Change: The Social Witness of Howard Thurman.* Martin Luther King, Jr Memorial Studies in Religion, Culture, and Social Development. New York: Lang, 1992.

Porter, Thomas W. *The Spirit and Art of Conflict Transformation: Creating a Culture of Justpeace.* Nashville: Upper Room, 2010.

Thurman, Howard. *The Creative Encounter: An Interpretation of Religion and the Social Witness.* New York: Harper, 1954.

Townes, Emilie Maureen. *In a Blaze of Glory: Womanist Spirituality as Social Witness.* Nashville: Abingdon, 1995.

Young, Michael P. *Bearing Witness against Sin: The Evangelical Birth of the American Social Movement.* Chicago: University of Chicago Press, 2006.

11

The Relationship
with Other Religions as Conversation

Donald M. Mackenzie

🎇 Interfaith dialogue can move us from a place of polite tolerance to deeper, more promising places of mutual understanding, appreciation, and thanksgiving. When this occurs, it usually reflects a willingness to become vulnerable in order to listen more effectively to the experience of those whose lives are sustained by other religious traditions while being willing to name what we experience as the essential truths that sustain us in our own religious tradition. This kind of listening and honest self-reflection with those of another religion can be extremely difficult. Many of us would much rather assume that our religious experience has little to gain from conversation with others, but as the poet Yehuda Amichai has said, "From the place where we are right, flowers will never grow in the spring."[1]

One fundamental assumption of this chapter, therefore, is that we discover the truth through relationships with others—all others, not simply those from our own religious tradition. At the same time, there is significant truth residing in the relationships themselves. Interfaith conversation at its best involves more than sharing information. It involves sharing ourselves. Most of the truths we try to proclaim are temporal while our relationships have a more eternal quality. Today we have problems and questions that will be gone tomorrow, but in a profound theological sense we will always have each other.

The business of identifying, defining, and protecting absolutes has, for many thousands of years, been a source of self-assurance and a testimony

---

1. "The Place Where We Are Right," quoted in Hiles and Hiles, eds., *An Almanac for the Soul*, 121.

to human power and stature. Religious people, with their texts and traditions, grow up within this mind-set. Because of this, religious communities often become very good at boundary management, religious education, self-assertion, self-defense, and institution-maintaining leadership. These practices often make it difficult for us to support one common purpose that I believe is fundamental to all major world religions—healing relationships, or what is commonly called "reconciliation."

In this chapter, I assume that interfaith dialogue seeks to reclaim the impulse toward reconciliation within all major world religions. It seeks to release us from a human and institutional tendency to focus on self-maintenance in a way that makes the relation-healing substance of our faith once again accessible. I speak about this out of my own experience of rediscovering this healing substance in my own faith through interfaith dialogue. And I believe that my experience has something to contribute to the substance of this book.

In this chapter, I do not want to describe theories or theologies of interfaith dialogue, or outline models for relating the world's religions. There are many good texts, by scholars such as John Hick, David Ray Griffin, and David Heim that wade into these deep waters.[2] Rather, I want to provide some idea of where we are, currently, as Christian people in relation to interfaith dialogue, and demonstrate the relevance of interfaith dialogue to the concept of conversation that is being promoted as a new understanding of ministry in this book. In this process, I will focus on the practices that my two interfaith partners and I have developed over the twelve years we have been working together. Following that I will identify key principles pertaining specifically to conversations that have become a part of the ministry and message of the "Interfaith Amigos," the name that has been given to our interfaith team. Then, I will outline the importance of conversation in interfaith dialogue highlighting aspects and dimensions of interfaith dialogue that contribute to the meaning of the term "conversation" as it is used in this book. I will end with a few cautions for those who pursue interfaith conversations.

Interfaith Dialogue: Where Have We Been?

Throughout the ages, people have looked with curiosity over the fences that separate cultures and religions. Trying to understand what other people believe, what gives other people purpose and meaning in life, is as old as meaning itself. Although originally there may have been some motivation to understand how enemies thought in order to provide intelligence

2. See for instance, Griffin, *Deep Religious Pluralism*; Heim, *Salvations*; Hick, *A Christian Theology of Religions*.

for military strategies, there has also been the hope that coming to a better understanding between and among peoples and nations could actually be a deterrent to conflict, and perhaps even war. The same hope has been true between and among people of different religions.

In religious experience, however, there is a deeper undercurrent than the desire to simply avoid conflict. The word "religion" derives in part from the word "religare," which translates "to bind fast" or to be under obligation toward another. In other words, this over-used word expresses a positive motivation to *connect* and to be bound together in relationship. Different religions vary (and different groups within religions vary), of course, with regard to this obligation to others, especially when these others belong to other religions. While many Christians have tried to be open to the experience of others, there has been a consistent conviction among most that the way of Jesus, the anointed one of God, is really the only way. While this conviction is changing for some,[3] it needs to be named. Although as Christians, we hear biblical texts and theological voices that echo this "one way" mentality, the truth is that everyone, no matter the religion or worldview, has a strong tendency to believe that her or his way is really the only way. One of the most malignant forms of this idea is reflected in the long history of the Christian supersessionist repudiation of Judaism. More recently, in today's global context, many Christians apply the "one way" doctrine to Islam.

Without wading into particulars, I want to emphasize two results of this way of thinking for us as Christians. First, this way of thinking, when dominant, breaks relationships before they can start. It leads to a deep-down belief that religions are really incommensurate and cannot learn from one another at the most profound levels. Second, this way of thinking leaves Christian people who are interested in interfaith dialogue feeling trapped by doctrine, by institutional control and a deep uncertainty about how to proceed. This feeling of being imprisoned by some of the teachings and traditions of the church reflects part of the need for conversation that is the substance of this book.

We now know, of course, that there are other forces, or what Christians sometimes call "principalities and powers" that seem to have a vested interest in keeping all religious people bound to the "one way" doctrine. Recent approaches to interfaith dialogue, especially among Protestant Christians, take into account the many ways that these forces function to inhibit conversation by adding economic and political ideologies and agendas into the

---

3. A poll taken by PBS and *U.S. News and World Report* in 2002 showed that of Christians, only 17 percent said that they felt that Christianity is the only way. 78 percent did not. The poll was reported in *The Christian Century* (May 8–15, 2002) and reported in Borg, *The Heart of Christianity*, 20.

mix. The film *Water* illustrates this kind of awareness beautifully. It focuses on what it is like to be a widow in India. At one poignant moment in the film, people are talking about why, in India, widows are beggars or prostitutes or both. One person says, "It is about our religion." Another says, "It is not about religion. It is about money disguised as religion."[4] The social and cultural authority granted to religion gives it the power to mask other agendas. As people begin to consider the substance of religion alongside the practices of religious institutions, and the ways that religions are sometimes used to further non-religious agendas, they recognize inconsistencies and realize more fully the need to get beyond "one way" doctrines, and thus the dire need for genuine interfaith dialogue.

Interfaith Dialogue Today

Defining "Interfaith Dialogue"

The phrase "interfaith dialogue" is familiar. To many people, however, it suggests a polite, tolerant, but often superficial exchange between two or more peoples of different religious and spiritual traditions. "Dialogue" is a slightly different word from "conversation," and it suggests a particular *kind* of conversation with a unique goal. This goal is not simply tolerance or respectful co-existence, but overcoming the barriers that separate us. In interfaith dialogue, this means overcoming the *religious* barriers that separate us.

In my experience, the best way to teach and learn the kind of conversation we call "interfaith dialogue" is through telling my own story, and then extrapolating principles and cautions from my living "case study." With those ends in mind, I now invite the reader into my interfaith story.

My Involvement in Interfaith Dialogue

In 1999, Rabbi Ted Falcon (affectionately known as "Rabbi Ted") and I were members of the Seattle Jewish-Christian Dialogue, an organized conversation among rabbis and ministers. This organization had a history dating back to a weekly television program called "Challenge," hosted by Fr. William Treacy and Rabbi Raphael Levine. Rabbi Levine began the program in 1960 to address the negative rhetoric in the public arena at that time about the possibility of a Roman Catholic becoming president of the United

---

4. *Water*, directed by Deepa Mehta and written by Anurage Kashyap, 2005.

States. The television program lasted for fourteen years. It created a willing culture for interfaith exploration in Seattle.

When the terrorist attack on the World Trade Center occurred, Rabbi Ted called Imam Jamal Rahman and invited him to participate in Shabbat worship that following Friday. Rabbi Ted wanted his congregation to hear a different story concerning Islam from the one so many of the newspapers and television stations were communicating. About six months following 9/11 Rabbi Ted called me to ask me if I would participate in an event to mark the first anniversary of the tragedy. I agreed and we held the event at my church, University Congregational United Church of Christ in Seattle.

As we were debriefing the program, the three of us looked at each other and said, "We can't stop now." We had no idea what that might mean except that we shared a conviction that overcoming the barriers that have historically separated our traditions might lead to more cooperation between us, so that we could effectively address some of the social and moral issues facing our community and our world. As we discussed these issues, we found that we were in significant agreement regarding three broad, shared hopes for our community and the world, tethered in different ways to our respective religious traditions: full access to all human and civil rights for everyone, the end to war and violence, and care for the earth.

We began by meeting weekly in order to get to know each other. Soon, we began to present programs on what we were learning about interfaith dialogue and about each other's traditions, institutions, and teachings. We journeyed to the Middle East together in November of 2005, and organized a weekly radio program from July of 2006 to July of 2007. As we continued our meetings we realized that the experiences we were having could be valuable to others and decided to write a book. The book was published in June of 2009, and we have been on the road much of the time since then presenting programs in the United States, the Middle East and Japan.[5]

Early Discoveries

At the beginning of our work together, we asked ourselves why it was that interfaith dialogue, while informative, was not leading us to deeper understandings of each other, and even to reconciliation. In spite of many attempts to learn about each other's traditions, the walls separating our

---

5. The first book we published is called *Getting to the Heart of Interfaith: The Eye-Opening, Hope-Filled Friendship of a Pastor, a Rabbi and a Sheikh*. We published a second book two years later titled *Religion Gone Astray: What We Found at the Heart of Interfaith*.

traditions seemed as high as ever. In spite of this, we shared an intuition that if we could get to know each other, if we could develop the sort of trust that comes not just with a strong professional association but with genuine friendship, we might be able to break through those walls. In other words, we felt that interfaith dialogue had to be built on and grow out of genuine dialogue regarding every aspect of our lives—family concerns, professional struggles and aspirations, interests and hobbies, and so on. We needed to get into one another's larger worlds in order to understand the ways that those worlds were shaped by religious desires and hopes. Although this was not always easy (you cannot force friendship), we felt that if we could at least *work at* friendship in this way, we might be able to get to a place where true interfaith conversations would emerge. Hopefully, reconciliation and a transformation of our ability to cooperate on the difficult moral issues we face as a world today would follow.

And so, we decided that our weekly meetings would have no specific agenda beyond conversation. We did not meet to compare notes about our traditions, nor did we meet to argue points of view. As time went by, each of us painted a deeper and more complex picture of our lives and made it available to the others. At the same time, we each began to discover ways our lives are similar, yet distinct from each other. These similarities and differences were often due to cultural and religious similarities and differences, and so we naturally began to discuss these powerful influences on our lives.

As we met, we knew that we were paving new ground, and though we felt deeply supported by the substance of our traditions, we were moving ahead without many models to show us the way. For unknown reasons, we decided that we had developed adequate trust and friendship to begin to re-perform elements of our conversations in public as a way to invite others into the conversation with us. And so we began to present interfaith programs and interfaith worship and as we did so, we began to encounter and understand new levels and aspects of each of our traditions. As we met and told our stories in private and in public, and led worship together, we realized that, if interfaith dialogue is to work, it is crucial to encounter at the deepest possible levels *the relationship between how we hold and are healed by our religions and how we understand and tell the stories of our lives.*

In November of 2005, we took a trip to the Middle East. About forty-five Christians and Jews went with us to see and feel a place held to be sacred by all three of our traditions. By visiting sacred sites, by reflecting on their different religious meanings and their importance to our own life stories, broader, common ground began to emerge for the "Interfaith Amigos." During this trip, we became serious about writing a book.

In that book, we recount one of the deepest experiences we shared on that trip. I tell this story only to provide one example of the kinds of difficult and ongoing conversations that exist at the intersection between our religious commitments and our life stories. This conversation began for us at the moment we passed through the barrier wall that separates Israel from the Palestinian Territories. It was a powerful experience for each of us, but in very different ways. Later, as we were co-writing the book, Jamal wrote in his account that he experienced the wall as repressive. When Ted read this, he was quiet for a moment and then he said, "If that is in the book, then I can't be in the book." In that moment, each of us knew that we had reached that place where interfaith dialogue has often been blocked. Each of us suspected that our work might have come to an end. But because we had come to know each other, it became possible for us to ask the question, "What is the opportunity in this problem? Are there other possible positive outcomes of this crisis?"

Those questions opened a door for us. That door led to a place that kept us connected—not through our ideas and doctrines, but through our commitment to relationship and to the place where healing and reconciliation might begin. Inside that door lay two important questions: "What does it feel like to be Ted; what does it feel like to be Jamal?" These are not therapeutic questions or questions pointing to the need to "fix" one another. They are communicational questions pointing to the need for empathy and role-taking (getting into each other's shoes). Only through this kind of role-taking can we enter places that, while completely different from the perspective of lived experiences, are nonetheless profoundly similar from the perspective of "affect" or the way one's life feels.

Ted and I knew that Jamal, in his statement, was not trying to be provocative or belligerent. He was describing something he had seen and felt. Jamal and I knew that Ted would not actually disagree with the substance of Jamal's statement. So why had Ted said what he did? Ted said that Jamal's statement had felt like an attack on Israel and, as Ted explained, an attack on Israel felt like an attack on Ted. Further, without more comment and reflection, Ted felt anxious he would be misunderstood by the Jewish community if he acknowledged Jamal's perspective. Jamal and I listened carefully to what Ted had to say and then Jamal was able to further explain his statement. He told us that he felt that, although Israel was a tiny entity in the midst of the Arab world, it was an entity with a mighty military machine aided by the resources of the Pentagon of the United States. As Ted listened, he was able then to put into words his different view. He told us that Israel was that tiny entity to be sure and that it is surrounded by a land mass 640 times the area of Israel, a mass that includes all of the Middle East, most of North Africa and the countries east of the Middle East including Kazakstan, Afghanistan, and Pakistan. And regardless of the origins of the conflict, the message of the Islamic world seems to be that Israel must be destroyed. Through the course of that conversation, we three began to get a deeper sense of how it felt to be Ted and a deeper sense of how it felt to be Jamal. Although motivated by very different histories and lived experiences, both felt threatened. Both experienced fear—of another religious and ethnic group, and of what would happen if they broke ranks from their own religious community. We took a deep breath and realized that we had reached a new place, and that it was likely that there would be many other similar places as we continued on our journey.

This, then, is the broad narrative framework for the principles I will outline below. Meaningful conversation between strangers is extremely difficult if not impossible. Clues might arise in an exchange between strangers that could lead to a meaningful conversation, but without getting to know each other, conversations that have traditionally characterized attempts to go deeper in interfaith dialogue, conversations concerning particular beliefs and practices, are likely to end in modest forms of knowledge and appreciation only. A certain level of trust that comes through that vulnerable willingness to tell our stories, our fears and our hopes, can help us, over time, to reach a place where conversations of substance can really happen, and where we can find the resources to *stay in conversation*, in spite of radically different experiences and perspectives.

Stages of Interfaith Dialogue

In our first book, *Getting to the Heart of Interfaith: The Eye-Opening, Hope-Filled Friendship of a Pastor, a Rabbi and a Sheikh*,[6] we named five stages of interfaith dialogue that we had found to be essential to a meaningful and substantive conversation concerning our traditions, their differences, and their similarities.[7] These stages, I believe, are relevant to the business of thinking more clearly about conversation as a root metaphor for ministry.

Stage One: Moving Beyond Separation and Suspicion. The first stage requires us to "get to know the other" so that we experience ourselves as in a relationship, rather than as separate entities. In a relationship, suspicion is less likely to take over. We are more prone to give one another "the benefit of

6. Since our first book Jamal has assumed the title "Imam," which means prayer leader. The title "Sheikh" which means elder, has political implications that for some were confusing.

7. Mackenzie, Falcon, and Rahman, *Getting to the Heart of Interfaith*, 8ff.

the doubt." The story of our near impasse as we discussed the wall separating Israel and Palestine is a good illustration of how important the experience of relationship can be for staying engaged and open to one another. A real commitment to staying in relationship helped us to move beyond that crisis into a deeper place.

Stage Two: Inquiring More Deeply. The second stage involves learning to identify the core teachings of our religious traditions. My interfaith partners and I distinguish "core teaching," "core values," and "core beliefs." A core teaching is something so central to the life, ministry, and message of the founder of a tradition that it must be understood to be a yardstick by which everything else in the texts and practices of that tradition can be measured. Core values such as cooperation, forgiveness, reconciliation and justice emanate from these teachings. Core beliefs focus on particulars that claim to support the substance of a tradition but may vary more widely in their interpretation and application. We also commonly use a fourth category designated by the word "faith." Faith designates our daily, "on the ground" way of making sense out of our religious experience. Faith is deeply informed and shaped by our spiritual growth and maturity, our religious identity, and our level of awareness of core teachings, values and beliefs within our religious tradition.

For instance, in our interfaith conversations, we have identified a core teaching of Judaism (ascribed to Moses in Deuteronomy 6:4) as Oneness (monotheism in its broadest and deepest sense), the teaching that there is only One and we are all a part of the One. At the level of one's daily experience of faith, this teaching conspires to make it difficult to distinguish between people and God, (loving God and loving neighbor) since Oneness is all-pervasive. Among other places, this Oneness rests at the heart of Kabbalistic Judaism, surfaces in the early texts and mystical traditions of Christianity, is integral to Sufism and to some mystical understandings of Islam.

In our conversations about Christianity, we have identified unconditional love as a core teaching of Jesus. While there is not one particular verse where this is said directly, we take the parable of the Prodigal Son (Luke 15:11–32) to be an illustration of that teaching, an illustration that helps us to understand other verses such as "Love your enemies and pray for those who persecute you," (Matt 5:44b) and "Love one another as I have loved you." (John 15:12). And while the scholarly evidence may be thin, we have decided that this love corresponds well, at the level of daily practices of faith, to the Hebrew word "*hesed,*" which is translated in Jewish Scripture variously as "loving kindness" and "steadfast love." It seems to us that Jesus' teachings accentuated love without conditions, often in very dramatic ways.

In our conversations about Islam, we have identified compassion as the core teaching of the Prophet Mohammed. The first verse of every one of the 114 chapters of the Qur'an but one begins with "In the name of Allah, the Most Compassionate, the Most Merciful." This compassion involves an open heart, and a willingness to try to mirror in our own lives the actions of God toward us. It also suggests an active empathy that embraces the lives of other people.

Discovering and clarifying these core teachings came as a result of increasingly open and critically reflective conversations, conversations in which we were challenged to speak of our own traditions, in which we learned about each other's traditions, and in which, by learning about other traditions we were encouraged to go more deeply into our own. Although critically reflective, engaged with the texts and theologians within our traditions, we could not have done this if we had been limited by the need to be the ultimate authority in our own traditions.

Through those all-important conversations about these core teachings, we realized that all three teachings exist, perhaps not as core teachings, but in significant forms in all three traditions. Identifying positive core teachings in each tradition gave each of us, in our interfaith dialogue, a unique footing in those conversations and the ability to contribute at least one positive perspective on a consistent basis as we continued to pursue difficult issues, seek our own spiritual growth, and deliberate about the common moral issues we want to address.

Stage Three: Sharing the Difficult Parts. Interfaith dialogue in stage three descends to a deeper level, one where it is possible to begin to break down the walls that keep us apart. At this stage, we begin to name the particular texts and practices in our *own* traditions where we believe that we ourselves have gone astray, where we have lost sight of the deeper, core teachings and purposes of our religions and the spiritual substance they were created to hold and convey. It is here that the very meaning of conversation is expanded and holds its deepest promise. By naming those things in our traditions that we identified as examples of going astray, things inconsistent with the focus of our traditions made known in our core teachings, we entered into a condition of vulnerability that without real conversations that developed trust between us, slowly over time, is not possible.

For the Interfaith Amigos, stage three was an enormous breakthrough. For us, it developed this way. One day in a conversation about the core teachings, which seemed in many ways to transcend the boundaries of our traditions, we started to talk about some of the particulars of our traditions. We realized three things. First, we realized that in each of our traditions there are particular texts and practices that are consistent with our core teachings. Second, we realized that these "consistent" texts can also be twisted or manipulated in ways that make them less consistent and more troublesome.

Finally, there are particular texts and practices in each of our traditions that seem to be inconsistent with our core teachings.[8] In Judaism, the idea of Shabbat clearly flows from and supports Oneness because of the way it encourages us to stop, to celebrate the very reality of creation, and to ask once again about our role in God's continuing work of creation. Shabbat encourages us to center ourselves in God's Oneness in ways that nurture our minds and spirits instead of numbing them, through such practices as prayer, meditation, and conversation. In Christianity, the idea of resurrection is consistent with the core teaching of unconditional love because it points to the belief that God's boundless love can always make everything new. In Islam, the concept of *ilm*, the second most frequently used word in the Qur'an after *Allah,* is consistent with the core teaching of compassion. *Ilm* refers to a holistic way of understanding religious experience that includes the work of the mind, the heart, and embodied feeling. Compassion, the core teaching of Islam can be neither understood nor practiced if experienced only at intellectual or emotional levels. It must be understood also at the level of feeling, of connecting to the deepest physical parts of our beings.

Each of these consistent particulars, however, can also be twisted into an inconsistent particular. Shabbat can become rigid and a way of dividing persons instead of uniting them in Oneness. An insistence on a particular kind of literal, supernatural, and physical interpretation of resurrection turns its meaning into a doctrinal litmus test to divide insiders and outsiders. And *ilm* can be interpreted as a kind of overly embodied and non-reflective religious experience that obscures the importance of critical thinking in the pursuit of compassion.

Descending to a still deeper level of critical reflection on our traditions, we identified four kinds of texts and practices that seem to be inconsistent with the core teachings of all of our traditions: exclusivity, violence, inequality of men and women, and homophobia. We realize, of course, that others working together in interfaith conversations might wind up with a different list.

For us, exclusivity seemed to be the defining category giving rise to the others we identified. In Judaism, Rabbi Ted pointed to the texts that identify the Jews as God's chosen people. He felt that these texts can be used to promote teachings and values in the Jewish community and elsewhere that are inconsistent with Judaism's core teachings. He argued, therefore,

8. Ibid., 16ff.

that this chosen-ness, in light of the core teaching of Oneness, should not signify a qualitatively better stature before God. Jews, he argues, are chosen for the way of Torah, Christians chosen for the way of the gospel of Jesus, and Muslims chosen for the way of the Qur'an.

As a Christian, I have identified several seemingly exclusive texts, but none more dominant than the text in John 14 in which Jesus is reported to say: "I am the way, the truth and the life." This text, I now argue, should be interpreted in light of the core teaching of unconditional love. The "I" does not refer narrowly to the historical Jesus, but more broadly to the incarnate Logos of God in John's gospel—the pattern and purpose of God incarnate, and thus to unconditional love itself in the world. In effect John's Jesus is saying: "unconditional love incarnate is the way, the truth, and the life."

In Islam, Imam Jamal points to troubling and often-quoted verses in the Qur'an (3:85) suggesting Islam is meant to supersede Judaism and Christianity. "If anyone desires a religion other than Islam (submission to Allah) never will it be accepted of him; and in the Herafter he will be in the ranks of those who have lost (all spiritual good)." Imam Jamal is quick to point out, however, that the prior verse says, "We believe in Allah, and in what has been revealed to us and what was revealed to Abraham, Isma'il, Isaac, Jacob and the Tribes, and in (the books) given to Moses, Jesus, and the prophets, from their Lord: We make no distinction between one and another among them, and to Allah do we bow our will (in Islam)" (3:84).

The challenge in Stage Three is to identify particulars consistent with core teachings and how those particulars can be twisted into negatives. Even more important, however, is the difficult work of identifying particulars that are easily interpreted in ways that are wholly inconsistent with the core teachings of one's tradition—especially particulars that divide us from our own core values, and from other religions. This requires a vulnerability that can be developed, over time, through conversations.[9]

Stage Four: Moving Beyond Safe Territory. In stage four we begin to experience the safety and freedom to share some of the really difficult aspects of our traditions and our own experience. In many respects, this breakthrough occurred for the Interfaith Amigos as we wrote the chapter about our trip to the Middle East. At this stage, empathic role-taking becomes central to interfaith conversations. Role-taking is the attempt to understand how it feels to be the other person in their religious context.[10]

9. For more on this, see Mackenzie, Falcon, and Rahman, *Religion Gone Astray*, 15ff.

10. See Flavell, *The Development of Role-taking and Communication Skills in Children.*

Psychologist D. W. Winnicott once spoke of this as the process of creating a "holding environment" in which negative feelings can be shared, old frameworks can be expressed and challenged, and new roles and frames can be explored.[11] In this holding environment we do three things. First, we *up-hold* one another, confirming who a person says they are and how they are currently making meaning in their lives without pushing for immediate change. Second, we *hold out* new possibilities. Without expecting the rejection of one's past, we "give permission" for each of us to let go of one way of thinking and adopt another. Third, we *hold on*, providing clear indications that we are not going to leave or abandon the conversation or relationship. We are in it for the long haul. Only is such a context will persons of faith find themselves able to share some thoughts and feelings that have remained hidden. Old wounds can be revealed, fears explored, unhealthy patterns of thought and behavior identified, double-binds experienced and pried open.

Stage Five: Exploring Spiritual Practices from Other Traditions. The final stage involves experiencing the spiritual practices and worship of different traditions. This stage is important to interfaith dialogue for several reasons. First, it gives us the opportunity to see and feel first hand both the universals and the particulars in our traditions. In worship we cannot avoid the experience of the connections and disconnections between religious experiences. For instance, confessing one's sins might be common to several traditions, but it will be expressed differently in each. In worship, these unique forms of experience are front and center. Second, seeing our dialogue partners at worship helps us to understand them better. We see them in a community of faith and practice, connected to one another, just as we are interconnected with others in our tradition. Third, worshiping together brings us closer together. It demonstrates respect for other religious experiences and the desire to learn from others. It lessens the chances of conflict in our local communities and increases the chances of cooperation. It helps us imagine creative responses to conflict and takes us deeper into our own traditions. Finally, worshiping together inevitably prompts myriad topics for further conversation, not about doctrine (though this may happen), but about the core religious experiences and practices within a religious tradition. Discussing these experiences and practices are among the best ways to move interfaith conversations forward.

These five stages of interfaith dialogue suggest elements of conversation that, I believe, are critical, not just for interfaith dialogue, but for the future of humanity. The stages represent ways to develop trust and to

---

11. See Winnicott, *The Maturational Processes and the Facilitating Environment*.

move toward the kind of genuine vulnerability that makes the discovery of troubled ground, shared ground and "new ground" possible.

Interfaith Dialogue and the Dynamics of Conversation

Several specific attributes of effective conversations can be suggested from our experiences with the stages of interfaith dialogue.

1. *Openness.* Conversation requires being open to the experience and expressions of meaning and purpose in the life of another person without negative judgment. There is an essential initial openness required. But, in order for that openness to be useful, there must also be an interest in and conviction that the story that can be heard from another person has positive value.

2. *Vulnerability.* Conversation requires a willingness to share life experiences and provide accurate insights into the ways in which one finds religious meaning and purpose. This often requires a measure of vulnerability that is not normally a feature of more superficial conversations.

3. *Critical Reflection.* Following initial sharing and listening, conversation requires critical thinking by those involved. What have we heard? What do we make of it? Where does it come from? What are its implications? Critical reflection sharpens the participants' understanding of what has been shared, permits insights to be summarized and connected with the core teachings and values of those with different backgrounds, and provides an opportunity for these insights to be taken more deeply into one's own story and expressions of religious meaning or purpose.

4. *Healing.* Interfaith dialogue assumes that conversation is not an option. It is a crucial foundation for creating healing and reconciliation in a conflicted world. This comes less from discovering new, timeless truths that connect us (as important as that may be) and more from creating ways of *communicating* that honor the integrity of the experience and insights of others, while creating new grounds from which we can work together toward common ends. As we "up-hold" each other with affection and respect, healing emerges at the heart of a relationship through a recurring dynamic of emptying oneself of fear, and filling oneself with care, compassion, and hope.

5. *Empathy.* In interfaith dialogue, conversation takes us into a way of being that is marked by role-taking and empathy. Empathic conversation involves the capacity to recognize the world of another, imagine that world as it is understood by the other, and communicate that

understanding to the other. Often, this fosters the kind of compassion that is so essential to healing and reconciliation. Empathy can be expressed in many different ways and, often, it comes in surprising ways.

6. *Story-telling.* Interfaith dialogue is grounded in story-telling. There are patterns and rhythms in our lives that we hold in common. Telling our stories can help to reveal those patterns and help us to see just how deeply we are related. When we tell stories, we provoke others to tell their stories. In this reciprocal process we open ourselves to receive insights from others into how they managed similar experiences, often in very different ways. These differences are often rooted in different religious experiences and traditions. This kind of reciprocal story-telling helps us to learn from each other and fosters cooperation and reconciliation in conversation.

Practical Implications for Ministry

Given the reality of pluralism in our communities, interfaith conversation can contribute to the minister's work as a conversation partner in several important ways.

Overcoming Exclusivity

The practice of interfaith conversation works against the natural tendency within organizations toward excluding others who seem different. Exclusive "our way is the only true way" thinking communicates that the experience of another person really has little or no value. Under such circumstances, conversation itself has no real value.

When a minister moves a congregation into interfaith dialogue, involving them in a journey into the lives and worldviews of those from other religions, congregations learn to find both universals that transcend the ordinary boundaries of our separate traditions, and particulars in *all* traditions, including their own, that often seem to create the barriers between and among persons from different religious backgrounds. This experience prompts those in the community of faith to re-think their exclusive claims and to consider what they might learn from all human others.

Shared Learning, Shared Knowledge

Interfaith dialogue is profoundly "pedagogical." Through reciprocal teaching and learning participants discover that conversation leads to a new place of knowledge. From a Christian perspective, this is reminiscent of the book of Acts, where Christians in the early church had a conviction that the production of knowledge about their new faith needed to be shared equally.[12] Much of the knowledge came through stories as well as through testimony relating to aspects of Jesus' teachings. But a significant portion of their knowledge arrived through struggling to understand their distinctiveness in relation to other religious traditions, especially first-century Judaism.

Interfaith dialogue adds this same dimension to Christian education. We minister in a context in which there is often a naïve belief that "all religions are the same." This promotes forms of participation within religious communities that can be shallow and un-reflective. Interfaith conversation quickly solves this problem and involves learners in a journey, not only seeking points of contact with other religions, but searching for a more profound understanding of their own traditions.

Learning Collaboration

Hierarchical thinking is immediately problematic in interfaith dialogue. It creates a false, over-zealous sense of one's value, and the value of one's traditions. Because interfaith conversation requires careful listening as well as speaking, and because interfaith conversation places tremendous value on experience, it calls into question the value of narrow hierarchical thinking in other realms of church life.

For instance, interfaith conversation points to the opportunity for ministers to honor each staff member, whether designated "associate," "assistant," "intern," "part time," or any other marker of hierarchy. In order to do this, a commitment must be made to the fact that every person has a story and brings wisdom to bear on situations. If conversations can be held with this in mind, unusual things can happen. Staff leadership that learns from interfaith conversation, therefore, then means two things: finding ways to invite experience from staff members to illumine a conversation and helping the conversation to reach a workable conclusion. Everyone's experience can be honored. Agreement, though crucial, is not as important as the process of listening, honoring, and seeking together an answer to a problem. It is the conversation that ultimately makes this possible.

12. Acts 2:42–47

Learning from the Religious Practices of Others

Instead of only learning in a rational-cognitive way from the codified doctrines and beliefs of another religious tradition, there is great value in engaging in conversations in which we learn from the spiritual practices of others. By spiritual practices, I mean practices of prayer, meditation, fasting, reading, reflecting on sacred texts, worship, service, community-building, and care. Interfaith dialogue teaches congregations to work from the inside-out in conversations, rather than from the outside-in—to access the deep, lived understandings and practices of another faith and engage in conversations that seek to build bridges there, rather than at the level of codified teachings only.

Conversing from a Spiritual "Center"

Interfaith conversations work best when entered by those who are living deeply into their traditions through practices of prayer, meditation, worship, and reflection. Such practices help them to speak from their center, or deepest place of belonging within that tradition. In other words, "centering" within a tradition is crucial to becoming a competent, imaginative, and creative conversation partner from within that tradition.

Cautions

Interfaith conversation is hard work. The needs of religious literacy[13] and spiritual growth through practices are not easily accomplished. Interfaith conversation is what my interfaith colleagues call "inconvenient work." It requires finding regular time to talk, worship, and learn about and in different faith communities. In some cases, it requires ongoing spiritual direction. There is no way around this. Interfaith conversation requires commitment, planning, and time. It does not seem immediately obvious in most congregations that this work should be on the congregation's agenda.

Interfaith dialogue is not an occasion for over-simplification. Critical thinking is necessary to help take interfaith conversations to those deeper places where the insights we have about what is "universal" and what is "particular" are genuine, true to the core teachings of a tradition, and can actually contribute to cooperation. There are times when interpersonal conversations must give way to conversations with books, articles, professors,

---

13. See Moore, *Overcoming Religious Illiteracy.*

and other resources within our traditions, in order for us to appreciate the complexities of what we often are quick to deem simple.

Patience is required. Interfaith dialogue cannot proceed too quickly. Relationships of any substance take time to develop the trust required to sustain them. At each juncture, interfaith conversation is a process that must be approached slowly, with openness to the new, a willingness to be surprised with outcomes different from expectations, and the expectation that our lives will actually be transformed.

Don't expect too much from the process. Interfaith conversations are incremental. Often changes seem small or insignificant. It is easy to lose heart if hopes are not met according to some inner time schedule. Try not to expect too much too soon. Celebrate small victories and don't be discouraged by setbacks.

Try not to set any difference aside as "irreconcilable." There are always areas of conversation that are difficult to understand and which can cause fear and doubt. But differences *always* have the potential to illuminate something in a new way, to provide a different perspective and to become a source of vitality and reconciliation. Learn to ask the question, "what is the opportunity in this problem."

Questions for Discussion

1. What are the essential elements of your own story, the blessings and the curses, the joys, the sorrows, the problems, the solutions?

2. What are your beliefs?

3. What are the relationships between and among the elements of your story and what you believe?

4. Do you feel that your "spiritual path" is the only way?

5. Is there anything that might change that?

6. What sort of experiences would make you feel that your life is honored and respected?

7. How would it feel for you to listen to the story and beliefs of another person without negative judgment?

Further Reading

Borg, Marcus J. *The Heart of Christianity: Rediscovering a Life of Faith.* San Francisco: HarperSanFrancisco, 2003.

Brown Taylor, Barbara. *An Altar in the World: A Geography of Faith.* New York: HarperCollins, 2009.

Crossan, John Dominic. *The Birth of Christianity: Discovering What Happened in the Years Immediately after the Execution of Jesus.* New York: HarperCollins, 1998.

Guthrie, Shirley C. *Always Being Reformed: Faith for a Fragmented World.* 2nd ed. Louisville: Westminster John Knox, 2008.

Volf, Miroslav. *Exclusion and Embrace: A Theological Exploration of Identity, Otherness, and Reconciliation.* Nashville: Abingdon, 1996.

Bibliography

Abraham, William J. *The Logic of Evangelism*. Grand Rapids: Eerdmans, 1989.

Airhart, Phyllis D. *Serving the Present Age: Revivalism, Progressivism, and the Methodist Tradition in Canada*. Mcgill-Queen's Studies in the History of Religion. Montreal, Buffalo: McGill-Queen's University Press, 1992.

Alinsky, Saul David. *Reveille for Radicals*. Chicago: University of Chicago Press, 1946.

———. *Rules for Radicals: A Practical Primer for Realistic Radicals*. 1st ed. New York: Random House, 1971.

Allen, O. Wesley. *The Homiletic of All Believers: A Conversational Approach*. Louisville: Westminster John Knox, 2005.

———. *Preaching and Reading the Lectionary: A Three Dimensional Approach to the Liturgical Year*. St. Louis: Chalice, 2007.

———. "Revelation." In *The New Interpreter's Handbook of Preaching*, edited by Paul Scott Wilson, 473–77. Nashville: Abingdon, 2008.

Allen, Ronald J. *Interpreting the Gospel: An Introduction to Preaching*. St. Louis: Chalice, 1998.

———. *Preaching and the Other: Studies of Postmodern Insights*. St. Louis: Chalice, 2009.

———. "Preaching as Mutual Critical Correlation through Conversation." In *Purposes of Preaching*, edited by Jana Childers, 1–22. St. Louis: Chalice, 2004.

———. *Thinking Theologically: The Preacher as Theologian*. Elements of Preaching. Minneapolis: Fortress, 2008.

Amichai, Yehuda. "The Place Where We Are Right." In *The Selected Poetry of Yehuda Amichai*. Translated by Chana Bloch and Stephen Mitchell. Berkeley, CA: University of California Press, 1996.

Anselm, *Proslogium, Monologium. Cur Deus Homo, Gaunilo's In Behalf of the Food*. Translated by S. N. Dean. 2nd ed. Chicago: Open Court, 1962.

Aquinas, Thomas. *The Summa Theologica of Saint Thomas Aquinas*. Translated by Fathers of the English Dominican Province. 5 vols. Notre Dame: Christian Classics, 1948.

———. *Summa Contra Gentiles*. Translated by Anton C. Pegis. Notre Dame: University of Notre Dame Press, 1975.

———. "The Nature of God." In *Summa Theologiae*. Translated by Timothy McDermott. New York: McGraw-Hill, 1963.

———. "The Trinity." In *Summa Theologiae*. Translated by T. C. O'Brien. New York: McGraw-Hill, 1963.

Augustine. *On Free Choice of the Will.* Translated by Thomas Williams. Cambridge: Hackett, 1993.

————. *The Trinity.* In *The Fathers of the Church (New Translation)*, vol. 45. Translated by Stephen McKenna. Washington, DC: Catholic University of America, 1963.

Ayres, Jennifer. *Waiting for a Glacier to Move: Practicing Christian Social Witness.* Princeton Theological Monographs. Eugene, OR: Pickwick, 2011.

Azariah, V. S. "The Problem of Co-operation between Foreign and Native Workers." In *The Ecumenical Movement: An Anthology of Key Texts and Voices*, edited by Michael Kinnamon and Brian E. Cope, 327–30. Grand Rapids: Eerdmans, 1997.

Bakhtin, Mikhail. "The Problem of Speech Genres." In *Speech Genres and Other Late Essays.* Translated by Vern W. McGee, edited by Caryl Emerson and Michael Holquist. Austin: University of Texas Press, 1986.

Balge, Richard D. "A Brief History of Evangelism in the Christian Church." Lecture. Wisconsin Lutheran College, 1978. Online: www.wlsessays.net/files/BalgeBrief.rtf.

Bass, Diana Butler. *Christianity after Religion.* San Francisco: HarperOne, 2012.

Battle, Michael. *Ubuntu: I in You and You in Me.* New York: Seabury, 2009.

Beaver, Susan. "Right-ish Relations: Wesley in the United Church." Unpublished.

Bell, Rob. *Love Wins: A Book about Heaven, Hell and Every Person Who Ever Lived.* San Franciso: HarperOne, 2011.

Berger, Peter. *The Sacred Canopy: Elements of a Sociological Theory of Religion.* New York: Anchor, 1967.

Bevans, Stephen. *Models of Contextual Theology.* Rev. ed. Maryknoll, NY: Orbis, 2005.

Birch, Bruce C. *What Does the Lord Require: The Old Testament Call to Social Witness.* Philadelphia: Westminster, 1985.

Boff, Leonardo. *Ecclesiogenesis: The Base Communities Reinvent the Church.* Translated by Robert R. Barr. Maryknoll, NY: Orbis, 1986.

————. *Trinity and Society.* Translated by Paul Burns. New York: Orbis, 1986.

Boisen, Anton. *Out of the Depths: An Autobiographical Study of Mental Disorder and Religious Experience.* New York: Harper, 1960.

Bonhoeffer, Dietrich. *Life Together.* New York: HarperOne, 1978.

Borg, Marcus J. *The Heart of Christianity: Rediscovering a Life of Faith.* New York: HarperCollins, 2003.

Bosch, David J. *Transforming Mission: Paradigm Shifts in the Theology of Mission.* American Society of Missiology Series. Maryknoll, NY: Orbis, 1991.

Brookfield, Stephen D. *The Skillful Teacher*, 2nd ed. San Francisco: Jossey-Bass, 2006.

Browne, Robert E.C. *The Ministry of the Word.* London: SCM, 1958.

Browning, Don S. *The Moral Context of Pastoral Care.* Louisville: Westminster John Knox, 1983.

Browning, Don S., and David A. Clairmont, editors. *American Religions and the Family: How Faith Traditions Cope With Modernization and Democracy.* New York: Columbia University Press, 2006.

Brueggemann, Walter. *Cadences of Home: Preaching among Exiles.* Louisville: Westminster John Knox, 1997.

————. *Journey to the Common Good.* Louisville: Westminster John Knox, 2010.

————. *The Practice of Prophetic Imagination: Preaching an Emancipating Word.* Minneapolis: Fortress, 2012.

————. *The Prophetic Imagination.* 2nd ed. Minneapolis: Fortress, 2001.

Brunner, Emil, and Karl Barth. *Natural Theology: Comprising "Nature and Grace" by Professor Dr. Emil Brunner and the Reply "No!" by Dr. Karl Barth.* Translated by Peter Fraenkel. 1946. Reprinted, Eugene, OR: Wipf & Stock: 2002.

Buber, Martin. *I and Thou.* Translated by Walter Kaufman. New York: Scribner, 1970.

Burrell, David. *Faith and Freedom: The Interfaith Perspective.* Malden, MA: Blackwell, 2004.

Carroll, Jackson. *As One with Authority: Reflective Leadership in Authority.* 2nd ed. Eugene, OR: Cascade, 2011.

Carter, Craig. *Rethinking Christ and Culture: A Post-Christendom Perspective.* Grand Rapids: Brazos, 2007.

Chaves, Mark. *Congregations in America.* Cambridge: Harvard University Press, 2004.

Chopp, Rebecca S. *The Power to Speak: Feminism, Language, God.* 1989. Reprinted, Eugene, OR: Wipf & Stock, 2002.

Clapp, Rodney. *A Peculiar People: The Church as Culture in a Post-Christian Society.* Downers Grove, IL: InterVarsity, 1996.

Clebsh, William A., and Charles R. Jaekle. *Pastoral Care in Historical Perspective.* Northfield, NJ: Aronson, 1975.

Clinebell, Howard J. *Ecotherapy: Healing Ourselves, Healing the Earth.* New York: Routledge, 1996.

Colson, Charles. *Countercultural Christians: Exploring a Christian Worldview.* Loveland, CO: Group, 2003.

Comstock, Gary. "Truth or Meaning: Ricoeur vs. Frei on Biblical Narrative." *Journal of Religion* 66 (1986) 117–40.

Cooper-White, Pamela. "Suffering." In *The Wiley-Blackwell Companion to Practical Theology,* edited by Bonnie J. Miller-McLemore, 23–31. Malden, MA: Blackwell, 2001.

Couture, Pamela. "The Blood that Tells (Knows) the Truth: Evil and the Nature of God." *Quarterly Review* 23 (2003) 347–59

———. *Child Poverty: Love, Justice, and Social Responsibility.* St. Louis: Chalice, 2007.

Coy, Patrick G. *A Revolution of the Heart: Essays on the Catholic Worker.* Philadelphia: Temple University Press, 1988.

Craddock, Fred B. *As One without Authority.* Revised with New Sermons. St. Louis: Chalice, 2001.

———. *Overhearing the Gospel.* Lyman Beecher Lecture 1978. Nashville: Abingdon, 1978.

Daley, Herman, and John Cobb Jr. *For the Common Good: Redirecting the Economy Toward Community, the Environment and a Sustainable Future.* 2nd ed. Boston: Beacon, 1994.

Dawn, Marva J. *The Sense of the Call: A Sabbath Way of Life for Those Who Serve God, the Church, and the World.* Grand Rapids: Eerdmans, 2006.

DiNucci, Daracy. "Fragmented Future." *Print* 53/4 (1999). Online: http://www.cdinucci.com/Darcy2/articles/Print/Printarticle7.html.

Doehring, Carrie. *The Practice of Pastoral Care: A Postmodern Approach.* Louisville: Westminster John Knox, 2006.

Dulles, Avery. *Models of the Church.* Expanded ed. Garden City, NY: Doubleday, 1987.

Dykstra, Robert C. *Images of Pastoral Care: Classic Readings.* St. Louis: Chalice, 2005.

Evans, Christopher H. *The Kingdom Is Always but Coming: A Life of Walter Rauschenbusch.* Waco, TX: Baylor University Press, 2010.

Faber, Heije, and Ebel van der Schoot. *The Art of Pastoral Conversation*. Nashville: Abingdon, 1965.

Fanon, Frantz. *Black Skin, White Masks*. Translated by Charles Lam Markmann. New York: Grove, 1967.

Farley, Edward. *Good and Evil: Interpreting a Human Condition*. Minneapolis: Fortress, 1990.

Flavell, John. *The Development of Role-taking and Communication Skills in Children*. New York: Wiley, 1968.

Fore, William F. "The Unknown History of Televangelism." *Media Development* 54/1 (2007) 45–48.

Fortune, Marie M. *Is Nothing Sacred? When Sex Invades the Pastoral Relationship*. 1992. Reprinted, Eugene, OR: Wipf & Stock, 2008.

Freire, Paulo. *Pedagogy of the Oppressed*. 30th Anniversary ed. Translated by Myra Bergman Ramos. New York: Continuum, 2000.

Fuller, Robert C. *Spiritual but Not Religious: Understanding Unchurched America*. New York: Oxford University Press, 2001.

Furr, Gary A., and Milburn Price, *The Dialogue of Worship: Creating Space for Revelation and Response*. Macon, GA: Smyth & Helwys, 1998.

George, Sherron Kay. *Better Together: The Future of Presbyterian Mission*. Louisville: Geneva, 2010.

Gerkin, Charles V. *Widening the Horizons: Pastoral Responses to a Fragmented Society*. Philadelphia: Westminster, 1986.

Gill-Austern, Brita L., and Bonnie J. Miller-McLemore, editors. *Feminist and Womanist Pastoral Theology*. Nashville: Abingdon, 1999.

Gooch, John O. *John Wesley for the Twenty-First Century: Set Apart for Social Witness*. Nashville: Discipleship Resources, 2006.

Grenz, Stanley J. *Theology for the Community of God*. Grand Rapids: Eerdmans, 1994.

Griffin, David Ray, editor. *Deep Religious Pluralism*. Louisville: Westminster John Knox, 2005.

Guiterrez, Gustavo. *A Theology of Liberation: History, Politics, Salvation*. Translated and edited by Sister Caridad Inda and John Eagleson. Maryknoll, NY: Orbis, 1971.

Gunton, Colin. *The Promise of the Trinitarian Theology*. 2nd ed. Edinburgh: T. & T. Clark, 1997.

Harmon, Steven R. *Ecumenism Means You, Too: Ordinary Christians and the Quest for Christian Unity*. Eugene, OR: Cascade, 2010.

Hartshome, Charles. *The Divine Relativity: A Social Conception of God*. New Haven: Yale University, 1948.

———. *Omnipotence and Other Theological Mistakes*. Albany: SUNY Press, 1984.

Hauerwas, Stanley, and William H. Willimon. *Resident Aliens: Life in the Christian Colony*. Nashville: Abingdon, 1989.

Heath, Elaine A. *The Mystic Way of Evangelism: A Contemplative Vision for Christian Outreach*. Grand Rapids: Baker Academic, 2008.

Heim, Mark. *Salvations: Truth and Difference in Religion*. Faith Meets Faith. Maryknoll, NY: Orbis, 1995.

Heurtz, Christopher L., and Christine D. Pohl. *Friendship at the Margins: Discovering Mutuality in Service and Mission*. Downers Grove, IL: InterVarsity, 2010.

Heyer, Kristin E. *Prophetic and Public: The Social Witness of U.S. Catholicism*. Moral Traditions Series. Washington, DC: Georgetown University Press, 2006.

Hick, John. *A Christian Theology of Religions: The Rainbow of Faiths.* Louisville: Westminster John Knox, 1995.

Hiles, Marv, and Nancy Hiles, editors. *An Almanac for the Soul: Anthology of Hope.* Healdsburg, CA: Iona Center, 2008.

Hiltner, Seward. *Preface to Pastoral Theology.* Nashville: Abingdon, 1958.

Hiltner, Seward, and Lowell G. Colston. *The Context of Pastoral Counseling.* New York: Abingdon, 1961.

Hodgson, Peter. *Winds of the Spirit: A Constructive Christian Theology.* Louisville: Westminster John Knox, 1994.

Holifield, E. Brooks. *A History of Pastoral Care in America: From Salvation to Self-Realization.* Nashville: Abingdon, 1983.

hooks, bell. *Teaching to Transgress: Education as the Practice of Freedom.* New York: Routledge, 1994.

Howe, Reuel L. *Partners in Preaching: Clergy and Laity in Dialogue.* New York: Seabury, 1967.

Johnson, Lydia F. *Drinking From the Same Well: Cross-Cultural Concerns in Pastoral Care and Counseling.* Eugene OR: Pickwick, 2011.

José "Chencho" Alas, El Salvador. Tannenbaum Center for Interreligious Understanding. https://www.tanenbaum.org/programs/peace/peacemaker-awardees/jos%C3%A9-chencho-alas-el-salvador.

Kasper, Cardinal Walter. *A Handbook of Spiritual Ecumenism.* Hyde Park, NY: New City, 2006.

Kiefert, Patrick R. *Welcoming the Stranger: A Public Theology of Worship and Evangelism.* Minneapolis: Fortress, 1992.

Kierkegaard, Søren. *Purity of Heart Is to Will One Thing.* Translated by Douglas Steere. New York: Harper, 1948.

Kim, Jung Ha. *Bridge-Makers and Cross-Bearers: Korean-American Women and the Church.* American Academy of Religion Academy Series 92. Atlanta: Scholars, 1997.

Knuth, Elizabeth T. "The Beguines." (December 1992). About.com. http://historymedren.about.com/gi/o.htm?zi=1/XJ&zTi=1&sdn=historymedren&cdn=education&tm=4&f=00&tt=14&bt=1&bts=1&zu=http%3A//www.users.csbsju.edu/~eknuth/xpxx/beguines.html.

Koenig, John. *New Testament Hospitality: Partnership with Strangers as Promise and Mission.* Overtures to Biblical Theology. 1985. Reprinted, Eugene, OR: Wipf & Stock, 2001.

Kornfeld, Margaret. *Cultivating Wholeness: A Guide to Care and Counseling in Faith Communities.* New York: Continuum, 2005.

Kujawa-Holbrook, Sheryl A., and Karen B. Montagno, editors. *Injustice and the Care of Souls: Taking Oppression Seriously in Pastoral Care.* Minneapolis: Fortress, 2009.

Küng, Hans. *The Church.* Translated by Ray and Rosaleen Ockenden. 1967. Reprinted, New York: Continuum, 2001.

Kysar, Robert. *Stumbling in the Light: New Testament Images for a Changing Church.* St. Louis: Chalice, 1999.

LaCugna, Catherine Mowry. *God for Us: The Trinity and Christian Life.* San Francisco: HarperCollins, 1973.

Lartey, Emmanuel Y. *In Living Color: An Intercultural Approach to Pastoral Care and Counseling.* 2nd ed. London: Kingsley, 2003.

LaRue, Cleophus J. *I Believe I'll Testify: The Art of African American Preaching*. Louisville: Westminster John Knox, 2011.

Latourette, Kenneth Scott. *A History of the Expansion of Christianity*. 5 vols. New York: Harper, 1937.

Law, Eric. *The Wolf Shall Dwell with the Lamb: A Spirituality for Leadership in a Multicultural Community*. St. Louis: Chalice, 1993.

Legge, Marilyn J. "Negotiating Mission: a Canadian Stance." *International Review of Mission* 93/368 (2004) 119–30.

———. "Seeking 'Right Relations': How Should Churches Respond to Aboriginal Voices?" *Journal of the Society of Christian Ethics* 22 (Fall 2002) 27–47.

Lewis, Harold T. *Christian Social Witness*. The New Church's Teaching Series. Cambridge, MA: Cowley, 2001.

Loder, James E. *The Transforming Moment: Understanding Convictional Experiences*. San Francisco: Harper & Row, 1981.

Long, Thomas G. *Beyond the Worship Wars: Building Vital and Faithful Worship*. Herndon, VA: Alban Institute, 2001.

———. *The Witness of Preaching*. Louisville: Westminster John Knox, 1989.

Lose, David J. "Beyond Our Wants." Online: http://www.workingpreacher.org/dear_wp.aspx?article_id=458.

———. *Confessing Jesus Christ: Preaching in a Postmodern World*. Grand Rapids: Eerdmanns, 2003.

———. "In God We Trust." Online: http://www.workingpreacher.org/dear_wp.aspx?article_id=407.

———. "God Bless You." Online: http://www.workingpreacher.org/dear_wp.aspx?article_id=450.

———. "Preaching 2.0." *Word and World* 30 (2010), 300–310

———. "Salt and Light." Online: http://www.workingpreacher.org/dear_wp.aspx?article_id=451.

———. "Perfect." Online: http://www.workingpreacher.org/dear_wp.aspx?article_id=456.

———. "Picture This." Online: http://www.workingpreacher.org/dear_wp.aspx?article_id=458.

Luther, Martin. "On Christian Liberty." In *Luther's Works*, vol. 31. Edited by Harold J. Grimm and Helmut T. Lehman. Philadelphia: Fortress, 1957.

Mackenzie, Don, Ted Falcon, and Jamal Rahman. *Getting to the Heart of Interfaith: The Eye-Opening, Hope-Filled Friendship of a Pastor, a Rabbi and a Sheikh*. Woodstock, VT: Skylight Paths, 2009.

———. *Religion Gone Astray: What We Found at the Heart of Interfaith*. Woodstock, VT: Skylight Paths, 2011.

Malefyt, Norma de Waal, and Howard Vanderwell. *Designing Worship Together: Models and Strategies for Worship Planning*. Herndon, VA: Alban Institute, 2004.

Marion, Jean-Luc. *God without Being*. Chicago: University of Chicago, 1991.

Marquardt, Manfred. *John Wesley's Social Ethics: Praxis and Principles*. Nashville: Abingdon, 1992.

Marsden, George. "Christianity and Culture: Transforming Niebuhr's Categories." *Insights: The Faculty Journal of Austin Seminary* 15/1 (1999) 4–15.

Martyr, Justin. *First Apology* in *Early Christian Fathers*. Translated by Cyril C. Richardson et al. Library of Christian Classics. Philadelphia: Westminster, 1953.

May, Rollo. *Power and Innocence: A Search for the Sources of Violence.* New York: Norton, 1972.

McClure, John S. *Other-wise Preaching: A Postmodern Ethic for Homiletics.* St. Louis: Chalice, 2001.

———. *The Roundtable Pulpit: Where Leadership & Preaching Meet.* Nashville: Abingdon, 1995.

McNeill, John T. *A History of the Cure of Souls.* New York: Harper & Row, 1951.

Messer, Donald, E. *Contemporary Images of Christian Ministry.* Nashville: Abingdon, 1989.

Miller, Barbara Day. *Encounters with the Holy: A Conversational Model for Worship Planning.* Herndon, VA: Alban, 2010.

Miller, Michael St. A. *Freedom in Resistance and Creative Transformation.* Lanham, MD: Rowman and Littlefield, 2013.

———. *Reshaping the Contextual Vision in Caribbean Theology: Theoretical Foundations for Theology.* Lanham, MD: University of America, 2007.

Miller-McLemore, Bonnie J., editor. *The Blackwell Companion to Practical Theology.* London: Wiley/Blackwell, 2011.

———. *Christian Theology in Practice: Discovering a Discipline.* Grand Rapids: Eerdmans, 2012.

———. "The Human Web and the State of Pastoral Theology." *The Christian Century,* April 7, 1993, 366–69.

Minear, Paul S. *Images of the Church in the New Testament.* Philadelphia: Westminster, 1960.

Moltmann, Jurgen. *The Trinity and the Kingdom: The Doctrine of God.* San Francisco: Harper & Row, 1981.

Monahan, Michael. "Emancipatory Affect: bell hooks on Love and Liberation." *The CLR James Journal* 17/1 (2011) 102–11.

Moore, Diane L. *Overcoming Religious Illiteracy: A Cultural Studies Approach to the Study of Religion in Secondary Education.* New York: Palgrave Macmillan, 2007.

Morton, Nelle, *The Journey is Home.* Boston: Beacon, 1986.

Nangelimalil, Jacob. *The Relationship between the Eucharistic Liturgy, the Interior Life, and the Social Witness of the Church According to Joseph Cardinal Parecattil Tesi.* Gregoriana Serie Teologia. Roma: Pontificia università Gregoriana, 1996.

Nicholls, Tracey. "Pedagogy of the Privileged." *The CLR James Journal: A Publication of the Caribbean Philosophical Association* 17/1 (2011) 10–36.

Niebuhr, H. Richard. *Christ and Culture.* New York: Harper & Row, 1951.

Nouwen, Henri. *The Living Reminder: Service and Prayer in Memory of Jesus Christ.* New York: HarperOne, 1984.

Nussbaum, Martha Craven. *Women and Human Development: The Capabilities Approach.* The John Robert Seeley Lectures. Cambridge: Cambridge University Press, 2000.

Nysse, Richard, and Donald Juel. "Interpretation for Christian Ministry." *Word & World* 13 (1993) 345–55.

Oates, Wayne E. *Protestant Pastoral Counseling.* Philadelphia: Westminster, 1962.

Old, Hughes Oliphant. *Worship: Reformed According to Scripture.* Louisville: Westminster John Knox, 2002.

Origin. *Contra Celsum.* Translated by Henry Chadwick. Cambridge: Cambridge University Press, 1980.

Pagitt, Doug. *Preaching in the Inventive Age*. Minneapolis: Sparkhouse, 2011.

————. *Preaching Re-Imagined: The Role of the Sermon in Communities of Faith*. Grand Rapids: Zondervan, 2005.

Palmer, Parker. *The Company of Strangers: Christians and the Renewal of America's Public Life*. New York: Crossroad, 1983.

————. *A Hidden Wholeness: The Journey Toward an Undivided Life—Welcoming the Soul and Weaving Community in a Wounded World*. San Francisco: Jossey-Bass, 2004.

————. *To Know as We Are Known: A Spirituality of Education*. San Francisco: Harper & Row, 1983.

Patton, John. *Pastoral Care in Context: An Introduction to Pastoral Care*. Louisville: Westminster John Knox, 2005.

Peterson, Eugene. *The Contemplative Pastor: Returning to the Art of Spiritual Direction*. Grand Rapids: Eerdmans, 1993.

Pew Research Center. "'Nones' on The Rise." The Pew Forum on Religion and Public Life. http://www.pewforum.org/Unaffiliated/nones-on-the-rise.aspx.

Pinnock, Clark. *Most Moved Mover: A Theology of God's Openness*. Grand Rapids: Baker, 2001.

Placher, William C. *Narratives of a Vulnerable God: Christ, Theology, and Scripture*. Louisville: Westminster John Knox, 1994.

Pollard, Alton B. *Mysticism and Social Change: The Social Witness of Howard Thurman*. Martin Luther King, Jr. Memorial Studies in Religion, Culture, and Social Development. New York: Lang, 1992.

Porter, Thomas W. *The Spirit and Art of Conflict Transformation: Creating a Culture of Justpeace*. Nashville: Upper Room, 2010.

Prenter, Regin. *Spiritus Creator*. Translated by John M. Jenson. 1953. Reprinted, Eugene, OR: Wipf & Stock, 2001.

Pruyser, Paul. *The Minister as Diagnostician: Personal Problems in Pastoral Perspective*. Philadelphia: Westminster, 1976.

Ramsay, Nancy, editor. *Pastoral Care and Counseling: Redefining the Paradigms*. Nashville: Abingdon, 2004.

Ramsey, Jr., G. Lee. *Care-full Preaching: From Sermon to Caring Community*. St. Louis: Chalice, 2000.

"Report of the Section on Unity: Third Assembly of the World Council of Churches, New Delhi, 1961." In *The Ecumenical Movement: An Anthology of Key Texts and Voices*, edited by Michael Kinnamon and Brian E. Cope. Grand Rapids: Eerdmans, 1997, 88.

Rienstra, Debra, and Ron Rienstra. *Worship Words: Discipling Language for Faithful Ministry*. Grand Rapids: Baker, 2009.

Rogers, Carl R. *Client Centered Therapy: Its Current Practice, Implications, and Theory*. Boston: Houghton Mifflin, 1951.

"The Role of Evangelism in the History of the United States of America." United States History. Online: http://www.u-s-history.com/pages/h3817.html.

Roof, Wade Clarke. *Community and Commitment*. New York: Elsevier, 1977.

Roozen, David A. "A Decade of Change in American Congregations: 2000–2010." Online: http://faithcommunitiestoday.org/sites/faithcommunitiestoday.org/files/Decade%20of%20Change%20Final_0.pdf.

Rose, Frank. *The Art of Immersion: How the Digital Generation Is Remaking Hollywood, Madison Avenue, and the Way We Tell Stories.* New York: Norton, 2012.

Rose, Lucy Atkinson. *Sharing the Word: Preaching in the Roundtable Church.* Louisville: Westminster John Knox, 1997.

Ross, Fiona C. *Bearing Witness: Women and the Truth and Reconciliation Commission in South Africa.* Anthropology, Culture, and Society. Sterling, VA: Pluto, 2003.

Runyon, Theodore. *The New Creation: John Wesley's Theology Today.* Nashville: Abingdon, 1998.

Saliers, Don. *Worship as Theology: Foretaste of Glory Divine.* Nashville: Abingdon, 1994.

Shouten, Norm. "Worship is a Dialogical Region." *Perspectives* 18/3 (2003) 6–11.

Stanton, Kim Pamela. "Truth Commissions and Public Inquiries: Addressing Historical Injustices in Established Democracies." JSD thesis, University of Toronto, 2010. University of Toronto Research Repository. https://tspace.library.utoronto.ca/bitstream/1807/24886/1/Stanton_Kim_P_201006_SJD_thesis.pdf.

Stevenson-Moessner, Jeanne, and Teresa Snorton, editors. *Women Out of Order: Risking Change and Creating Care in a Multicultural World.* Minneapolis: Fortress, 2009.

Stone, Bryan P. *Evangelism after Christendom: The Theology and Practice of Christian Witness.* Grand Rapids: Brazos, 2007.

Suchocki, Marjorie Hewitt. *Divinity and Diversity: An Affirmation of Religious Pluralism.* Nashville: Abingdon, 2003.

———. *God, Christ, Church: A Practical Guide to Process Theology.* New Revised Edition. New York: Crossroad, 1992.

Tanner, Kathryn. *Theories of Culture: A New Agenda for Theology.* Guides to Theological Inquiry. Minneapolis: Fortress, 1997.

———. "Trinity." In *The Blackwell Companion to Political Theology,* edited by Peter Scott and William T. Cavanaugh. Malden, MA: Blackwell, 2004.

Temple, William. *Social Witness and Evangelism.* The Social Service Lecture. London: Epworth, 1943.

Thandeka, *Learning to be White: Money, Race, and God in America.* New York: Continuum, 2000.

Thompson, William D., and Gordon C. Bennett. *Dialogue Preaching: The Shared Sermon.* Valley Forge, PA: Judson, 1969.

Thurman, Howard. T*he Creative Encounter: An Interpretation of Religion and the Social Witness.* 1st ed. New York: Harper, 1954.

Tillich, Paul. *Systematic Theology.* Vol. 1. Chicago: University of Chicago, 1951.

———. "The Theology of Pastoral Care: The Spiritual and Theological Foundations of Pastoral Care." Advisory Committee on Clinical Pastoral Education, 1958.

Tisdale, Leonora Tubbs. *Preaching as Local Theology and Folk Art.* Fortress Resources for Preaching. Minneapolis: Fortress, 1997.

Townes, Emilie Maureen. *In a Blaze of Glory: Womanist Spirituality as Social Witness.* Nashville: Abingdon, 1995.

Tracy, David. *The Analogical Imagination: Christian Theology and the Culture of Pluralism.* New York: Crossroads, 1981.

———. *Blessed Rage for Order: The New Pluralism in Theology.* New York: Seabury, 1975.

———. "Theological Method." In *Christian Theology: An Introduction to Its Traditions and Tasks,* edited by Peter C. Hodgson and Robert H. King, 35–60. Rev. ed., Minneapolis: Fortress, 1985.

Truth and Reconciliation Commission of Canada. Online: http://www.trc.ca/websites/ trcinstitution/index.php?p=26.

———. "Final Report." http://www.justice.gov.za/trc/report/index.htm.

United Church of Canada. 41st General Council. Online: http://www.gc41.ca.

Ward, Keith. *Divine Action*. London: Collins, 1990.

———. *Why There Almost Certainly Is a God: Doubting Dawkins*. Oxford: Lion, 2008.

Watson, David Lowes. *God Does Not Foreclose: The Universal Promise of Salvation*. Nashville: Abingdon, 1990.

Webb, Stephen H. *Jesus Christ, Eternal God: Heavenly Flesh and the Metaphysics of Matter*. Oxford: Oxford, 2012.

Wesley, Andrew. "Questions on Forgiveness." Ara Pacis Initiative. http://www. arapacisinitiative.org/en/forgiveness-and-reconciliation/264-rev-andrew-wesley.

Wesley, John. *The Works of John Wesley*. 5 vols. Edited by Albert C. Outler. Nashville: Abingdon, 1985.

White, Susan. *Foundations of Christian Worship*. Louisville: Westminster John Knox, 2006.

Whitehead, Alfred North. *Process and Reality*. Corrected ed. Edited by David Ray Griffin and Donald W. Sherburne. New York: Free Press, 1978.

Williamson, Clark M. *Way of Blessing, Way of Life: A Christian Theology*. St. Louis: Chalice, 1999.

Williamson, Clark M., and Ronald J. Allen. *The Vital Church: Teaching, Worship, Service, Learning*. St. Louis: Chalice, 1998.

Willimon, William, *Pastor: The Theology and Practice of Ordained Ministry*, Nashville: Abingdon, 2000.

———. *Who Will Be Saved?* Nashville: Abingdon, 2008.

Wimberly, Edward P. *African American Pastoral Care*. Rev. ed. Nashville: Abingdon, 2008.

Winnicott, D. W. *The Maturational Processes and the Facilitating Environment: Studies in the Theory of Emotional Development*. Madison, WI: International Universities Press, 1965.

World Lutheran Federation. "Nairobi Statement on Worship and Culture." 1996. Online: http://www.worship.ca/docs/lwf_ns.html/.

Yoder, John Howard. *The Politics of Jesus*. Grand Rapids: Eerdmans, 1994.

Yong, Amos. *Hospitality and the Other: Pentecost, Christian Practices, and the Neighbor*. Faith Meets Faith. Maryknoll, NY: Orbis, 2008.

Young, Michael P. *Bearing Witness against Sin: The Evangelical Birth of the American Social Movement*. Chicago: University of Chicago Press, 2006.